Digital and Social Media Marketing

Digital and Social Media Marketing: A Results-Driven Approach is an exciting new industry-led, research-informed and results-driven guide to digital commerce. Its examples draw from European SMEs to offer a unique perspective for those learning about digital marketing. Having been developed in close collaboration with the Search Engine Marketing Trade Association (SEMTA), it is a reliable source of prevailing industry standards for practitioners at the cutting edge of their trade.

Unlike other digital marketing texts, this accessible textbook gives special consideration to the need for continuous planning, implementation, observation and improvement upon the digital strategy implementation. Equally unique is the book's Digital Business Maturity Model, and the Buyer Persona Spring, which offer organisations a clear roadmap for understanding their relative levels of technology adoption and digital strategy development.

Embracing the true spirit of digital and social media marketing, the book will be the first of its kind in this field with digital learning materials, case studies and exercises available in a supporting #passion4digital community and a related Massive Open Online Course (MOOC).

This book will provide a hands-on, accessible and user-friendly platform to turn skills and knowledge into strategic advantage. Ideal for postgraduate learners, instructors interested in providing a unique and up-to-date learning experience and for SMEs and practitioners aiming to be at the cutting edge of Digital and Social Media Marketing.

Aleksej Heinze is Senior Lecturer at the University of Salford, UK.

Gordon Fletcher is Senior Lecturer at the University of Salford, UK.

Tahir Rashid is Senior Lecturer at the University of Salford, UK.

Ana Cruz is a Lecturer in Marketing at the University of Sheffield International Faculty, CITY College, Greece.

This book takes a practical and strategic outlook to digital marketing with an easy to follow step-by-step approach. Each chapter has several business case studies that help give insights into real-world issues and scenarios, which can be used by both academic and business readers.

—Joanne Kuzma, Principal Lecturer in Computing,
University of Worcester, UK

This book is a great resource for both students and businesses. The case studies are fresh and topical and the latest findings from research are woven into this very stimulating text. Digital marketing is examined from a strategic and a practical perspective with both authority and creativity.

—Kate Dobson, Lecturer Consultant,
University of Worcester, UK

Digital and Social Media Marketing: A Results-Driven Approach is a wonderful book that really communicates great concepts and practical techniques for helping companies and students understand how to approach digital commerce and transformation. Heinze, Fletcher, Rashid and Cruz nailed it with the "Marketing first" approach.

—Carla Dawson, Co-Founder of onmarc.com

This book gets into almost every aspect of modern marketing, and the Buyer Persona Spring really helps to keep the focus on building conversations and engagement. I would highly recommend it to anyone getting into marketing.

—Susan Patch, Marketer, E-Learning
Squared, Canada

Digital and Social Media Marketing

A Results-Driven Approach

Edited by Aleksej Heinze, Gordon Fletcher, Tahir Rashid and Ana Cruz

Routledge
Taylor & Francis Group

LONDON AND NEW YORK

First published 2017
by Routledge
2 Park Square, Milton Park, Abingdon, Oxon OX14 4RN

and by Routledge
711 Third Avenue, New York, NY 10017

Routledge is an imprint of the Taylor & Francis Group, an informa business

British Library Cataloguing in Publication Data
A catalogue record for this book is available from the British Library

Library of Congress Cataloging in Publication Data
A catalog record for this book has been requested

ISBN: 978-1-138-91790-3 (hbk)
ISBN: 978-1-138-91791-0 (pbk)
ISBN: 978-1-315-68876-3 (ebk)

Typeset in Bembo
by Apex CoVantage, LLC

Visit the companion website at www.mastersindigitalmarketing.org/book

Printed and bound by CPI Group (UK) Ltd, Croydon, CR0 4YY

Contents

Boxes

Case studies

Figures

Tables

Contributors

Alexander Christov, University of National and World Economy (UNWE), Bulgaria

Ana Cruz, University of Sheffield International Faculty, CITY College, Greece

Alex Fenton, Salford Business School, University of Salford, UK

Gordon Fletcher, Salford Business School, University of Salford, UK

Rimantas Gatautis, Kaunas University of Technology, Lithuania

Verena Hausmann, Universität Koblenz-Landau, Germany

Sayed Ali Hayder, Salford Business School, University of Salford, UK

Aleksej Heinze, Salford Business School, University of Salford, UK

Sophie Iredale, Salford Business School, University of Salford, UK

Ashley Jones, Events Director, Social Chain, UK

Stelios Karatzas, University of Sheffield International Faculty, CITY College, Greece

Bartłomiej Kurzyk, University of Łódź, Poland

Mostafa Mohamad, Salford Business School, University of Salford, UK

Tahir Rashid, Salford Business School, University of Salford, UK

Milanka Slavova, University of National and World Economy (UNWE), Bulgaria

Ivan Stoychev, University of National and World Economy (UNWE), Bulgaria

Anna Tarabasz, University of Łódź, Poland

Elena Vitkauskaitė, Kaunas University of Technology, Lithuania

Martin J Williams, Managing Director, UKcopywriting.com, UK

Sue Williams, Universität Koblenz-Landau, Germany

Acknowledgements

We would like to thank our international advisory board members and all the contributors who have offered their feedback on the ideas of this book:

Barry Adams – Managing Director – Polemic Digital – UK

Dawn Anderson – Director – Digital Marketing & SEO Search Strategy Consultant – Move It Marketing – UK

Olga Andrienko – Head of Social Media – SEMrush – Russia

Tomasz Bartosz Kalinowski – Project manager, University of Łódź – Poland

Anjlee Bhatt – Chief Conversationalist and Caffeine Enthusiast – Pressed Media – UK

James Bowman – Business Manager – Integral Healthcare Partnership – UK

Christina Chokoeva – Marketing Manager – DINO Ltd – Bulgaria

Aisha Choudhry – Head of Search – Fast Web Media – UK

Vida Davidaviciene – Head of Department of Business Technologies – Vilnius Gediminas Technical University – Lithuania

Carla Dawson – Digital Marketing Strategist – xdawson.com – Argentina

Ian Dodson – Co-Founder and Director – Digital Marketing Institute – Ireland

Richard Dron – Technical Innovation Officer – Salford Business School – UK

Alex Fenton – Lecturer in Digital Business – Salford Business School – UK

Joana Ferreira – Digital Marketing Manager – Fast Web Media – UK

Richard George – Managing Partner – MEC Manchester – UK

Briony Gunson – Digital Content Account Director – MEC Manchester – UK

Christopher Hackett – Data and Solutions Engineer – Fast Web Media – UK

Sophie Iredale – Researcher – Salford Business School – UK

Emilis Jarockis – Co-Founder and Marketing Manager – Sinergija verslui – Lithuania

Chris Kent – Digital Marketing Strategist, Chartered Marketer & Author of *21st Century Marketing* – Isle of Man

Błażej Kupaj – Sales and Marketing Manager – Lacan Technologies – Poland

Georgi Malchev – Managing Partner – Xplora.bg Company – Bulgaria

Cathal Melinn – Digital Media Manager – Digital Marketing Institute – Ireland

Susan Patch – Marketer – E-Learning Squared – Canada
Adrian Solomon – Project Manager of South East European Research Centre – Greece
Colin Telford – Managing Partner of The Candidate Ltd – UK
Diana Tolockaite – Digital Marketing Executive – Fast Web Media – UK
Jo Turnbull – Organiser of Search London – UK
Regimantas Urbanas – Marketing Manager, Baltics – Google Lithuania, UAB – Lithuania
Rolandas Urka – Co-Founder and Director – Sinergija verslui – Lithuania
Elena Vasilieva – Project Manager of Salford Business School, University of Salford – UK
Marc Wilson – Business Manager – Focus Independent Adult Social Work CIC – UK

Students

Mariam Ali – Student at Salford Business School – UK
Elsa Bota – Student at University of Sheffield International Faculty, CITY College – Greece
Cariad Fiddy – Student at Salford Business School – UK
Emily Goddard – Student at Salford Business School – UK
Nadia Latif – Student at Salford Business School – UK
Lia Nersisyan – Student at University of Sheffield International Faculty, CITY College – Greece
Felicia Siavalas – Student at University of Sheffield International Faculty, CITY College – Greece
Shazia Ullah – Student at Salford Business School – UK
Mohammed Waqar – Student at Salford Business School – UK

Lifelong Learning Programme

This book has been funded with support from the European Commission. This publication [communication] reflects the views only of the author, and the Commission cannot be held responsible for any use which may be made of the information contained therein.

Definitions of terms

Affiliate marketing – is a commission-based arrangement where referring sites receive a commission on sales or leads sent on to merchants' e-commerce sites. Commissions can be fixed per lead or action or an agreed-upon percentage of the purchase.

AIDA model – Attention, Interest, Desire and Action model. This model was developed in 1893 in traditional advertising content evaluation and refined by many, including Elmo Lewis (1872–1948). It is used to evaluate the quality of marketing communication content, which should attract the Attention of the audience by focusing on the benefits of the product or service, raise the audience's Interest, offer evidence that it will meet their needs, hence raising their Desire, and finally, have a call-to-Action which could be tracked for measuring the success of content engagement.

Anchor text – text that appears as a web link to a human web page user as well as a search engine.

Black hat SEO – method of gaming the search engine algorithm to achieve high search engine ranking by breaking the search engine guidelines, for example through buying incoming links from spammy and irrelevant websites. Black hat SEO is also referred to as spamdexing, search spam, web spam, search engine spam or search engine poisoning, amongst others.

Buyer persona – is a fictitious representation of your customer which is based on your market research data and usually includes demographics, locations, national and regional culture, socio-economic background, decision-making patterns, their 'pain points' and 'hot points', the keywords they might use on search engines and social networks that they might engage with, and other information that helps marketers to focus content towards buyers' needs.

Collaterals – or marketing collaterals is the set of media assets produced for communicating messages about a product or service. This could include, for example, web pages, social media hashtags, apps, traditional print brochures, leaflets and video.

Critical mass – the minimum size of a community needed to sustain a community or make a community viable.

Customer – an individual who has made a purchase from you in the past if you are a business or – for a non-transactional organisation such as a health advice centre – a recorded interaction where value has been exchanged, such as advice given or medicine prescribed.

Digital marketing strategy – is a long-term set of priorities (over three to five years) for engagement of an organisation using relevant channels, content and data with the specific buyer persona.

EEA – the European Economic Area is the largest economic marketplace in the world and creates an economic bond amongst EEA country member states.

Emergent strategy – development of a pattern of activities which start with actions and practices that over time become successful routines, and are documented in contrast to a prescriptive strategy where a long-term plan is developed which informs a pattern of regular activities.

EU – the European Union unites most of the European countries in a politico-economical bond.

Fold – on a web page an imaginary line where the screen ends and a user has to scroll to see further content. The name is carried on from newspapers, where usually you can only see one section of a paper before it is folded.

Hashtag – a word or a number prefixed with a # sign which is used to develop topics on social media networks. For example, the hashtag for this book is #passion4digital.

Hot point – the issues and topics that are considered important by the target audience, for example, efficiency in customer service. See also 'pain point'.

HTML – Hypertext Markup Language. A standardised language to tag content on web pages which facilitates the World Wide Web (WWW) in order to make it accessible to web browsers and other web content readers such as search engines.

Keyword – a significant search query which comprises one word or a series of words that are used by search engine visitors, and has been methodically determined considering the Relevance, Specificity, Popularity and Competition for this term.

Keyword map – a list of keywords methodically developed for a particular organisation, which take into account organisational strategy and its services and products when it comes to deciding the focus of the web properties to be developed.

Long tail keyword – a search term that comprises three or more words which are used by individuals who are closer to their purchase decision compared to those who use a 'short tail keyword'. For example, 'Nikon D3200 Digital SLR Camera in Black' is a long tail keyword.

Metadata – information that is used to describe data; for example, a book has metadata that includes a book title, the author and the year of publication. A web page metadata includes similar fields, including two very important fields for search engines – page title and page description. If a web page has metadata defined for a page title and description, these tend to be displayed on a search engine results page (SERP).

Organic SEO – a method where search engine rankings are improved using methods that do not rely on payment for individual visitor clicks. This method relies on strategies such as content marketing, where the emphasis is placed on developing relevant and useful content which attracts external links and social shares and is developed around strategic keywords.

Paid Search Marketing – pay-per-click or PPC is part of Search Engine Marketing. It differs from 'organic' or 'natural' Search Engine Optimisation (SEO), as it involves paid advertising. In essence, PPC is a text-based ad with a link to a company page that is displayed to a user when their keyword query matches a phrase chosen by the advertiser. The advertiser pays a fee for predefined actions by the user. Although this is usually a click on the ad, there are other charging methods, as PPC may additionally involve advertising through a display/content network of third-party sites – these are described as cost-per-click (CPC), cost-per-mille (CPM) or cost-per-action (CPA).

Pain point – issues that are considered common challenges by our buyer persona, for example, high energy costs. See also 'hot point'.

PPC – see Paid Search Marketing.

PPC SEO – a method of optimising the paid advertising campaigns. This relies on strategies such as click-through optimisation, which increases the number of relevant people clicking on an ad as a reduced cost to the advertiser.

Primary keyword – a search term that is used as a 'focus keyword' on a particular digital profile page and describes the main aspect of the content being developed. For example, a web page should have one primary keyword and two or three secondary keywords.

Prospects – individuals who have the potential to become your customers. The main, simple difference between a prospect and a customer is that the customer has made a purchase from you in the past whilst the prospect has not.

rel=nofollow – an HTML tag used by some search engines to determine if a link should be used as endorsement and hence increase the ranking authority of a web page.

Secondary keyword – a search term that is used as a supporting term on a digital profile page and does not describe the main aspect of the content, as opposed to the primary keyword.

Seed keyword – a search term that is entered into a keyword research tool with the intention of discovering related terms.

SEO – Search Engine Optimisation. A method of improving the position of an online profile such as a website or a social media profile in SERPs.

SERP – Search Engine Results Page – the web page that displays the results to a search query and usually lists the top ten answers. The web pages generated by a search engine are based on its index of the Web at the time of a search query.

Short tail keyword – a search query term that comprises one or two words. Typically these terms are used by individuals who are in the early stages of their search for information, compared to those who use a 'long tail keyword'.

Sitemap – a protocol used by the major search engines to read the web pages of a website. The sitemaps.org website outlines the standards used: www.sitemaps.org/

SMART objective – a Specific, Measurable, Attainable, Realistic and Timely statement that breaks down a wider aim. Objectives can be set at an organisational, business or campaign level. Once objectives are set, these are reviewed on a regular basis in order to learn from them before they are revised for the next round of continuous improvement.

SPAM – generally used in an email context where a large quantity of unsolicited emails is received. However, SPAM also occurs on online forums where repeat and often off-topic messages are posted simply for the gain of visibility, as well as links from the forum. In a search engines context, SPAM is considered to be any action that violates the fair use guidelines of a search engine and tends to include actions which are exclusively made to game the search engine ranking algorithm.

Thin content – a web page that does not add any value for the visitor. It tends to have a lot of adverts and no original content. The number of words is always a determinant factor for the thinness of a page, but web pages with a low number of words (under 500) would likely be considered thin.

UK – United Kingdom.

URL – Universal Resource Locator – it is the unique address of a web page on the World Wide Web.

USA – United States of America.

Section I

Introduction

A visual introduction to Digital and Social Media Marketing

Gordon Fletcher, Salford Business School, University of Salford, UK

This book takes a practical approach. Regardless of whether you are running a flower shop in Krakow, a bookstore in Glasgow or a multinational in Thessaloniki, there will be useful lessons to be found throughout the book. Being practical also means that this book is 'always strategic' about digital marketing. Attention is always turned towards those who buy your goods or services and how you can have ongoing sustainable interaction with them.

The importance of marketing is significant for all facets of an organisation. In this book we present an approach to digital business that is described as 'marketing first'. For your organisation this will come to place digital marketing at the heart of everything you do and will contribute to all of the key business decisions that you make. A marketing first approach to digital business shapes and changes your organisation to respond to changing business practices, global markets, including new competitors, and the increased expectation of transparency and engagement from your customers. It is not simply about generating a short-term boost in sales. All of the actions described in the book have an impact on the way that a business functions and, over time, contribute to a realignment and digital maturing of your organisation. As a business recognises the pivotal importance of data in the operation of all its functions, the business itself changes as it progresses through the Digital Business Maturity Model (Figure 0.1) – a model that we explain in detail in later chapters.

This chapter introduces the concepts of Digital and Social Media Marketing through a visual device that we describe as the 'Buyer Persona Spring' (Figure 0.2). Step by step through this chapter we will explain the value and purpose of the Spring and each of its elements with the goal of connecting you – and your organisation – in an ongoing and sustainable way with your customers.

The Spring will also guide you through the rest of this book as we explain the key concepts and activities that are currently used in Digital and Social Media Marketing. This structured explanation of the concepts will give you a clear basis for understanding and applying the marketing actions that we recommend as world leading practice throughout the rest of this book.

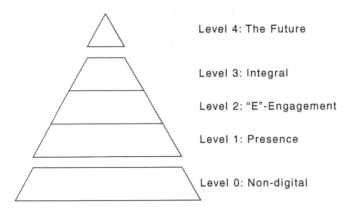

Level 4: The Future

Level 3: Integral

Level 2: "E"-Engagement

Level 1: Presence

Level 0: Non-digital

Figure 0.1 The Digital Business Maturity Model

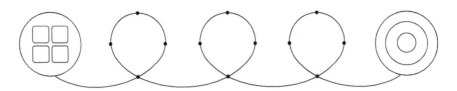

Figure 0.2 The Buyer Persona Spring

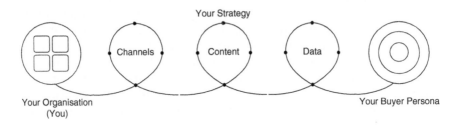

Figure 0.3 The Buyer Persona Spring now labelled

The Spring (Figures 0.2 and 0.3) is composed of three key elements. On the left is the organisation (you) attempting to engage and interact with your customers who are represented at the right-hand side of the Spring. You, your organisation and your customers are complex in their own right and composed of many parts. We will describe these parts in detail later. The device that connects you to your customers is the Spring itself, which has three loops representing the three key strategies of all digital marketing. These strategies cover channels, content and data. By using the Spring to structure your thoughts, this book sets out to help you understand your own organisation and your customers as well as the complexities of maintaining communications with them in a digital era.

The starting point for understanding digital marketing is found in the answer to the question, 'What is a buyer persona?'. To understand all of your customers we describe and speak to them collectively through the buyer persona. The buyer persona recognises that you are not just speaking on a one-to-one individual basis with each customer but instead are speaking with definite groups of customers who share similar qualities, attributes and attitudes. The buyer persona is a representation of all your customers and consumers that you describe (in detail) as part of your strategic planning. In the era of digital communications the buyer persona also recognises that your customers are never all the same and that their combinations of interests and motivations vary slightly, between themselves and over time, in relation to you and your products and services. In the rush to become digital, the era of mass-consumerism and mass-consumption has quietly disappeared and been overtaken by the rising stars of e-commerce, custom-made goods and short-run production. Your buyer persona enjoys and appreciates being spoken to as an individual – even if they are a construct of your own market research – and responds positively to your considerations.

Making the buyer persona the focus of your attention is acknowledgement that all marketing – but especially digital marketing – is about building ongoing positive and context-driven relationships. You want your organisation's brands and your products and services to engage with your buyer persona. Your buyer persona will be a narrative about the optimal buyer, it is an identity that is recognisable to your consumers and customers and talking to your buyer persona will create a recognisable and meaningful conversation for them. The buyer persona is an important recognition that successful digital marketing requires you to work with all those who 'engage with' you rather than solely 'those who buy your products and services'. Through your digital marketing strategies and your engagement with your buyer persona you are engaging not only with buyers but also potential buyers, influencers, previous buyers (who can become influencers) and potentially even competitors.

The buyer persona is visually represented in this book by a series of intersecting circles that describe the various roles and identities that are often used in digital marketing texts (Figure 0.4). 'Users' are the outermost wrapper category for the buyer persona. This is the most inclusive category of individuals that effectively includes everyone who can be engaged through digital channels. The implication in the label is that an individual 'uses' digital media. This is also tacit recognition that the 'digital' of digital marketing has made 'marketing' a two-way conversation which diminishes the value of broadcast approaches. However, increasingly the impact of the digital channels and content, as well as the importance of data-driven experiences, are also felt by those who do not engage regularly with digital media. Ineffective and purely tactical marketing

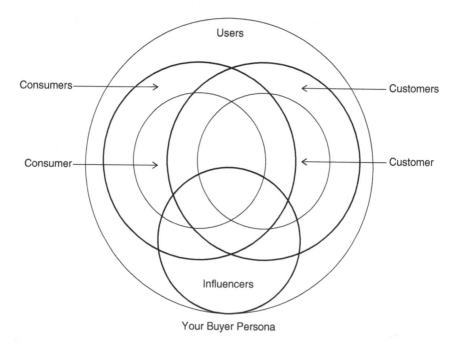

Figure 0.4 Inside the buyer persona

tends to address this category of users. In contrast, strategic approaches to digital marketing recognise much clearer differentiation of 'users'. Influencers are the individuals who influence the buying decisions for themselves and others. In the context of digital channels, influencers include product reviewers and bloggers as well as the closer and more traditional influence of, for example, friends and family. Influencers overlap with all the other categories within the buyer persona, not as a result of their comparative importance but rather their complex relationship with all aspects of the buyer persona. This complexity translates – in marketing terms – into the difficulty that organisations have in engaging with these individuals in an appropriate manner.

Within the buyer persona are the consumers and customers. Customers are those who buy your goods and services and are distinct from consumers, who actually consume and gain benefit from and realise the value of your goods and services. It is likely that in many if not most cases these two categories will overlap, but as any retailer of children's toys, for example, will recognise, these roles can often represent an important distinction. Within the circles of the consumers and customers, two further circles represent the individual consumer and customer. These inner circles remind us that consumers and customers themselves are also differentiated between individuals within these categories. Your goal in working with the buyer persona is to gain advantage through digital technologies to individually address a specific point of inter-section within the circle of users that may incorporate influencers, consumers and customers, and which is recognisable to those who buy and consume your goods and services.

We use an unlabelled symbol of the buyer persona (Figure 0.5) throughout the book to reinforce the focus of our discussions and its relationship to the other elements of the Buyer Persona Spring.

0.1 You and your buyers

Explaining the buyer persona's role within the Buyer Persona Spring requires a return to the beginning, with an examination of your relationship with the people who buy your goods and services – your customers.

The buyer persona has a more complex meaning than that of buyer, con-sumer or customer. In a simple world, the relationship between you and your buyers can be represented by a single straight line (Figure 0.6).

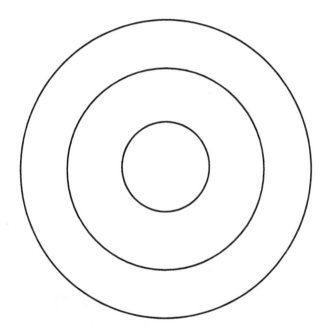

Figure 0.5 The buyer persona symbol

Figure 0.6 The simplistic relationship between your organisation and the buyer

You sell goods (or services) to a buyer. This is a single transaction that is repeated with each buyer. Some buyers may return to you to buy again, but this simple relationship model only regards a return buyer as yet another buyer. In this model every transaction you have with a buyer is regarded as the same relationship repeated again and again over time (Figure 0.7).

The relationship shown in Figure 0.7 is unlikely to be sustainable unless it is modelling a specific combination of circumstances. The most likely circumstance that echoes the model of Figure 0.7 will be found where you may have the privilege of being the sole supplier of goods or services as a result of location, time, convenience or the type of product or service that is being sold (Figure 0.8).

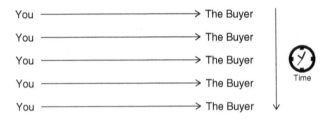

Figure 0.7 The simplistic relationship between you and the buyer repeated over time

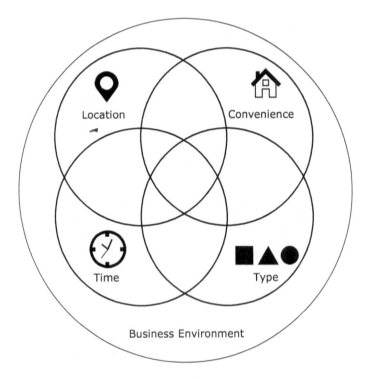

Figure 0.8 The parameters for being a sole supplier

For example, a late-night store, a highly specialised business-to-business (B2B) product or a business in a highly regulated industry could all exploit one or more parameters of being a sole supplier. However, even if this is your current business situation or you benefit from holding multiple parameters for being a sole supplier, it cannot remain the case permanently. Already, in most sectors, more consumers have access to mobile commerce and global alternatives that enable far greater choice and options than ever before. Even traditional business models, for example, taxis and bed and breakfasts, have felt the influence of digital technology through the Uber and Airbnb apps. With their underlying business models built around the sharing economy and channels that rely upon social networking, their challenge to traditional models is their resistance to being pinned down as a conventional single competing company. These challenges reduce the privilege offered by any combination of specific parameters for continuing to be a sole supplier.

In the competitive global environment and with the acknowledgement that your organisation must sensibly and regularly engage with the buyers of your goods or services, you are already recognising the need and importance of marketing to the entire business. This recognition is the basis for our description of a 'marketing first' approach to digital business. The briefest of mentions in the previous paragraph to mobile commerce and global alternatives has already pointed towards a need for your marketing to be digital, as that is the direction in which your entire business needs to move. Digital marketing will enable this to happen proactively rather than being faced with the prospect of becoming a casualty of the change prevailing in all business sectors. A marketing first approach to digital business is the most accessible opportunity for you to be able to take on and overtake your slower-moving competitors.

To reflect the necessary two-way ongoing and communicative nature of the relationship that you must build with your customers, a second arrow is added (Figure 0.9) to our original simple relationship (Figure 0.6). In traditional marketing this extra arrow can be used to reflect a wide range of meanings. The two-way relationship reflects the influence of marketing communications on the buyer, marks the combination of push and pull factors that influence buyer behaviour and is a recognition that it is easier to encourage return custom from previous buyers than to continuously initiate new relationships (Figure 0.7). More implicit in this two-way relationship is the recognition that you actively learn from your interactions with buyers and modify your approach as a result of reflection and learning. All of these implied understandings that are embedded in a relatively simple diagram (Figure 0.9) are already pushing you towards an 'always strategic' perspective.

Of course, if this two-way diagram (Figure 0.9) represented the sum total of the relationship between a buyer and a business, then the organisation could

You ⟵⟶ The Buyer

Figure 0.9 A simple communicative relationship between you and the buyer

manage the majority of its marketing activities through continuous direct conversations with each of its buyers individually. Some (very small) businesses can
still continue to do this. Imagine, for example, the conversations of a local baker,
the local milkman or a local retailer of high-value jewellery, who all choose
to solely serve their local community. In the most straightforward of ways the
local baker in this example will receive return customers because of their conversations and interactions. However, as soon as the lines of communication
become more complex or become mediated by digital technologies, the business becomes busier. If a business has growing ambition, then this face-to-face
relationship and approach to marketing require the support of well-planned,
more wide-ranging and more strategic forms of engagement.

A common response by some businesses to the complexity of engaging with
their customers and prospective customers is to try as many different activities
and actions (offline and online) as possible (Figure 0.10). The ensuing whirl-
wind of activity may produce results, but without getting any clear feedback or
measures of the results the chances of repeating or learning from these actions
are small. The activity represents an entirely tactical approach to marketing with
varying results and no reflection on the outcomes achieved by the activities that
have been undertaken.

Even in the digital domain, where the measurement of activities is significantly more accurate than traditional marketing, there are numerous examples
of businesses employing this 'pay, spray and pray' approach across a range of
channels to try to communicate with an ill-defined audience that may or may
not include their target customers. Importantly, and more specifically, the application of analogies to traditional television or newspaper marketing actions to
the digital domain increasingly does not hold up well.

However, without a clear understanding of digital marketing it is unsurpris-
ing that many large and well-established businesses have applied the (to them)
familiar techniques of traditional marketing and mass-consumer advertising.
A false assurance has been offered to these businesses that maintaining old strategies is also the lowest-risk strategy. Some online channels encourage previous
levels of spending by offering apparently familiar sales packages.

At the same time, for many smaller organisations and businesses, the developing sophistication of digital marketing has resulted in many seeing their own
online activities as experiments in a new and untested domain. Neither the
small nor large business scenarios described here reflect a strong understanding
of the benefits or differences of digital marketing. For the small business, the
majority of the models and tools for strategic marketing continue to have value
and meaning in a digital domain. With the addition of the digital context, an

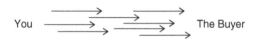

Figure 0.10 Purely tactical marketing activities

Table 0.1 The digital marketing challenge matrix

Digital marketing challenges	Barriers (to digital marketing)	Benefits (of digital marketing)
Small business	Expense to engage Lack of human resources No strategic view	Competitive advantage Expand markets Diversify products/services Target buyers
Large business	Broadcast media perspective 'Lock in' with agencies Low expectation of feedback	Data-driven decisions Iterative planning and learning Focus on buyer persona

organisation's marketing function has the capacity to provide greater levels of analytical feedback and rapid responses than have ever been possible with traditional methods. For small businesses, their marketing challenge is the same as it has always been: committing to the ongoing investment of resources that allow them to become strategic (Table 0.1).

For larger businesses with established approaches to their marketing, digital marketing offers the ability to be more sophisticated in addressing their core audience (the buyer persona) with differentiated and carefully positioned content and opportunities for conversation. This change also introduces the importance of data and the embedding of a learning cycle into marketing activity, which for some organisations is a major challenge to their existing practice (Table 0.1).

0.2 Your complex organisation

Your complex organisation (Figure 0.11) must interact with your buyer persona. Your buyer persona is the narrative that represents – through a single persona – the many buyers who want your products and services and who seek an association with your brand. As a strategically oriented organisation, the buyer persona is the focus of attention for your digital marketing actions, but you must also have some self-awareness of your own organisation. In the Buyer Persona Spring, your complex organisation is presented as a series of overlapping circles (Figure 0.12).

The outside circle of the organisation represents the market (or markets) within which you exist. Most organisations will recognise this in a straightforward way as being what they 'do', their profession or the things that they sell. Digital business does challenge these initial labels because all digital businesses 'do' data. However, this particular challenge and consequent change of perspective is a discussion for later chapters.

You and your competitors are positioned within your market. The acknowledgement here of competitors and markets is recognition of the many external factors that have an impact upon your plans for interacting with your buyer persona. The market itself is also affected by other factors beyond just your

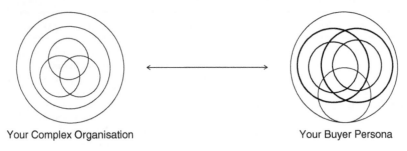

Your Complex Organisation   Your Buyer Persona

Figure 0.11 The complex organisation and the buyer persona

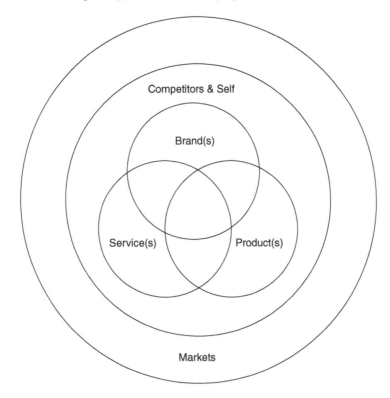

Figure 0.12 Your complex organisation

activities and those of your competitors. An understanding of these factors can be gained through a PESTLE (Political, Economic, Social, Technical, Legal and Environmental) analysis of the external environment. Both you and your competitors have a range of goods and services that you are offering to your buyer persona. If you are successful or at least sustainable as a business you are also

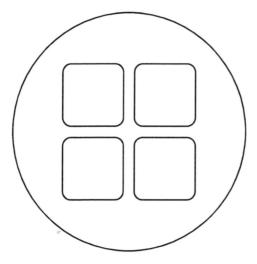

Figure 0.13 Your organisation

meeting some specific needs of your current buyer persona. Even if you currently only offer tangible goods, the organisation diagram (Figure 0.12) does acknowledge your future as a digital business with the potential for new services that are driven by your data. Overlapping with your goods and services is your brand (or brands). Brands can communicate with the buyer persona in a way that is distinct from the goods and services themselves. The meaning that brands convey through their presentation is an important start and end point for feeding back from the buyer persona.

Your organisation is dynamic, with continuously shifting relationships with the buyer persona. Being strategic means that you learn from the buyer persona and respond to the changing external environment with data-driven evidence-based decisions.

We represent your organisation throughout this book with a simplified icon (Figure 0.13).

0.3 The Buyer Persona Spring and action-based learning

The final element of the Buyer Persona Spring is the connecting spirals – considered overall, this is the strategy that connects your organisation with your buyer persona. The iterative nature of successful strategic digital marketing means that the buyer persona as well as your tactics and techniques are all regularly reviewed. This iterative strategic approach to marketing and business is the key concept embedded in the Buyer Persona Spring.

Each of the spirals contained within the Buyer Persona Spring visually represents the action learning cycle (Figure 0.14). The cycle is a continuous process of planning, acting, observing and reflecting. After the completion of each cycle, the reflection and learning resulting from the process inform any changes needed for subsequent plans. The action learning cycle is a well-established and recognisable theory of learning that has direct application to business planning and, through this link, digital marketing. The action learning cycle is generally represented with directional arrows indicating that reflection will always lead onwards to the next stage of planning.

The action learning cycle is by definition an iterative process and is never accurately conveyed as a single cycle of action. Instead, the action learning cycle should be represented as a continuous – possibly never-ending – process (Figure 0.15).

In the Buyer Persona Spring we overlay the principles of the action learning cycle to reflect the need to plan and enact marketing activities (Figure 0.16). The Buyer Persona Spring and the action learning cycle can then be read in parallel. This continuous iterative loop of activities will also be familiar to those with experience of Agile software development, which advocates a similar

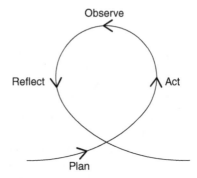

Figure 0.14 Action learning cycle

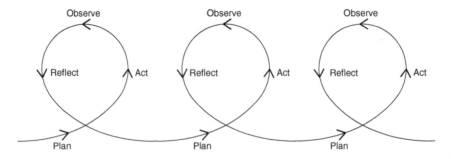

Figure 0.15 The repeating action learning cycle

Figure 0.16 An individual loop in the Buyer Persona Spring

iterative, continuous and consciously self-reflective strategic approach to core processes and activities. With a strategy in place to reach the buyer persona, specific plans can then be made. Planning for digital marketing sets SMART (Specific, Measurable, Attainable, Realistic and Timely) objectives (discussed in Chapters 1 and 2) that will determine the outcomes necessary to measure and assess the success of specific actions. Planning will start with the definition of campaigns and then, within those campaigns, the specific tactics required will be identified. The tactics and campaigns will need to be observed and monitored. At the end of the timeframe determined by the SMART objectives there will be an opportunity to assess and reflect upon the success of the plan. This reflection will then feed back into the overall strategy and subsequent planning. In effect, at this point the next cycle has been initiated. In distinction from the action learning cycle, the cycle of activities in the Buyer Persona Spring is not always one-directional. Your assessment may require only small revisions to your tactics or campaign. In a practical sense this involves one or two steps backwards rather than pressing onwards to a completely new strategy. Similarly, the Buyer Persona Spring recognises that changes and alterations in your strategy may be compatible with your current campaigns and tactics, effectively creating a repeat of the same loop.

As with the action learning cycle, the Buyer Persona Spring is a continuous process (Figure 0.17). Each iteration of the spring allows an opportunity for you to revise your strategy and to accommodate changes in the buyer persona or your organisation. Within each iteration there are opportunities – upon reflection and assessment – to modify or tweak your tactics and campaign based on immediate feedback from the data that you will continuously collect.

For successful digital marketing we identify three key priorities (or substrategies) that are each taken up by the continuous cycles of the Buyer Persona Spring. These three priorities are Channels, Content and Data (Figure 0.18). The ordering of these three sub-strategies also represents an increasing sophistication as your organisation moves towards increasing digital business maturity.

Figure 0.17 Iterative loops within the Buyer Persona Spring

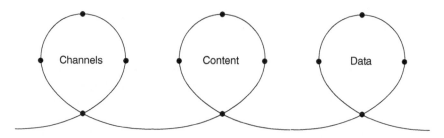

Figure 0.18 The three key sub-strategies of digital marketing

Figure 0.19 The Buyer Persona Spring

Channel sub-strategies deal with the specific channels through which your organisation represents itself. Channels include your essential website presence as well as any more specialised presence channels you might have, such as a *DeviantArt* account for creative businesses.

The Content sub-strategy decouples specific platforms from the content that your organisation produces and how it disseminates this content. The Content sub-strategy will inevitably overlap with the Channel sub-strategy, but it will also tackle other systems where your organisation may not have direct control or access.

The broader Data sub-strategy will take your organisation to more sophisticated levels of digital maturity through recognition of the pivotal importance of all types of data. The Data sub-strategy will overlap with the Content

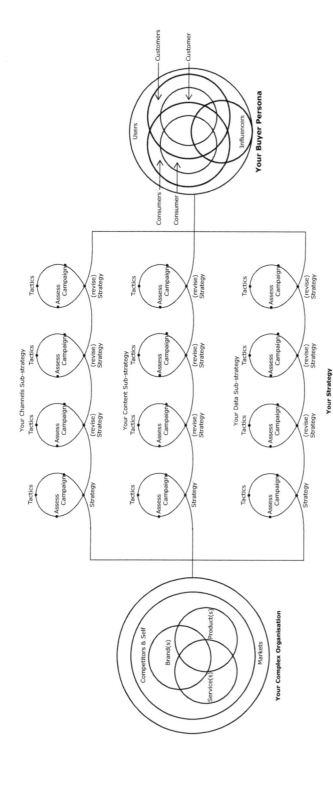

Figure 0.20 The complete Buyer Persona Spring

sub-strategy and then extend to encompass all data that can be accessed and interrogated by the organisation. The Data sub-strategy will itself directly contribute to the iterative basis of the Buyer Persona Spring and inform the evolution of all three sub-strategies – as well as your overall strategy – as they all engage your buyer persona.

0.4 The Buyer Persona Spring

In combination, the organisation, the buyer persona and the three sub-strategies of digital marketing represent the Buyer Persona Spring (Figure 0.19). The relationship and interactions between the organisation and the buyer persona are two-way, iterative, dynamic and strategic. The specific planning, interactions and activities that are the basis for your organisation's digital marketing activities are defined and shaped by existing and relatively familiar tools of business analysis in the form of PESTLE and SWOT (Strengths, Weaknesses, Opportunities and Threats) analyses and setting SMART objectives, with success being measured through key performance indicators (KPIs).

The full model of the Buyer Persona Spring (Figure 0.20) recognises that each strategy must run in parallel (and in harmony) with the others, and that each strategy is iterative and actively incorporates feedback into subsequent planning and activities. However, the Buyer Persona Spring containing a single set of loops (Figure 0.19) is used throughout the following chapters as a simpler representation of the challenges and opportunities that become available as you step through the development of a digital marketing strategy for your organisation in subsequent chapters.

Ultimately, success – measured by comparing your organisation's performance against that of your competitors and the outcomes that you will define in your marketing strategy – will conceptually draw the Buyer Persona Spring closer to your organisation. This will only be achieved with the parallel alignment of the three priorities – of content, channels and data – and the alignment of the actions you implement to address these priorities with your own organisation's position, your overall strategy and the relevance of your buyer persona.

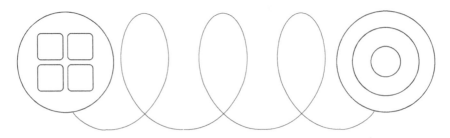

Figure 0.21 The Buyer Persona Spring – success

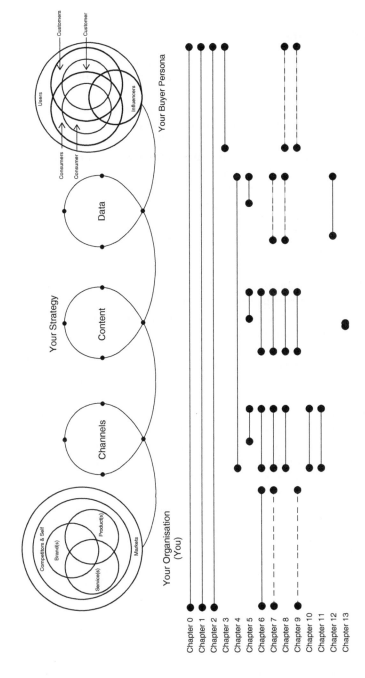

Figure 0.22 The book's chapters mapped to the Buyer Persona Spring

Symbolically, this tight alignment will contract the Buyer Persona Spring and draw your organisation closer to your buyer persona.

0.5 Book structure

- Chapter 1 describes digital marketing in terms of the concepts, key technologies, technology adoption in organisations and the recognition of success.
- Chapter 2 explains how digital technologies can be utilised in an organisational context to serve specific business needs.
- Chapter 3 explains how to understand digital consumers. Understanding consumers enables the description of the buyer persona to capture the drivers behind digital consumer decision making.
- Chapter 4 develops a digital strategy. By understanding the digital consumer, an organisation can then develop a strategy that sets objectives and uses tactics to achieve its aims.
- Chapter 5 discusses campaign planning and management as a key tactic for implementing a digital strategy.
- Chapters 6, 7, 8, 9 and 10 are interrelated chapters that provide more details on the specific actions required to implement digital campaigns.
- Chapter 6 describes the issues of digital presence.
- Chapter 7 details the practice of search engine optimisation (SEO) and explains how digital presence should be optimised to obtain strong search engine results.
- Chapter 8 focuses on social media and the behaviour of online communities.
- Chapter 9 focuses on content marketing and the importance of amplifying such content.
- Chapter 10 considers pay-per-click (PPC) advertising as a means of driving customers towards an organisation's digital presence.
- Chapter 11 incorporates the actions of mobile marketing and describes the peculiarities of working within a mobile environment.
- Chapter 12 looks at campaign evaluation, including the benefits of and cautions in using web analytics.
- Chapter 13 considers future users and future marketing issues.

1 Understanding Digital and Social Media Marketing concepts

Rimantas Gatautis, Kaunas University of Technology, Lithuania

1.0 Learning objectives

In this chapter you will learn how to:

- use the terms and understand the concepts of digital marketing;
- recognise the patterns of success and failure in digital marketing;
- position individual organisations – including your own – within the Digital Business Maturity Model;
- identify and understand the buyer persona;
- apply the models and tools used for planning digital marketing campaigns.

1.1 Understanding Digital and Social Media Marketing

This chapter outlines the key concepts and marketing actions that can make organisations more effective, more impactful, more sustainable, and more strategic within a 'marketing first' digital business model. This perspective is an important conceptual starting point, as it recognises marketing as an integral business function and a key mechanism that drives a business towards a fully digital approach. Figure 1.1 shows the more traditional viewpoint of marketing texts that separate business functions – including digital engagement – into discrete parts of an organisation. This perspective is taken in contrast to Figure 1.2, which presents the strategic and integrated marketing perspective taken throughout this book. The Buyer Persona Spring reflects the strategic perspective necessary for successful digital marketing – and for successful digital business overall. The representation of the organisation in the Buyer Persona Spring acknowledges the influence of external factors, including competitors, and connects with the buyer persona itself through an iterative, self-reflective cycle of campaigns in combination with the use of specific digital marketing tools and techniques.

The essential first step in taking a strategic 'marketing first' approach to digital business is to demystify the current jargon connected with Digital and Social Media Marketing, and to link the meanings of these words with more recognisable business terms and concepts. After providing a knowledge of current terminology, the chapter goes on to discuss the general principles relating to

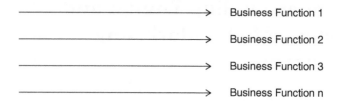

Figure 1.1 A traditional view of marketing, digital and other functions within a business

Figure 1.2 Visualising the conceptual understanding of business used in this book

digital marketing success and failure, and presents this assessment in relation to a business's overall digital business maturity. This chapter builds on Chapter 0, with continuing emphasis on the importance of the buyer persona for understanding the relationship of customers to the goods and services offered by your organisation. The Buyer Persona Spring is then returned to later in this chapter and throughout the rest of the book. This chapter concludes with a summary of the tools used for planning and delivering strategic Digital and Social Media Marketing. The purpose and value of these planning tools are also presented in relation to the overall Buyer Persona Spring model.

1.2 How to speak Digital and Social Media Marketing

As with many emerging areas of business, the terms employed to describe Digital and Social Media Marketing actions and planning have multiple and sometimes contradictory meanings. For clarity, the key terms are applied consistently throughout this book using the definitions below:

- *Digital technologies* describes the complex combination of hardware, software, Internet access and social networks that now represent the familiar forms of computing that are part of many people's everyday lives in Europe and other advanced economies.
- *Information and communication technologies* (or *ICTs*) is a more traditional term for digital technologies. The term is generally used in a more restrictive sense than 'digital technologies' to primarily describe the hardware and sometimes the software used for storing, processing and sharing digital

information. In this sense, the most commonly used examples of ICTs are personal computers (PCs), laptops, tablets and mobile phones (specifically smartphones). These devices in combination with common software such as web browsers, word processors and spreadsheets represent the most recognisable ICTs.

- *The Internet* is the largest and most commonly used network for digitally mediated communications. The Internet is a globe-spanning network of computers that links a range of digital technologies including mobile phones, computers and increasingly other things such as domestic appliances (e.g. fridges), wearable devices, and cars in a way that enables interchangeable communication. Increasingly, this wider connectivity of non-traditional items to the Internet is commonly labelled the 'Internet of Things'.

- *The World Wide Web* (or *WWW*, or just *'the Web'*) is often confused with the Internet as the global network of interlinked computers providing digitally mediated communications. However, more precisely, the Web is a very specific but very popular service delivered through the Internet. The simplicity of authoring a web page – creating web content – combined with the embedding of web browsers – accessing web content – in most Internet-enabled devices makes the Web the second most popular Internet service after email.

- *Web 2.0* was popularised by Tim O'Reilly – the founder of the technical publishing company, now O'Reilly's Media – and refers to websites and applications that allow the interactive creation and sharing of information. The importance of Web 2.0 technologies is found in their enabling of two-way forms of communication, where anyone can create, share, collaborate and communicate. This definition contrasts with Web 1.0 – a *post hoc* label that identifies earlier forms of web presences as being based on one-way and broadcast forms of communication usually undertaken by the website owner in order to address an audience, without any opportunity for their interaction or engagement. Web 2.0 is a watershed development for digital marketing, as genuine audience interaction through a web interface allowed marketing actions to fully apply the principles of traditional marketing and then exceed traditional marketing's ability to measure, assess and evaluate individual actions.

- *Social media* is the collective term for technologies that allow digitally enabled communication between many users. It is often characterised by platforms such as *Facebook* and *Twitter*. However, the term also includes other communications technologies – including blogs, *YouTube* and *Snapchat* – that take advantage of the interconnectivity of the Internet and the interactivity of Web 2.0 technologies to enable creation and sharing.

- *Digital Economy* was a term first introduced by Tapscott (1995) in his book *The Digital Economy: Promise and Peril in the Age of Networked Intelligence*. The digital economy refers to the commercial opportunities facilitated through electronic commerce in the widest sense, including the entire supply chain and all the associated ancillary business services that enable these transactions and actions. The Internet Economy, Net Economy and Web Economy are also sometimes used as a synonym for Digital Economy.

- *Digital business, electronic business* or *e-business* broadly refers to the activities of an organisation that uses digital technologies. Electronic business or e-business first emerged in reference to isolated functions within traditional businesses. Over time the term has become more widely applied to businesses and business environments that have evolved from electronic commerce through to full engagement with the digital economy. Digital business is no longer an isolated domain confined to specific business functions within a larger organisation. Instead, digital business has become central to core business processes undertaken within an entirely digital workflow.
- *Social commerce* is a term first introduced by *Yahoo!* in 2005 and refers to the e-commerce that uses social media channels to enable online buying and selling.
- The *marketing function* is a core business function in any organisation. Marketing is the continuous iterative process of listening to customers, understanding their needs and offering products or services that satisfy these needs.
- *Digital marketing* describes the primary use of digital technologies to support the marketing function of an organisation. In organisations that understand the marketing function, digital techniques are combined with traditional forms of marketing activity. However, in digital business, traditional activities are led by, guided by and integrated with digital marketing. Synonyms for digital marketing include electronic marketing, online marketing and Internet marketing. Digital marketing includes the delivery of online content to customers in order to attract and engage them in activities associated with the business's goods and services.
- *Search engine marketing* – also referred to as search marketing or SEM – is a particular aspect of digital marketing that aims to understand and consciously guide the behaviour of prospective buyers when they are using search engines. Search engine marketing then incorporates the development of content to trigger positive responses from search engine algorithms as well as to engage individuals.

  There are two primary types of search engine marketing. The first is described as search engine optimisation (SEO), organic SEO or natural search, and focuses on improving the content of a website to be appealing first to its intended audience and, as a consequence, to search engine algorithms. The second form of search engine marketing is described as paid search engine marketing or pay-per-click (PPC). PPC is the core activity of *Google's* search advertising business. Organisations with a level of digital business maturity will employ a mixture of both forms of search engine marketing.

- *Social media marketing* is the aspect of digital marketing that focuses on understanding and engaging the buyer persona through social media use. Social media marketing involves activity on a consciously selected combination of social media networks that are most relevant to your buyer persona. Social media marketing follows search engine marketing in having both organic and paid approaches that are distinct. As more social media channels seek to monetise their business models, the paid aspect of social media marketing will become more dominant.
- *Mobile marketing* refers to an organisation's digital marketing activities that facilitate customer engagement through mobile devices including smartphones, tablets and other mobile computing devices. As digital business itself becomes predominantly mobile, this form of marketing will become increasingly part of mainstream (digital) marketing.
- *Mobile commerce* includes any form of commerce that is specifically transacted through mobile devices. Specific forms of commerce may be more appropriate for certain sectors where purchases are more immediate and smaller in scale, for example, takeaway food delivery, public transport tickets and access to physical tourist and public attractions. Mobile commerce is growing at a significantly faster pace than other forms of electronic commerce.

These core terms relating to search engine, social media and digital marketing are clearly interrelated concepts that cannot be read in isolation from the overall activities, strategy or vision of any organisation. Figure 1.3 shows the close connection between and interrelationships of these terms.

1.3 Success and failure in digital marketing

Through a combination of continuous change, the introduction of new technologies and the business immaturity of existing technologies, the adoption of search engine and social media activity into an organisation's marketing mix has not always been successfully realised. The Buyer Persona Spring is a dynamic model that delivers success and manages potential failure to minimise any detrimental impact on the organisation. Recognising the hallmarks of success and failure in all types of organisations is an instructive process in developing your own organisation's digital strategy.

During the period of the so-called *dot-com bubble* or *Internet bubble*, which occurred between 1997 and 2000, thousands of Internet-based companies failed. This period of recent history is an ever present warning to all businesses about the importance of using, and actively engaging in, robust business planning and management techniques irrespective of whether they are being applied to a traditional or digital business.

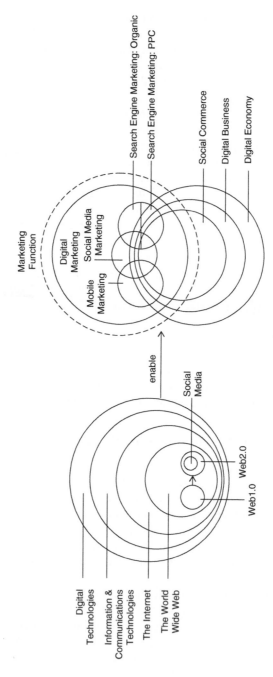

Figure 1.3 A visualisation of the interrelationship between the key terms used in this book

Recognising patterns of failure

An indicative company failure during the dot-com bubble was *Boo.com. Boo.com* aimed to create a global online fashion store and brand that served the needs of contemporary consumers. However, having spent $US 188 million in six months it was declared bankrupt in May 2000. The key factors in *Boo.com*'s rapid failure was its over-ambition – in a relatively unknown market, the lack of sufficient capital to sustain it through its establishment period and most significantly the degree to which it failed to exert clear managerial control. The company planned to reach $US 100 million in sales in the first year, but did not consider the sheer number of customers it would need to achieve this volume of sales, the cost of attracting each new consumer and the average cost of each transaction.

The company's attempt to use the most innovative and sophisticated technological solutions was, on reflection, a high-risk strategy that also contributed to its failure. *Boo.com* offered each customer the ability to virtually model the items of clothing they were considering buying. The technology behind the virtual showroom was resource intensive and required high-speed Internet connectivity, which – in 2000 – was not widely available. *Boo.com* was also overly ambitious in developing its international reach. The company tried to start up simultaneously in 18 countries – a task that was at the same time beyond the capabilities of *Amazon* or *Google.* A further impact on *Boo.com*'s chances of success was a six-month technical delay in the development of the online platform. During this initial delay the company also committed to maintaining significant stock levels and paying its employees' salaries. As a fashion retailer, the stock quickly became dated and the staff could not do any meaningful work that contributed to company revenues while the platform was unavailable. *Boo.com* went into receivership with $US 25 million of debt.

There are many other possible case studies of failed Internet ventures. Some of these failures were based on managerial or financial factors, others related to poor marketing decisions or a lack of understanding regarding their buyer persona. *Pets.com, Startups.com* and *Lastminute.com* all faced similar challenges to *Boo.com* and, in turn, each organisation failed to successfully exploit digital technologies in a way that was relevant and that realised genuine value for their buyer personas.

More recent examples of poor decision making in social media are *Belvedere*, a French Vodka company that posted corporate messages on its *Facebook* and *Twitter* pages promoting the company's products. Unfortunately, the message included a scene of simulated sexual assault and resulted in significant negative feedback from *Belvedere* community members. Following the initial reaction of users, *Belvedere* removed the advertisement and posted a lightly worded apology, which stated:

> *'We apologize to any of our fans who were offended by our recent tweet. We continue to be an advocate of safe and responsible drinking.'*

However, this statement was seen by users as being too weak an apology. The former senior editor of *The Atlantic*, Megan McArdle, summarised the community's concerns very clearly in a single tweet:

> *'Fascinated by Belvedere Vodka's non-apology apology, which seems to assume that most of their customers think rape is awesome.'*

The examples of *Belvedere* and *Boo.com* provide some initial guidance for planning your own organisation's strategy. Both examples reveal the close and constant interplay between technology and people. In digital marketing, people and their opinions, emotions, ethics and attitudes inevitably dominate over technology – no matter how advanced or simple to use. The experiences of these organisations can be summarised as the five signals for imminent strategic failure in a digital business. Your organisation needs to consciously avoid these signals.

Table 1.1 Signals of failure for a digital strategy

Signals to avoid	Response and remedy
1. Lack of a digital strategy or operational plan	Primarily characterised by impulsive digital marketing actions with no assessment of the costs or risks. For example, a website requires continuous maintenance to keep the content relevant and the site secure and each social media profile must be constantly monitored.
2. Lack of sufficient skilled staff for digital activities	Digital marketing and digital business is a constantly changing field. There is a need for continuous learning and a holistic understanding of all digital activities in relation to the buyer persona.
3. Lack of high-level organisational sponsorship	The senior leadership responsible for driving the vision and mission of the organisation can undervalue the role of digital technology within the business. Digital developments extend beyond marketing or IT. In order to set the right strategic aims and to support the creation of effective digital strategies, new organisational structures as well as infrastructures are needed. The structures will necessarily incorporate multidisciplinary teams to understand the buyer persona and respond with the most appropriate solutions.
4. Lack of originality	Often the organisational approach to digital business is one of 'me too'. Time and effort must be dedicated to understanding the buyer persona and how an organisation's goods and services are offered.
5. Lack of agility	Digital technologies and the buyer persona can both change rapidly. Organisations must be technologically proactive to market conditions in order to continue to deliver unique value to their buyer persona.

Recognising patterns of success

Case Study 1.1 *Happeak*

Alongside the history of digital business failure there are also many examples of success that extend far beyond the large and 'new' global brands of *Google, Amazon, eBay* or *Alibaba*.

Happeak began as a boutique shop in the old town of Vilnius (Lithuania) in 2008. In 2010 it launched its own product line for children and moved to a large shopping centre. Today *Happeak* is a well-known local brand for children's clothing, gradually increasing its exports to other European countries including Finland, Latvia, Italy and the UK.

For *Happeak*, the digital environment is an integrated one that incorporates advertising, e-commerce and engagement with the buyer persona. The company's owner finds it is easy to use digital marketing to incorporate activities in this way, as it requires no intermediaries to manage, and costs can be controlled and kept to a minimum. Most of the day-to-day time allocated to digital marketing in *Happeak* involves keeping content up to date and engaging with customers. Because of the integration and transparency of the business's activities, digital marketing offers a tangible return on investment (ROI).

For *Happeak*'s owner, the key benefits brought by being digital are:

- the relatively low cost base compared to the fixed costs of physical premises;
- the possibility to reach new and geographically diverse customers;
- a dynamic relationship between *Happeak* and the buyer persona;
- quick response times to enquiries and questions.

Dambrauskė, the owner of the company, observes that,

> When expanding a business to use digital channels it is important to have a long-term plan that is based on research evidence. It is also important to constantly evolve and listen to the customers – who are always right.

The largest investment for the business has involved online purchasing facilities. Dambrauskė recognises that,

> Our business is not just e-commerce; we have an online shop and a physical store. We have a typical e-commerce challenge – to

convince the prospective buyer that you are a reliable and trustworthy organisation. It is also difficult to achieve success on the digital market if your product prices are higher than the average price.

However, e-commerce technology is only the mechanism for transacting sales. A lot of effort is also dedicated to attracting consumers. *Happeak* uses social networks, *Google* AdWords and joint projects with partners to drive consumers to the e-commerce aspects of the business. *Happeak* has a very active *Facebook* page that is used for intensive interaction with individual customers. The company also uses *Pinterest.*

According to Dambrauskė, *Pinterest* 'is not a business tool – it is a nice addition to image-making'.

Pinterest and *Facebook* as well as *Twitter* and other social networking tools are used actively and constantly by *Happeak*, a minimum of three or four times each week.

Happeak's owner observes,

If you choose e-business, then do it very carefully. I would suggest your business must be accompanied by digital opportunities. People like to search online, but most often buy personally. But at least digital will give you the opportunity to reach new markets and attract new clients. Revenues will follow.

Happeak highlights the importance of social media as pivotal channels for digital marketing. However, the adoption of social media has created hype similar to that seen in the dot-com boom of the late 1990s. Advocates for the primacy of social media have claimed that these networks are more important than an organisation's website. However, this type of 'social media first' approach creates an atmosphere of continuous catch-up. Every time a new social media network becomes popular, the organisation is necessarily forced to add another channel of communication. The human and financial effort invested into building an individual social media profile is also subsequently lost when a network becomes less relevant to the target customers. Avoiding the dangers of overhyped media is part of an organisation's sustainable strategy for digital business in general and social media specifically.

Sustainable digital business strategies will usually include investment in a website and a blog, and the repurposing of this content for amplification on the most relevant social media platforms. As your organisation moves towards data-driven decision making, social media network activity and engagement will both become good indicators of the trust that is extended towards your organisation. High levels of trust require a sustained investment of time and effort by your organisation, with the risk that a single wrong action has the potential to seriously damage all your previous positive efforts.

Learning from previous mistakes in social media communication, including those of *Belvedere Vodka* and *Boo.com* as well as the success experienced by *Happeak* and more recognisable global digital brands, highlights five rules for social media success:

1   The buyer persona can be accurately targeted using social media channels.
2   The buyer persona expects sincere two-way communication with 'their' brands.
3   The buyer persona will immediately react to poor messages that denigrate 'their' brand – including messages from the brand itself.
4   The buyer persona will quickly spread negative word of mouth about 'their' brand if they are mistreated.
5   The buyer persona will resist the most blatant advertising messages on social media.

The range of online activities used by *Happeak* highlights seven important considerations for organisations evolving to become digitally mature businesses (Table 1.2).

A McKinsey report also discussed by Hirt and Willmott (2014) outlines seven traits for a successful digital organisation that should inform the development of your own digital business strategy.

1.   Be unreasonably aspirational. Many organisations treat digital activities as an extension to their existing business. Be aspirational in the use of digital channels and respect these as value creation channels.
2.   Acquire new capabilities. You do not necessarily need to concentrate on developing digital talents internally. As an alternative, attract digital talent from other industries or from the crowd.
3.   'Ring fence' and cultivate talent. Digital talents need 'space for creativity'. If your talent is buried in daily updates, development documentation or uninspired corporate communications, they may 'wither'.
4.   Challenge everything. Being successful means questioning everything – goals, situation, solution, means and platform. Successful organisations generate unique value for the buyer persona by stepping away from historical norms.
5.   Be quick and data driven. The digital environment is a rapidly changing environment; however, it is also a data-rich environment. Always endeavour

Table 1.2 The seven steps towards improving digital engagements

Stage	Actions
Plan	Activities should be planned as campaigns that are implemented, tracked and evaluated so that future activities benefit and build upon the lessons learned.
Budget	Budget to establish and support the ongoing technical operation of the organisation's digital environments. Budget to ensure ongoing security and correct functionality.
Manage	Day-to-day content management of an organisation's digital environment does not require major technical knowledge but it must be managed.
Buyer Persona	The initial buyer persona should focus on local users. But remember that there are no geographical limits and your content also has a global reach.
Share	Content, including the organisation's website, must share information about the company, its products and its services.
Engage	Use a relevant mix of content and engagement, including the Web, as well as social networks, and review sites that are used by the buyer persona. Attract, inform and persuade. Create a community for the buyer persona.
Align	Online and offline marketing and engagement actions should be aligned.

to make data-driven decisions. If the data is unavailable, then question its absence.

6. Follow the money. Digital transformation doesn't always mean investing in new revenue streams. You can also save money. Integration, co-creation and crowdsourcing may all generate more efficient ways of working.
7. Be obsessed with your buyer persona. Your buyer persona has constantly increasing expectations. The good service you previously offered may now be the 'norm' or even below average for the sector.

All of these traits of successful digital business can be summarised by the simple statement: 'Be Strategic'. As a supporting statement, 'Be Holistic' emphasises the need to consider all of your organisation's activities in your drive to become a sustainable 'marketing first' digital business.

1.4 The Digital Business Maturity Model

The history of digital and social media marketing to date can be categorised into four distinct phases. These phases also reflect the continuous evolution of digital business. Each phase can be hallmarked by the principal technologies that were used to deliver marketing messages and the relationship of these technologies to the overall development and popularity of the Internet. The quickest method for identifying the developing digital sophistication of a business overall can be discerned in the look, feel and user interactions of their web pages.

- Phase one: Brochureware
  This initial phase of development introduced the first websites. The model for marketing activity at this stage was to create the digital analogies of printed brochures. Early restrictions on commercial activity through some networks meant that even brochureware could be seen as a risky activity. Some organisations still retain this mindset and take a largely broadcast-based approach to their digital marketing messages that offers no form of two-way communication with customers.
- Phase two: Tradigital
  Tuten and Solomon (2012) label the second period of digital marketing 'Tradigital'. This phase is based around concepts of push marketing that were already well established within traditional marketing. Tradigital used new tools to share content that are similar in style and intent to television and direct mail marketing campaigns. This period is characterised as one of digitally enabled mass and targeted marketing activities, such as banner advertising, microsites, email campaigns and search marketing.
- Phase three: Social media marketing
  The development of social technologies – often described as Web 2.0 – brought marketing actions based around a pull approach, with organisations utilising, for example, online social networks and the capability to encourage sharing, rating and reviewing to enhance other digital marketing activities (Pomirleanu et al., 2013).
- Phase four: Engagement marketing
  Engagement marketing is characterised by the development of engaging content and the use of tools and techniques that bring prospects into deep contact with the organisation. These engagements can include augmented reality, gamification and 'smart-everything' through the burgeoning Internet of Things. New technologies that rely on high-speed mobile Internet connections, including wearables and drones, open up the prospect for still more digital marketing techniques.

Through this phased evolution, content has become more customised and interactive as well as increasingly immersive. Irrespective of the increased technical capacity required by new marketing techniques – such as customised video content – the aim of each marketing action still remains to capture and engage the attention of the buyer persona.

The changes in approach and perspective, brought about through increasingly sophisticated forms of digital marketing, also mean that organisations are becoming more digitally mature overall. With increasing digital marketing activity there is an opportunity to recognise the pivotal role that data plays in the overall management of an organisation. The self-aware and digitally mature business is then able to rapidly and proactively respond, through data-driven decision making, to the ever-changing circumstances of the buyer persona.

The uptake of digital business practices includes the measurement of business performance and produces organisational change. The Digital Business Maturity Model (Figure 1.4 and Table 1.3) presents broad phases of development without proposing a single deterministic route or process of adoption. Many external influences act upon the development of individual digital business maturity, including existing policy frameworks, industry sector levels of competitiveness and business collaboration, relative levels and quality of education and training, the presence of an entrepreneurial culture and the robustness of national and regional ICT infrastructures. This means that your individual steps as an organisation towards full digital business maturity will vary in the details. However, the most ready route to digital maturity for a small business is achieved through taking a 'marketing first' approach to digital business.

The majority of organisations currently conduct their digital marketing activities within Level 1 and Level 2 of the Digital Business Maturity Model. More highly developed stages of the model move your organisation towards becoming a complete digital business, a situation that will become increasingly important for your organisation to achieve in order to remain competitive. Constant experimentation and evaluation is crucial for successful digital marketing and digital business, as there is an external backdrop of new tools

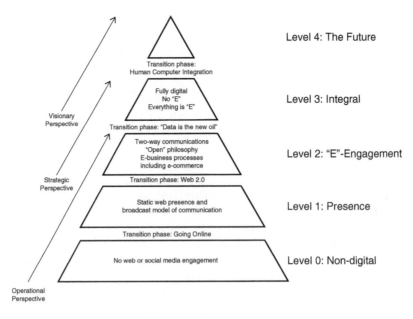

Figure 1.4 The Digital Business Maturity Model

Table 1.3 A description of the Digital Business Maturity Model

Phase	Description of phase
Level 0 – Non-digital	'Traditional' business. These businesses are not online in any meaningful way. Any presence may have been created robotically by one of the many online business directories that pollute *Google* and the other search engine results pages (SERPs). However, a business owner has no control over or input into the information being presented about their own organisation.
Level 1 – Presence	The presence level of digital business uses digital technologies to broadcast untargeted messages to an ill-defined audience. No active interaction or two-way communication can be observed at this level.
Level 2 – 'E'-engagement	An organisation has an operational information system that allows some reporting and integration of activities between multiple channels. Increasing efforts to achieve operational efficiencies and gain competitive advantage through the analysis and interpretation of data.
Level 3 – Integral	Most of the organisation's functions are digital. Decision making in these digital businesses is data-driven and value is being created through use and re-use of the organisation's digital assets.
Level 4 – The future	A fully integrated data-driven digital business with day-to-day functions being driven by predefined business rules and potentially the application of artificial intelligence.

and techniques that are continuously becoming available to all organisations, including your competitors. Until each new tool or technique is tried, experimented with and documented, there is no evidence to understand the individual use case or the prospective specific benefits to your organisation. Knowing when to stop using a tool or a technique is equally important, as digital marketing and digital business become increasingly sophisticated and integrated within the overall operations of a digital business. All of these decisions should also be part of your long-term strategic planning rather than simply reactions to immediate environmental change, the availability of new tools or the actions of your competitors.

1.5 The buyer persona

As digital environments present ever more opportunities for marketing and business generally, it is increasingly important for your organisation to understand your buyer persona. All organisations aim to achieve favourable behaviours from their intended consumers and customers. These behaviours can vary from heightened awareness to a purchase decision and repeat custom. Understanding and responding to these behaviour patterns and the decision-making journey is how you create new opportunities for your organisation. We represent these opportunities in the Buyer Persona Spring as the focus and drive of your activities. The buyer persona builds on the research and writings of a range of different authors who have all tackled the question of understanding consumer decision making and the journey that consumers take towards a positive outcome for your organisation.

The classic marketing approach defines the consumer journey or consumer decision-making activities as a linear process undertaken over several stages (Figure 1.5).

However, several alternatives to this model have been proposed to identify consumer behaviour within digital environments. Marsden (2011) supports the classical approach, but suggests that the behaviour is more cyclical and that it iterates over three phases.

According to Marsden (2011), the journey starts from the recognition of a problem and is followed by a consideration set or a dynamic decision loop. Consideration leads to purchase and post-purchase decisions that form a loyalty loop. Marsden (2011) builds his proposition on Edelman (2010) and McKinsey's consulting research by explaining a shift from the traditional linear approach to a more complex consumer decision-making journey that emphasises the cyclical nature of consumer decisions.

Owyang (2012) also supports a cyclical representation of the consumer journey, and sees the journey as dynamic and being influenced by a number of factors, including:

- recent development and advancement in technology deployment;
- change of media;
- increasing power of word of mouth.

A more recent approach to understanding the consumer journey is offered by Bosomworth (Smart Insights, 2015) and is based on the ZMOT (Zero Moment of Truth) theory developed by *Google* and McKinsey's research.

According to Bosomworth (Smart Insights, 2015), the consumer journey is emotional and triggered by various factors, including advertising, friends' comments and word of mouth. This positions Digital and Social Media Marketing

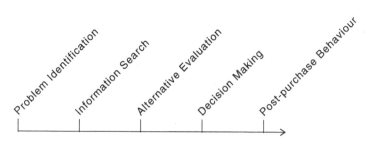

Figure 1.5 Consumer decision making

actions as having an important role in the initiation and leading of consumers through the entire journey.

For Bosomworth (Smart Insights, 2015), a trigger is followed by a consideration moment, as every consumer is individual in their preference and needs. The consideration moment relates to the information that is required to make decisions. At this point, a consumer will deploy search engines, social networks and their own personal networks in order to obtain this information. When a purchase decision is taken, it is followed by a second moment of truth, which is when consumers start consuming or utilising a product or service and then form their own opinion. The second moment of truth may then also serve as the trigger or ZMOT for another consumer. Solis (2014) similarly describes an Ultimate Moment of Truth (UMOT):

> The UMOT signifies the instant when a customer creates content based on an experience with the product or service and publishes it in their community or network of preference for others to find. The intention of doing so is a combination of self-expression and the desire to inform others. This experience then becomes discoverable for anyone who searches that network. And in many cases, these experiences also populate *Google*'s search results. Said another way, the Ultimate Moment of Truth becomes the next person's Zero Moment of Truth.
>
> (Solis, 2014)

An alternative approach to understanding the consumer journey is to consider how consumers behave within online ecosystems. Online ecosystems, or click-ecosystems, describe a consumer's behaviour or movement between search engines, media sites, other intermediaries and competitors. All of these approaches attempt to systematise the relationship you have with your customers. By systematising the relationship, it becomes more manageable and able to be controlled.

The challenge for your organisation is to understand what influences individuals to show interest in your goods and services. Who is buying your goods and services? Who is using them? What are the influencers that bring customers back to you, particularly given the vast array of global alternatives now available to them?

Understanding this combination of behaviours means developing and understanding your buyer persona. The buyer persona is your account of your ideal customer and consumer. This account of the buyer persona is descriptive and detailed. It will include a description of the preferences, interests and background of your ideal customer. The buyer persona recognises the situation in which this customer is positioned in terms of demographics, location, situation and aspirations. However, the account is fact-based and must draw on evidence from your own organisational experience as well as relevant details gathered from external sources. While the majority of your customers, consumers and influencers will never completely align with your buyer persona, by consistently addressing the buyer persona you will create a genuine rapport with a range of customers and consumers who recognise and identify with the buyer persona you have defined, and this will, in turn, build a meaningful trust-based engagement with them that persists over time.

1.6 Tools for Digital and Social Media Marketing

There is a number of recognisable and common tools that enable strategically working with the buyer persona.

PESTLE

A key tool for developing an understanding of your organisation within the wider external environment is the PESTLE analysis. The acronym is an abbreviation of:

- P for Political
- E for Economic
- S for Social
- T for Technological
- L for Legal
- E for Environmental.

Further refinement of the PESTLE acronym has included an additional E to cover Ethical considerations. For each of these parameters, the impact of any changes is evaluated in relation to your organisation's current situation. The PESTLE analysis is a dynamic tool and one that offers the opportunity to conduct a regular sense check of the external environment against the needs and expectations of your buyer persona in relation to your current goods and services.

SWOT Analysis

The SWOT analysis is a well-known tool for assessing the internal and external circumstances of an organisation. For many organisations, the SWOT analysis is a mechanism for conducting a ready assessment of their situation in relation to the market generally and their competitors. The SWOT analysis is presented as a 2x2 grid. Half of the grid relates to the internal situation and half relates to the external situation. Split in the other direction, half of the grid relates to positives and half relates to negatives (Table 1.4).

Table 1.4 The principles of a SWOT analysis

SWOT analysis	Positive factors	Negative factors
Internal factors	**Strengths**	**Weaknesses**
External factors	**Opportunities**	**Threats**

The aim of a SWOT analysis is to recognise, as an organisation, what you are good at, and to balance this against what others are better at than you are (Table 1.4).

As with the PESTLE analysis, the SWOT analysis is dynamic and, with ever-changing circumstances, should be utilised regularly by your organisation to maintain a strategic perspective on your objectives.

Ansoff Matrix

Analysis of your own organisation's current situation, and the impact of the ever-changing external situation, provides the foundation for developing your digital business maturity. Both the PESTLE analysis and the SWOT analysis set you up to examine the opportunities and prospective future direction for your organisation. Arguably, the most widely used strategic framework for assessing new opportunities is the Ansoff Matrix (Ansoff, 1957) (Table 1.5). The Ansoff Matrix is based on identification of product and market opportunities that are both existing and new. The Ansoff Matrix produces a visual assessment of the four resultant combinations that can then be used to determine potential strategic directions for the organisation.

Examples of each quadrant in the Ansoff Matrix:

*   Market penetration decision – continue to perform in an existing market with an existing product, e.g. opening e-commerce channels to sell existing products.
*   Market development decision – access new market segments with existing products, e.g. localised website, e-commerce, delivered in several languages to reach consumers in other countries or using other platforms such as *eBay* or *Amazon* to offer products through other channels.
*   Product development decision – establish new products or services and offer them to an existing market, e.g. create a product information service for your specific market sector that provides answers in real time.
*   Diversification decision – create new products that are offered to new markets, e.g. a virtual service for new international markets.

The Ansoff Matrix guides organisational strategic planning and decision making by disentangling the complexity of prospective future business directions in an orderly and structured way. The Ansoff Matrix, however, offers no guidance as to how to set out your objectives or to measure the success of your strategic decisions.

Table 1.5 The Ansoff Matrix

Ansoff Matrix	*Existing products*	*New products*
Existing markets	**Market penetration**	**Product development**
New markets	**Market development**	**Diversity**

An increasingly common framework for setting out what you hope to achieve by becoming a mature digital business is described by defining SMART objectives. SMART refers to Specific, Measurable, Attainable, Realistic and Timely. With your knowledge of

- your current situation as an organisation, obtained through a SWOT analysis,
- your assessment of the external environment – drawn from a PESTLE assessment,
- coupled with the prospective directions you have identified – through the use of an Ansoff Matrix,

you are now in a position to define your objectives. The setting of SMART objectives provides a realistic and manageable framework that enables, even encourages, achievable ambition. SMART objectives also set out the limits of your ambition in a way that can be measured and that ensures success can be recognised when it has been achieved (Figure 1.6).

Organisations focus on three specific aspects of performance to measure their success in a digital environment. These contexts are often referred to as the three Vs (Visibility, Value, Volume) and can become the basis for individual SMART objectives within your organisation:

- Visibility: If your organisation focuses your digital marketing efforts on building awareness for the buyer persona, typical metrics measuring success in this area relate to the number of visitors brought to your own digital properties through different digital channels. Measurement of this V includes, for example, presence on search engines for relevant search terms, total number of visitors over a certain period, number of visitors from a particular channel, bounce rate and the number of returning visitors.
- Value: If your organisation is focusing your efforts on selling to your buyer persona, the typical metrics for measuring success are the cost to acquire customers, total conversions, customer retention rate and average order size.
- Volume: If your organisation is concerned with building direct relationships through the buyer persona, the typical metrics for assessing success are the number of customer engagements, the overall customer experience and customer reviews.

The selection and combination of appropriate metrics depends on your organisation's digital marketing strategy and current level of digital business maturity. Typically, small businesses tend to use simple metrics and tools. However, more ambitious and longer-term goals require more sophisticated metrics and measurement methods.

The sophistication and complexity that higher ambitions place upon your organisation can be managed by tackling the issues in smaller and more

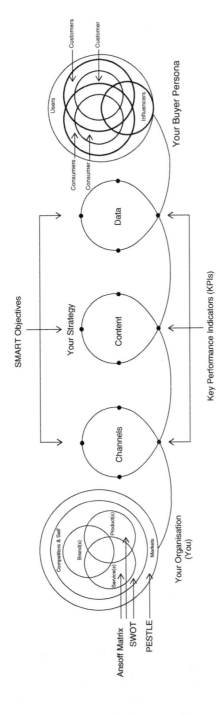

Figure 1.6 The relationship of strategic analysis tools to the Buyer Persona Spring

manageable pieces. This book applies the well-established concepts of action learning to understand digital marketing as a business activity that must be constantly evaluated and maintained. This iterative cycle of activity is a principle that is embedded in the Buyer Persona Spring. This means that your organisation's digital marketing plans can be strategically committed to and then broken down into discrete time-constrained campaigns. Each of these campaigns is a project which then has its own indicators of success. The four stages of action learning allow you to systematically undertake your digital activities in a way that can be managed and assessed. These four stages are Planning, Action, Monitoring and Evaluation:

1   Planning – at the outset, your organisation uses market research to inform the structure and purpose of a campaign and plans the start and end date. Key activities are defined, including the channels that will be used, and how these activities will be tracked is set out. The objectives of the campaign are specified, and the manner by which these will be measured and evaluated is identified at the same time. How campaign success will be evidenced is made clear with the definition of key performance indicators (KPIs).
2   Action – the activities are implemented based on the plan.
3   Monitoring – feedback from the action is captured. The already defined indicators of success are observed for the campaign. These indicators can take many forms, including the total number of visitors, completed actions or closed sales. Other indicators might include positive and negative comments from buyers or visitors.
4   Evaluation – based on the agreed KPIs and the feedback data that has been captured, consideration is then given to what should be stopped, modified, increased or continued as an activity.

This cycle of planning, action, monitoring and evaluation is repeated continuously. The process is systematic, with the primary objective of improving the engagement, communication and interaction with the buyer persona. The activity that is undertaken to achieve this objective is done in ways that can be evidenced, are measurable and most importantly are positive, and that produce value for the organisation.

The tools of business analysis and their benefits for forming a digital marketing strategy are examined in greater detail in Chapter 2.

1.7 Summary

This chapter outlines the key concepts and marketing actions that can make organisations more effective, more impactful, more sustainable and more strategic within a 'marketing first' digital business model. Digital technologies are becoming an integral part of an organisation's activities as well as in modern consumer life. Many organisations face digital transformation challenges and are seeking the best opportunities to utilise digital technologies and digital marketing benefits.

The key lesson of this chapter is that there is no 'one size fits all' approach when it comes to developing digital marketing communications. Indeed, a number of factors determined by your buyer persona need to be considered over the long term. This perspective is itself an important conceptual starting point, as it recognises marketing as an integral business function and a key mechanism that drives a business towards a fully digital approach.

The Buyer Persona Spring reflects the strategic perspective necessary for successful digital marketing. The representation of the organisation in the Buyer Persona Spring acknowledges the influence of external factors, including competitors, and connects with the buyer persona through an iterative, self-reflective cycle of campaigns in combination with the use of specific digital marketing tools and techniques.

Digital approaches to business remain challenging, and must compete with the opportunities in the physical world. Therefore, organisations must clearly demonstrate the value of their digital offerings to consumers and select appropriate metrics to understand when and if their efforts bring benefits to the organisation. A strategic, iterative and reflective approach is the only way to reduce risk and to continue to keep digital marketing innovations relevant to any organisation.

1.8 References

Ansoff, H.I. (1957) Strategies for diversification. *Harvard Business Review, 35*(5), 113–24.

Edelman, D.C. (2010) Branding in the digital age. *Harvard Business Review, 88*(12), 14–18. Palgrave Macmillan. doi: 10.1108/eb040166.

Hirt, M. and Willmott, P. (2014) Strategic principles for competing in the digital age. *McKinsey Quarterly* (May), 1–13.

Marsden, P. (2011) *F-commerce. Selling on Facebook: The opportunities for consumer brands.* Syzygy Group.

Owyang, J. (2012) *Strategy: Lead the dynamic consumer decision journey.* www.altimetergroup.com

Pomirleanu, N., Schibrowsky, J.A., Peltier, J. and Nill, A. (2013) A review of Internet marketing research over the past 20 years and future research direction. *Journal of Research in Interactive Marketing, 7*(3), 166–81.

Smart Insights (2015) *ZMOT.* www.smartinsights.com

Solis, B. (2014). *Defining the zero moment of truth.* www.briansolis.com/2014/09/new-era-seo-zero-moment-truth-defined-shared-customer-experiences/

Tuten, T.L. and Solomon, M.R. (2012) *Social media marketing.* Pearson Education; FT Prentice-Hall.

2 Identifying business needs

Milanka Slavova, University of National and World Economy (UNWE), Bulgaria

2.0 Learning objectives

In this chapter you will learn how to:

- recognise external factors that impact on your digital marketing strategy;
- recognise internal factors that may influence your digital marketing activities;
- translate the aspirations of your long-term plans into practical projects;
- develop an organisational culture of continuous improvement;
- re-evaluate your current business model from a buyer persona perspective.

2.1 Digital marketing strategy

A long-term strategic marketing plan is essential to the success of your digital business. A strategic perspective (three to five years) ensures that your organisation does not become solely reactive to the decisions of your competitors or the introduction of unexpected technologies or tools. A good strategy – for any purpose – will be sufficiently robust to resist the short-term impact of external changes in the market. At the same time, your strategy should be sufficiently flexible to enable a planned, considered response to external changes that can bring additional benefit and value.

Before you can implement a digital marketing strategy, you need to identify your organisational needs. Understanding these needs will then shape the actions you implement while ensuring that they are precisely suited to your organisation and meet the needs of your buyer persona. The Buyer Persona Spring recognises that both your organisation and your buyer persona are complex. As a result, the relationship that you build between the two must be dynamic and sufficiently flexible.

You must first analyse the external situation and the internal environment of your organisation (Figure 2.1). With this insight you can then identify your buyer persona, including the products and services that are wanted and needed. Once you have an understanding of the buyer persona and your own organisation in place you can define strategies for bringing the two together. By

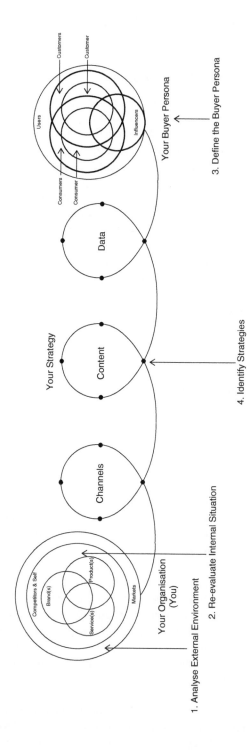

Figure 2.1 Creating a digital marketing strategy

completing this series of actions you will have placed your organisation in a strong position to use digital marketing successfully.

2.2 Analysing the external environment

The external environment includes all the external forces that influence your organisation and its activities. These external forces cannot be directly controlled, but they can be identified and analysed. By doing this analysis, you will understand the influencers on your customers' changing needs, be able to take advantage of new opportunities ahead of your competitors and anticipate problems in advance. For example, when the demand for online shopping began to grow, many direct selling companies needed to respond, but in a way that minimised the negative impact on their sales force in physical stores. Some organisations created a solution by offering different product lines for digital sales from those available offline.

To give structure to the analysis of the environment, many marketers suggest a separate examination of the macro- and micro-environmental factors (Kotler and Armstrong, 2012). Macro-environmental factors include demographics, economics, technology, political and legal forces and social factors, while micro-environmental factors include suppliers, resellers, customers, competition and the general public.

Analysing the macro-environment

The tool most often used to explore the macro-business environment is PESTLE, which includes external legal, environmental and, according to some authors, ethical forces.

The demographic environment

People are your market, and they adjust their attitudes, perspectives, ethical position and worldviews constantly. Whether it is caused by changing age structures in particular regions, geographic population shifts, shifting levels of education, improving digital skills or shifting opinions about ethical behaviours or population diversity, your market is always in flux.

At one end of the generational spectrum are the Millennials or 'Generation Y'. According to most marketing analysts, Millennials are generally regarded as born-to-digital customers who expect more of everything, including more control over their experience with products and services. At the other end of the spectrum, the requirements of an aging population for digital products and services are different again. In some markets, 'silver surfers' are one of the growing demographics who might be physically restricted in mobility but who are affluent and digitally connected.

There are also those who are excluded from the digital world because of low levels of digital skill and little direct access to the digital economy. This lack of access and skill is often a result of disadvantages, such as poor levels of education, unemployment and other forms of economic or social inequality.

Understanding how your target audiences are engaging with your products is essential. It allows you to adapt your offering accordingly and informs the construction of your buyer persona. This approach to marketing research is called *user experience testing and observation.*

One example of this approach to marketing research is the way that the Royal College of Art, UK worked with Samsung to solve the problem that older people have in setting up a smartphone. Their design solution emerged from co-creation sessions with older people and resulted in the use of a hard-back 'storybook' containing the SIM card and battery within its pages, which guided the user through an understandable narrative to set up their phone (Myerson, 2014).

The potential for the aging population in the digital economy sees companies design digital services that correspond to the cognitive abilities of the older generation, and highlights that, if you understand how your market is engaging with your organisation and its products and services, you are in an ideal position to better meet their needs.

The political environment

The political situation in your target market plays a role in shaping your buyer persona. The European Union (EU) has attempted to harmonise national practices to encourage trade within Europe, but every country still has specific issues that require consideration.

From legal regulations, such as safety, tax laws, social security expenses and retirement age, to aspects such as privacy laws, you need to know the rules of the countries you are working in. For Digital and Social Media Marketing, the most significant rules and regulations are connected with issues of privacy, data collection and how customer information is used.

For example:

- In the USA, the Federal Trade Commission (FTC) requires Internet businesses to post a privacy policy that explains how the company uses any collected personal information.
- In the UK, the Committee of Advertising Practice (CAP) is regulated by the Advertising Standards Authority (ASA), which includes general rules that state advertising must be responsible, and must not mislead or offend, and has specific rules that cover advertising to children and ads for specific sectors like alcohol, gambling, motoring, health and financial products.
- The EU Consumer Rights Directive (European Commission, 2014) is designed to protect consumers when shopping online. Prices have to be clearly displayed and businesses have to explicitly disclose the total cost of the product or service as well as any extra fees or delivery charges.

The political decisions of governments can also influence the access that customers have to digital channels. These are decisions often brought about as the result of social unrest. For example, in 2015 Turkey banned access to *Twitter* and *YouTube* after users published images of a prosecutor held hostage by far-left militants.

The economic environment

The economic environment includes rates of growth, inflation, interest rates, exchange rates and the level of unemployment. Generally, during periods of economic growth, the demand for an organisation's products and services expand, while during stages of decline sales will decrease primarily because consumer income shrinks. Lower income levels are also a hallmark for wider economic downturns.

Understanding the economic environment enables an organisation to position itself, in relation to their buyer persona, with accuracy and to maximum effect. The global scope of digital marketing tools enables an organisation to address a changing economic situation with immediate beneficial impact. For example, a florist based in Poland, where the economy is in a downturn, might consider targeting the wedding market in Germany, where the economy may be growing or at least showing a lesser downturn than Poland.

An important reason for doing an economic analysis is to understand the impact of these forces on consumer purchasing power and the ways in which different groups of buyers consume. A major trend in the post-2008 economic crisis was price-conscious purchasing. Digital technologies, including the introduction of fully digital supply chain management, allow dynamic pricing based on current availability and quantity. This is a practice already used by most airlines as well as many hotel groups and chains. A similar impact to price-conscious purchasing was felt in high street stores. Customers are freely offered an opportunity to see the goods and try them out, but the practice of 'showrooming' means that once a customer has identified the product they are interested in they will then often go online and place the order with a cheaper online retailer before even leaving the physical premises of a high street store. Attracting and retaining the price-conscious customer requires pricing strategies that bring them longer-term economic benefits. This may come in the form of, for example, rewarding the return visitor, offering monthly payment schemes, 24-hour sales or discount codes. Understanding the economic influences of customers will also shape your buyer persona.

The technological environment

Consideration of the external technical environment is a key factor for digital marketing. In markets where digital penetration is high, consumers spend more time online and willingly engage in a wide variety of activities, including the creation of content. Consumers participate in more online social networks that, in turn, influence their purchasing behaviour. Mobile devices also allow consumers to communicate from everywhere and to access content in a variety of formats – video, audio, images and text. Physical location is no longer a constraint on consumers – their online communities and preferences increasingly make a greater impact on their decision making than specific physical influencers.

To speak to the customer in a digitally enabled world, you need to bring value to them in new ways, engage them with your brand and your organisation and increase the immediacy of the exchange (see Case Study 2.1).

Case Study 2.1 *Chobolabs* targets hard-core gamers using mobile devices

Established in 2011 by Bulgarians Deyan Vitanov and Petar Dobrev after selling a successful philanthropic start-up.

The goal of *Chobolabs* was to create a platform that would keep hard-core gamers 'on the edge of their seat'. Passionate gamers, Vitanov and Dobrev were frustrated by the lack of apps for their favourite games and believed that competitive multiplayer games could become a reality on mobile devices. Their aim was to create a 'unicorn' in Silicon Valley – an innovative start-up with a market value of over $US 1 billion dollars.

Vitanov and Dobrev developed a game engine that works on all platforms – iOS, Android, Windows and the Web. Unlike their competitors, the young entrepreneurs did not copy game designs from PCs or consoles. Their approach was based on the idea that 'mobile demands original thinking' because the display is smaller and customers are accustomed to using a touch screen. Aware that many hard-core gamers did not trust the mobile multiplayer games, Vitanov and Dobrev were convinced that mobility was a major advantage because it allows playing everywhere.

In 2014 *Chobolabs* attracted investors after demonstrating their idea and a rough prototype. The company successfully completed a $US 1.3 million round of funding to finance its first game. At the time of writing, *Chobolabs* are looking for engineering talents from all over the world, intending to create a team of 15 developers in Bulgaria and 10 in the USA.

Chobolabs intend to provide the game for free and to make profit on the sale of additional in-game items such as weapons and clothes. They plan to add a social flavour to the product by letting users play with friends, have a clan and organise tournaments with cash awards.

Currently, the platform is under continuous testing. Without any marketing efforts the beta version has been downloaded 300,000 times.

Source: www.chobolabs.com

Digital technologies enable you to quickly and continuously connect, collaborate and conduct business with your customers. To get the most out of them you need to understand the technological environment within which your organisation and your buyer persona operate. You need to understand how your customers access the Internet, how, what and when they purchase and the type of online experience they desire.

What works for one organisation will not necessarily work for another. For example, apps work well for companies who have a lot of repeat business. A florist specialising in weddings is likely to only encounter their customers once or twice in a lifetime. An app will bring little additional value to this small number of transactions. In contrast, a florist dealing regularly with wedding planners might find that an app can add significant value. Connecting the technological environment with the specifics of your organisation and the development of your buyer persona will contribute, in turn, to the strategies that you employ to bring your organisation and buyer persona closer together through the Buyer Persona Spring.

The opportunities that digital technologies enable will only continue to further empower the customers by allowing the individualisation of offerings on a global scale. This level of engagement will also increasingly become the expected norm. By learning your customers' online habits, your buyer persona will become more detailed and this will, in turn, enable your organisation to find new methods for appropriate engagement.

Environmental factors

Environmental factors include issues and phenomena such as natural resources, global warming, pollution control and the conservation of energy as well as other scarce resources.

Many organisations already use digital marketing to encourage environmentally friendly behaviour and to promote their own environmental efforts. For example, in May 2014 Unilever officially launched a digital marketing platform to promote its environmental protection efforts in China (Yining, 2014). The 'Small Action, Big Difference' campaign encouraged Chinese consumers to reduce energy consumption by turning off lights and printing documents on both sides of the paper. Consumers could access their profile and see their contributions on the popular social networks Weibo and WeChat as well as the campaign's official website (Yining, 2014).

Changes in ethical, social and cultural aspects

New social and cultural trends need to be continuously scanned to align digital marketing with the behaviours and expectations of consumers. Social and cultural changes can create shifts in consumer attitudes that can become opportunities or threats and sometimes both. There are many tools to help you systematically assess ethical, social and cultural changes, including analysis services such as *Think with Google*, *Google Trends* and *SocialBakers* as well as digital marketing communities such as #passion4digital and businessculture.org.

Although these aspects are closely related and generally change at a slow pace, they are each distinct and should be considered separately in your external analysis. Social aspects relate to the structures that guide our day-to-day lives including our education system, how we manage an organisation and the availability of public health care. Cultural aspects relate to those parts of our experience and knowledge that we share with each other. In traditional cultures, we might describe specifically shared practices as customs or traditions. In contemporary culture, we might similarly share a love of football (irrespective of the team we support). Ethical aspects relate to the boundaries of what we believe is acceptable, both socially – such as being late for a meeting – and culturally – such as sharing too much about our personal life at a pub. Ethical boundaries shift continuously, even when social and cultural norms may remain relatively static.

The most evident shift in ethical perspectives from a digital marketing perspective can be seen in the increasingly open default policies relating to the sharing of personal information by *Facebook*. The default privacy settings are a matter of company policy that reflect current commercial agendas and social understandings of doing digital business. The willingness to accept these by the users of the social network reflects prevailing cultural attitudes to sharing personal information. Tension, complaints or resistance all reflect the boundaries of what is generally regarded as ethical behaviour. When legislation has been implemented or advocated around issues of data privacy and sharing, this is a social control introduced to match the boundaries of generally accepted ethical behaviour and to restrict commercial activities that go beyond these boundaries.

Understanding the social, cultural and ethical environment that you are working in will also help to define your own organisation's ethical worldview – an increasing expectation of customers that has been brought about by the increased transparency created by digital communications – and that of your buyer persona.

Analysing the micro-environment

Micro-environment analysis involves examining those forces that are closer to the organisation and have a direct impact on creating and delivering value to the customers. Popular models for studying some of those forces and their impact on the organisational strategies are Michael Porter's Five Forces Model and stakeholder analysis. The micro-environment is generally easier to identify and respond to as an organisation.

The Five Forces Model is a framework for industry analysis that explores the impact of 1) current competition, 2) new entrants, 3) substitutes, 4) buyers and 5) suppliers. Examining the five forces allows the company to define clearly its strengths and weaknesses and to choose an appropriate strategy that will lead to new positioning or the utilisation of industry change. The impact of digital technologies can be integrated into all aspects of the model. Figure 2.2 shows the classic model.

Rivalry among existing competitors

As the most powerful of the five competitive forces, rivalry has a big impact on the attractiveness and profitability of your organisation. The digital economy leads to accelerated rivalry but simultaneously offers ways of gaining a competitive advantage through differentiation, tailored offerings and individual customisation. By understanding the strengths and weaknesses of your major competitors, you also learn how your organisation can gain a competitive advantage.

A well-known example of this assessment and response to rivalry is Airbnb. As a competitor to conventional accommodation providers, Airbnb offers an accommodation service by creating 'a platform of trust' that allows property owners to rent out spare rooms, homes, castles and yurts. Technology – in the form of an app and a website – connects prospective renters to every property owner directly. The company founders realised that if the system can be trusted, it will match accommodation needs and opportunities in a way previously only possible through family and friends and on a scale not possible without the Internet.

The example of Airbnb takes the advantages of holiday accommodation provided by 'friends and family' to the next level using digital channels and, as a result, introduces a significant game-changing rivalry to the traditional hospitality industry. One of the major successes of the company was during the 2014 World Cup, when 120,000 people placed by Airbnb stayed in Brazilian homes instead of hotels. A similar approach could be implemented in a variety of markets, including the childcare example of *Yoopies* described in Case Study 2.2.

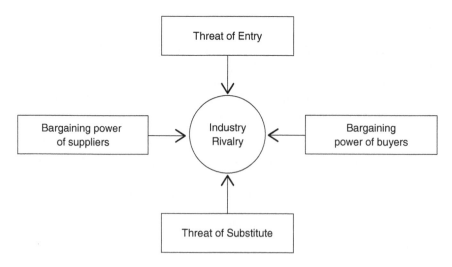

Figure 2.2 Industry Analysis Model (adapted from Porter, 1979)

Case Study 2.2 *Yoopies.* Digital intermediary for quality childcare

Established in November 2011, *Yoopies* is a social platform that allows parents to easily find a babysitter. It was created by Benjamin Suchar after he observed the problems his sisters and friends were experiencing finding a reliable babysitter.

Yoopies promotes its services through social networks, search engine optimisation (SEO) and search engine marketing (SEM), and word of mouth. The target market for the company is urban parents. According to its founder, the major differentiators between *Yoopies* and its competitors are the quality of profiles and the parents' network.

Yoopies enables parents to find the perfect babysitter according to 50 criteria including availability, distance, experience and qualifications. The company certifies babysitters by checking their ID and their qualifications and by conducting a personal interview with every babysitter that is certified. Parents can search for recommendations and review trustworthy babysitters in their network of friends and family. For example, by linking their *Facebook* account to their *Yoopies* account, parents develop their network and receive more feedback and comments on babysitters (Cymerman and Suchar, 2013).

Yoopies' business model requires parents to subscribe to the website. The first contact with a babysitter is free. The subscription starts at €4.90 per month for an annual subscription and €9.90 for a monthly subscription to access all contacts in unlimited ways. The company offers preferential rates on products, services and activities related to children for their premium subscribers (https://yoopies.fr/).

After only 18 months *Yoopies* became the leading childcare provider in France, with a double-digit monthly growth. In four years, it had expanded to eight European countries (France, Spain, Italy, Belgium, Switzerland, Australia, Germany and the UK) and by the end of 2015 the company had ten employees.

The goal of *Yoopies* is to become the European leader in linking home services that are based on trust (Boogar, 2014). In 2014 the company acquired Yokoro, a marketplace for homecare services including babysitting, cleaning, tutoring and personal assistance.

Source: Boogar, 2014

The threat of new entrants

The threat of new organisations entering the industry is high when the barriers to entry are low. This is especially relevant when digital technologies are constantly disrupting established business models by allowing new types of competitors to appear.

An example of a disruptive technology-based 'new entrant' is the Estonian peer-to-peer money transfer service TransferWise. Regarded as one of Europe's digital icons, the company built a web platform allowing customers to transfer money quickly and at less cost than any of its traditional competitors, particularly high street banks.

The threat of substitute products and services

A substitute has the same, or a very similar, function to your existing product or service but it is presented or performed in a different way. The readiness of customers to buy substitutes on the basis of a benefit or quality-to-price ratio determines the degree of risk posed to your own products and services. It is relatively easy to overlook the threat of substitutes when it comes from a different industry or when the threat is based on a new technology. A relevant example for digital business is the interrelated functions of smartphones and cameras. Smartphones decrease the appeal of low-end digital cameras and other specialised devices, such as cheap video cameras. However, at the prestige end of the market, higher-end digital SLR cameras still attract consumers who are eager to capture professional-quality images and video not possible on consumer-grade mobile phones.

The substitution to the photography industry is a result of mobiles being – as the MIT Technology Review says – 'the Swiss Army knives of consumer electronics' that perform decently on many tasks. The ubiquity, ease of use and extensibility – through the use of apps – of smartphones offered a substitute product for low-end cameras that effectively destroyed the market for these single-purpose devices.

The bargaining power of suppliers

Suppliers are an essential contributor to the success of your organisation. A supplier's power can manifest itself through access to limited resources or through the capital and ongoing costs of switching to another supplier. In the digital economy, the power of many traditional suppliers decreases as new options emerge and as supply requirements change. Suppliers also appear who offer new but essential goods and services, such as providers of the data storage, connectivity, sensors and embedded operating systems that all form the potential basis for new data-driven services for your organisation or for your customers and their product experience.

As a contemporary example, in the search industry, *Google* now dominates the supply of website visitors through the provision of search results. The relationships with end users and their knowledge of consumers' product usage are the basis for their business power (Porter and Heppelmann, 2014).

Another recent example of a change in suppliers' services is Massive Open Online Courses (MOOCs), which are capable of offering global access to university courses for a virtually unlimited number of students. Traditionally, the choice of a higher education provider would have been geographically constrained, except for the most wealthy.

The bargaining power of buyers

Buyers can exert influence and control over an industry when there is little product differentiation and substitutes can be easily found. This circumstance particularly applies to products and services where buyers are price-sensitive and where switching between choices does not result in significant cost to the customer. Digital technologies have the capacity to increase or decrease the bargaining power of buyers.

Digital technologies empower customers by making them more informed, allowing them to easily compare the benefits and prices of products and services, communicate through different channels, share information and participate together in company processes like new product development (see Case Study 2.3). However, in contrast, digital technologies also allow producers to 'disintermediate' – to remove intermediates who increase the price of a product or a service as a result of increased transaction costs. Reducing the length of the supply chain and targeting precisely the buyer persona are key strategies of digital business that are making a major impact in most industries.

Case Study 2.3 *LEGO®*. Ideas innovation and crowdsourcing re-energised the company

In the 1990s and early 2000s, as children started to prefer video games and computers to plastic blocks, *LEGO* was close to bankruptcy.

Their solution was the implementation of open innovation and crowdsourcing. In 2008 *LEGO* launched the online platform *LEGO* Cuusoo, allowing *LEGO* fans to become actively involved in the new product development process, both in the idea generation and the screening.

With *LEGO* Cuusoo, users could produce a page describing their new concept and then share it with others to elicit their reactions. *LEGO* fans could collaborate with others on *LEGO* projects. The *LEGO* Review Board, composed of designers, product managers and other key team members, would evaluate projects that reached 10,000 supporters for playability, safety and fit with the *LEGO* brand and winners would receive 1 per cent of the total net sales of the product.

One of the first products based on this open innovation and crowdsourcing was the Hayabusa 369-piece building set, a model of the world's first mission probe to collect samples from the surface of an asteroid and return them to Earth.

At the end of April 2014, LEGO renamed the platform *LEGO* Ideas, and continues to encourage fans to submit 'projects'.

Sources: Mejia (2014) and Ideaconnection (2013)

With an understanding of the external and internal situations within which your organisation is positioned, you have already filled in some key aspects of your Buyer Persona Spring (Figure 2.3). With this recognition, you are also in a

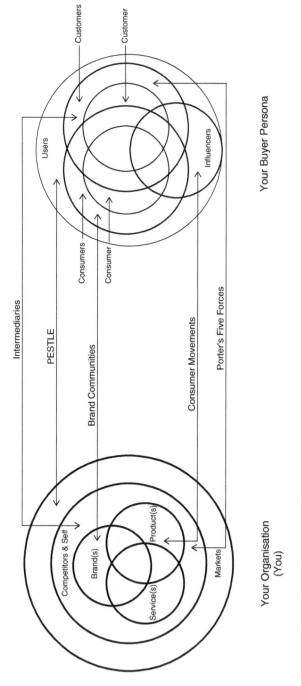

Figure 2.3 The Buyer Persona Spring in relation to existing models, tools and potential sources of support

position to recognise external organisations that can support the development and achievement of your digital business strategy.

Marketing intermediaries

Marketing intermediaries include resellers, physical distribution firms, marketing services agencies and financial intermediaries. Intermediaries help your organisation research the market, and promote, sell and distribute your products and services to your buyer persona.

Financial intermediaries include banks and insurance companies. Increasingly, services and interactions in this sector are mediated through digital technologies (see Case Study 2.4).

Intermediaries reduce the need for your organisation to try to do everything. The disruptive organisational environment introduced by digital technologies requires new technologies to be implemented quickly and demands new types of business service providers. Most organisations do not have the internal resources to manage this rapid pace of change.

Recent research shows that while a business is actively investing in building the necessary digital capabilities and skills, it runs the risk of wasting investment when it tries to accomplish everything by itself (May and Fersht, 2014). To avoid this, large companies like Procter & Gamble, Mondelez and Unilever use mobile and social start-ups or technology vendors to enrich their marketing strategies with creative energy.

Case Study 2.4 *Talkwalker.* Marketing intermediary

Luxembourg-based *Talkwalker* is a marketing intermediary that helps companies track and optimise their social performance.

Established in 2009 by young engineers, *Talkwalker* is an easy-to-use, powerful social media search, analytics, measurement and monitoring engine. According to its *Twitter* certification page, *Talkwalker* is used by companies 'to find key influencers, top conversations, trending topics, for risk management, business intelligence and measuring the effectiveness of social campaigns and presence (187 languages)'. *Talkwalker* currently has 62 employees and opened an office in New York City in early 2015.

The company launched a platform for a variety of analytics and insight online (www.talkwalker.com). Its search index covers 150 million sources. The algorithm makes it possible to analyse and interpret any website. Carson (2014) explains that *Talkwalker* can pull in information from customer reviews on *Amazon* even though the structure of the web-site is quite complex. The services of this intermediary include listening, sentiment analysis, analytics and insight, mention alerts and many other features that allow companies to get a full picture of the brand and its competitors online. The analysis offered by *Talkwalker* even covers less popular social networks. The company integrates these results and then makes the results available to all clients.

The company received buzz in the marketspace for *Talkwalker* Alerts, which allow a high level of customisation and which are fast emerging as a reliable alternative to *Google* Alerts.

The approach the company has chosen is to keep the simplicity of the platform while adding features. Its second version was launched in June 2014. At the end of 2014, *Talkwalker* became one of the first five European companies to earn *Twitter* certification.

Sources: Carson (2014), Price (2013) and *Talkwalker* (2014)

Utilising marketing intermediaries is also your route to move the advice and guidance found in this book from a do-it-yourself 'kitchen table' level to a pro-fessional service. The principles and concepts outlined in all of the chapters can be applied directly by your own organisation – if you are small or if you have your own marketing department – or separately – under your instruction – by a marketing company, once you have grown big enough.

Consumer movements

Consumer movements unite consumers to protect their rights. Digital tech-nologies are democratising consumer movements by blurring the difference between an expert and an ordinary consumer with in-depth knowledge. Digital technologies allow individual consumers to communicate with any organisation and enable continuous access to company information. Accord-ing to Jobber and Ellis-Chadwick (2012), marketing management should consider consumer movements and online brand communities as an oppor-tunity to create new product offerings to meet the needs of what can become emerging market segments.

2.3 The practicalities: identifying micro- and macro-conditions

After exploring the external environment, it will be clear that there are many opportunities for your organisation. But what do you do next? Determining your next steps requires an internal analysis of your organisation, to connect the external opportunities with the strengths of your organisation.

Internal analysis

Right now, your organisation has both tangible and intangible assets that you can apply to digital solutions. Your tangible assets might include equipment, cash availability and human resources each with their own particular knowledge and skills. Your intangible resources might be intellectual property rights, tacit knowledge, brand equity or reputation.

When your resources are integrated and organised to perform effectively and efficiently they become capabilities. Your core capabilities will be unique and will differentiate your organisation from your competitors.

To start your internal analysis, you need to identify the strengths and weaknesses of your current business model and business strategy, and then decide what needs to be adjusted or changed to align with the identified opportunities and threats.

Business model and business strategy

The terms 'business model' and 'business strategy' are often confused. Your business model is the way your organisation creates and offers value to your customers. Your business strategy is represented by all the methods your organisation uses to realise your business model. There are plenty of companies that operate the same business model but their strategies can vary significantly.

An example in the digital domain is the difference between *MySpace* and *Facebook*. Both organisations employ the same business model – they are social network brokers that facilitate personal connections between users. The major source of revenue for both of these brokers is the sale of advertising space targeted to users' interests.

However, the strategic approach each company took was different. *MySpace*'s strategy was to target a music-focused community, while *Facebook* started with a university audience and then opened its membership to everyone, offering flexibility for the users to define their own communities. *Facebook* became a leading global network, eventually attracting many *MySpace* users. The ability to customise and to target specific interests defined by the members of the site itself proved to be the key differentiator and source of value that made *Facebook* the preferred option.

Digital health check

A digital health check determines how effectively your organisation is using digital technology. The health check consists of a list of questions concerning digital business and marketing performance:

- Digital thinking – What managerial support is in place for the digital business strategy? To what extent is digital technology an aspect of daily work? Where and to what extent is digital technology used in communications channels?

- Digital infrastructure – What hardware and software is in place? Does your organisation have guidelines, policies and processes to support digital projects? Does your organisation have a digital strategy?
- Digital tools – What provision is there to create and support digital teams, projects and training?
- Digital decision investment – How much investment is required for your organisation's Digital and Social Media Marketing to achieve its objectives?

A digital health check can tell you which level of the Digital Business Maturity Model your company is at, and also what is needed to achieve the next level (Fletcher, 2014). A marketing-led digital approach will lead your organisation towards a wider and more complete transformation.

There are two major characteristics which organisations that have transformed and reached high levels of digital maturity have in common: a preparedness to invest in digital initiatives, and senior leadership with a clear vision that engages the whole organisation and sustains the transformation.

High-tech companies are some of the most mature digital companies, while others such as the pharmaceutical industry are just beginning their journey towards digital maturity (Westerman et al., 2013).

Value stream mapping

Value stream mapping is a diagnostic tool for analysing the value created by an organisation and how it delivers value to customers. Traditionally, this a technique used in manufacturing facilities and supply chains, but it is now increasingly applied more widely to service industries.

To begin, the organisation selects a process and breaks it down into a series of discrete steps. Within every process there are some steps that add value and some that do not. Both cost money and time. The steps that produce waste or do not add value are then examined in order to make improvements.

Value stream mapping conducted by Boston Consulting Group (BCG) on digital advertising agencies found that 80 per cent of the time was spent on non-productive activities, while only the remaining 20 per cent was spent on activities that were regarded as adding value, such as strategic targeting, data-driven innovation and performance optimisation. In response to these results, organisations involved in the study deployed a unified technology platform that provided a single user interface which assisted in eliminating the wasteful processes.

Collaborations and partnerships with technology providers, advertisers and media owners can also decrease unproductive internal activities.

Strengths, Weaknesses, Opportunities and Threats (SWOT) analysis

External and internal data can be used to conduct a Strengths, Weaknesses, Opportunities and Threats (SWOT) analysis (Table 2.1).

The opportunities presented through digital technologies can be overwhelming for many organisations. A SWOT analysis can assist in managing digital transformation as a prioritised list of projects.

The SWOT analysis enables you to make a comprehensive list of all the internal and external strengths, weaknesses, opportunities and threats. This enables your strategic planning to be based on informed decisions that increase your strengths, reduce your weaknesses, capitalise on opportunities and mitigate threats.

These actions are achieved by developing specific projects and campaigns that deal with each identified parameter. For example, if a new technology is identified as an opportunity, its implementation within your organisation would become a project commencing with feasibility testing against your buyer persona. A SWOT analysis can also be done for competitors to identify areas where your organisation could gain competitive advantage.

With a completed SWOT analysis, you have the basis for digital strategy development. The successful digital strategy will not solely be a set of digital tools working in isolation, but rather a set of processes, tools and communications that work towards a common organisational objective.

For example, consider a SWOT analysis for your e-commerce website (Table 2.2) – its strengths could be customer-centric design and messaging, useful and relevant content and a quick and easy checkout process. Weaknesses might include a confusing structure and navigation or a lack of mobile support. The opportunities could be emerging new and untapped markets and new technologies to improve the user experience. The threats will often include the emergence of new competitors, rival new design concepts and new regulations. Combining these elements of your SWOT analysis, some strategic options might be to improve market penetration by implementing full mobile support for the current customers or to enter new markets with customised content and easier checkout processes.

After having completed and interpreted your SWOT analysis, your organisation needs to determine a digital marketing strategy. One way of planning this

Table 2.1 The SWOT Matrix

SWOT analysis	Positive factors	Negative factors
Internal factors	**Strengths**	**Weaknesses**
External factors	**Opportunities**	**Threats**

Table 2.2 Simplified SWOT analysis of an e-commerce website

SWOT analysis	Positive factors	Negative factors
Internal factors	**High-quality content**	**Not mobile friendly**
External factors	**New markets**	**New e-commerce technology**

is to use the Business Model Canvas, which will emphasise how to best take advantage of the business environment.

Business Model Canvas

Digital business models challenge many traditional physical business models in three ways: 'ownership' of the consumer experience; business process consistency across all channels; and use of customer data across the entire organisation (Weill and Woerner, 2013). New business models focus on three core principles:

- The content – what product, for what market, with what technologies.
- The experience – empowered customers co-create products, share information and require more of everything.
- The platform – the technologies that enable access to your product or service.

One of the popular frameworks for the development of a business model is the Business Model Canvas, which helps your organisation align activities and to look for new areas of growth. The Business Model Canvas consists of nine building blocks that produce a snapshot of the business model in a single image and focuses on interactions rather than a specific product or service (Figure 2.4).

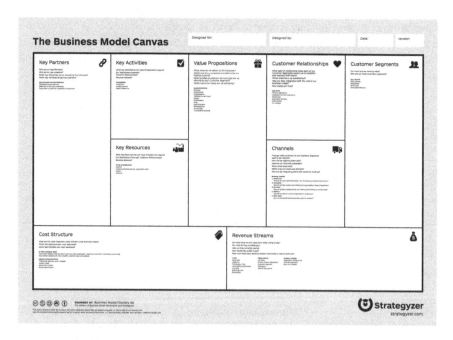

Figure 2.4 Business Model Canvas (Wikimedia, 2015)

The building blocks for the Business Model Canvas are:

- *Customer Segments.* Who are the individuals and the organisations for which you create value?
- *Value proposition for the customer segments.* What are the products and services that you offer to those customers? Which problem does your product solve? What benefits are provided? What is the minimum viable product – the core features that allow the product to be deployed?
- *Channels through which the organisation reaches its customers.* What are the touchpoints through which your organisation interacts with customers? What kind of channels does your organisation use? Which are the best and the most cost-efficient ones? Do these channels correspond to customer needs?
- *Customer relationships.* In what ways do you acquire customers? What is the cost for your organisation to get and keep customers?
- *Revenue streams.* How does your organisation capture value? What is your pricing strategy?
- *Key resources needed.* What infrastructure allows your company to develop, deliver and capture value? What are the key resources needed for your distribution channels, customer relationships and revenue streams?
- *Key activities.* Which activities allow your organisation to create value? What are your key activities within distribution channels, customer relationships and revenue streams?
- *Key partners.* Who helps your organisation? Which partners and suppliers provide resources and activities that are important for your organisation?
- *The cost structure of the business.* Which cost elements in your organisation are connected with activities and resources? Which resources or activities are the most expensive?

The building blocks of your Business Model Canvas will be the synthesis of your previous analysis of external and internal factors. Completing the canvas will engage many people in your organisation (all of them, if you are a small organisation) and will be a dynamic process. With a complete Business Model Canvas you will understand your complex organisation and will have key intelligence for identifying many aspects of your Buyer Persona Spring (Figure 2.5).

2.4 Summary

As we've seen, identifying the long-term vision of where you want your organisation to be and breaking down this vision into manageable projects allows you to create a managed pathway to long-term success. Continuously using market research and staying updated on shifting influences in the external environment will enable your organisation to create a productive internal learning culture that encourages proactive relevant and sustainable innovation. The methodical approaches to planning and organising described in this chapter make it is easier

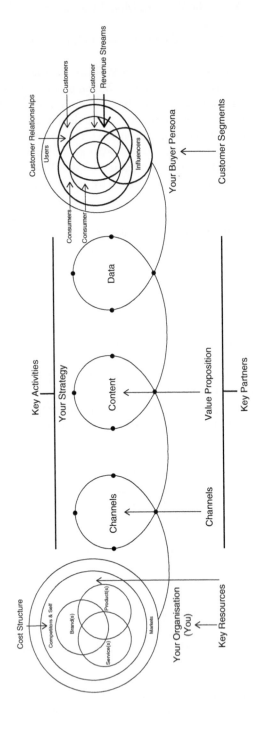

Figure 2.5 Elements of Business Model Canvas in relation to the Buyer Persona Spring

for multiple stakeholders in your organisation to share a consistent vision and to achieve clearly defined strategic goals.

Techniques such as value stream mapping allow an organisation to evaluate the day-to-day operation of an organisation from a customer perspective. With this technique, you can identify the individual activities that add value, for which customers, and see how these activities could be improved.

While digital technologies offer you a confusing multitude of ways in which you can engage with your customers, the opportunity to use these technologies alone is not sufficient justification to deploy them in your organisation. Only by identifying the overall key priorities for your organisation are you able to prioritise investment in individual technologies. By taking a continuously iterative action research approach to planning and evaluating your organisation's activities you will succeed.

2.5 References

Boogar, L. (2014) *European babysitter marketplace Yoopies acquires Yokoro to expand into homecare.* www.rudebaguette.com/2014/03/20/european-online-babysitter-platform-yoopies-acquires-yokoro-expand-homecare-marketplace/

Carson, E. (2014) *Talkwalker: Delivering extensive social media analytics to Europe and beyond.* www.techrepublic.com/article/talkwalker-delivering-extensive-social-media-analytics-to-europe-and-beyond/

Cymerman, J. and Suchar, B. (2013) *J'aime les startups.* www.jaimelesstartups.fr/yoopies/; https://yoopies.fr/

European Commission (2014) *The directive on consumer rights.* http://ec.europa.eu/justice/consumer-marketing/rights-contracts/directive/index_en.htm

Fletcher, G. (2014) *Digital Business Maturity Model: The future of #Digital Business.* http://blogs.salford.ac.uk/business-school/digital-business-maturity-model/

Ideaconnection (2013) *LEGO Cuusoo: Innovating with the crowd.* www.ideaconnection.com/open-innovation-success/Lego-Cuusoo-Innovating-with-the-Crowd-00376.html

Jobber, David and Ellis-Chadwick, Fiona (eds) (2012) *Principles and practice of marketing.* Maidenhead: McGraw-Hill Education.

Kotler, Philip and Armstrong, Gary (eds) (2012) *Principles of marketing.* Global Pearson.

May, N. and Fersht, P. (2014) *Disrupt or be disrupted: The impact of digital technologies on business services. A study of digital's impact on business services.* www.accenture.com/t20150523T032510__w__/us-en/_acnmedia/Accenture/Conversion-Assets/Microsites/Documents11/Accenture-Digital-Technologies-Business-Services.pdf

Mejia, L. (2014) *Turn your LEGO fantasies into reality with LEGO Cuusoo.* http://readwrite.com/2014/02/11/lego-cuusoo-dream-projects

Myerson, J. (2014) *Making digital technology more inclusive.* www.ageuk.org.uk/profes sional-resources-home/knowledge-hub-evidence-statistics/debates-on-ageing/digital-technology/

Porter, M. (1979) How competitive forces shape strategy. *Harvard Business Review,* 57, 86–93.

Porter, M. and Heppelmann, J. (2014) *How smart, connected products are transforming competition.* https://hbr.org/2014/11/how-smart-connected-products-are-transforming-competition

Price, G. (2013) *Need a Google Alerts replacement? Meet Talkwalker.* http://searchengineland.com/talkwalker-google-alerts-replacement-153305

Talkwalker (2014) *Twitter for business.* https://biz.twitter.com/partners/certified-products/talkwalker

Weill, P. and Woerner, S. (2013) Is your organization ready for total digitization? *Harvard Business Review*, 24 July, https://hbr.org/2013/07/is-your-organization-ready-for

Westerman, G., Tannou, M., Bonnet, D., Ferrais, P. and McAfee, A. (2013) *The digital advantage. How digital leaders outperform their peers in every industry.* http://ebooks.capgemini-consulting.com/The-Digital-Advantage/#/21/zoomed

Wikimedia (2015) *Business Model Canvas.* https://commons.wikimedia.org/wiki/File:Business_Model_Canvas.png

Yining, D. (2014) *Unilever promotes environmental protection efforts.* www.shanghaidaily.com/business/consumer/Unilever-promotes-environmental-protection-efforts/shdaily.shtml

Section II

Building your digital marketing strategy

3 Understanding your buyer persona

Ana Cruz and Stelios Karatzás, University of Sheffield International Faculty, CITY College, Greece

3.0 Learning objectives

In this chapter you will learn how to:

- identify online consumer behaviour;
- develop a buyer persona;
- appreciate a customer journey through to online purchase;
- find digital 'trust touchpoints' and 'pain touchpoints' for consumers;
- make content go viral;
- recognise the importance of ethically and morally driven consumer behaviour within digital environments.

3.1 Understanding online consumer behaviour

Understanding individuals, groups or organisations when they engage in the process of selecting, purchasing, using or disposing of products, services, ideas or experiences to satisfy their needs and wants is the essence of understanding consumer behaviour (Solomon et al., 2013). This understanding needs to be at the heart of any effective marketing strategy. To a large extent, the scale of consumer response to your strategy will determine whether or not your organisation will survive and thrive. Understanding the behaviours of your consumers makes good business sense and is a vital part of a successful digital marketing strategy. Once you have developed a strong understanding of your consumers, you also have the key components for building your buyer persona.

The rapid uptake of digital devices as everyday items that are always on and always with us means that the same technology provides a comprehensive platform to measure and understand more completely the way consumers behave during the purchasing process. Before starting to develop a marketing strategy, a buyer persona and a robust digital presence, it is essential that your organisation identifies who you are marketing to and who are your customers.

Table 3.1 reveals some of the different categories used to identify markets as well as providing some immediately useful examples.

Table 3.1 Market segmentation variables

	Category	Description	Examples
Consumer markets	Demographics	Segmentation based on the characteristics of the population	Age Gender Social class Ethnic group Generation (Generation Y, Generation X, Millennials) Income Family life cycle (e.g. single, married with no children, full nest, empty nest, solitary survivors) Region
	Geographic	Segmentation based on the geographical location of the population	Region: by country, continent, state Population density: urban, suburban, rural
	Psychological	Group segments according to their lifestyle, activities, interests and opinions	Lifestyle AIO (activities, interests, opinions) Personality
	Behavioural	Segmentation based on actual consumer behaviour towards products and brands	Benefits sought Brand loyalty Usage (light user vs heavy user) User status (potential, first time, regular) Readiness to buy
Business-to-business (B2B) markets	Geographic	Segmentation based on the location. Important, as shipping costs may have an impact on pricing and purchasing behaviour	Cluster geographically as companies may have similar needs
	Company type	Segmentation based on factors with potential impact on purchasing behaviour	Company size (large, small and medium enterprises (SMEs), micro) Industry (e.g. services or manufacturing) Decision-making unit (people involved in the purchasing process and decision making) Purchasing criteria
	Behavioural	Similar to consumer behavioural segmentation in consumer markets. Purchasing procedures may also be worth considering	Usage (light user vs heavy user) User status (potential, first time, regular) Readiness to buy Purchasing procedures (e.g. tenders, negotiations)

By being specific about the categories that you want to work with, your organisation can then focus on defining your primary target market through the creation of a buyer persona.

3.2 The buyer persona

The use of personas is not new. The concept was widely used in direct marketing long before it was adopted in digital marketing. Personas are useful in considering goals, desires and the limitations of brand buyers and users. This understanding needs to guide decisions about product offering, service, interaction and the user's journey towards purchasing (or repeat purchases). Data about customers is usually abstract, in that it identifies key demographic attributes such as age and location. The use of buyer personas goes further by placing a personal and human story around the consumer that gives a focus for defining the marketing content that is required, as well as the tone, style and delivery strategy for that content. Identifying a buyer persona is key to enabling your organisation to organise your marketing strategy so that you can efficiently reach those who are most receptive and more likely to become long-term customers, advocates and influencers.

Key aspects of your buyer persona include:

- **Who** – A short biography of your ideal customer, including where they work, their responsibilities and their commitments to family and friends.
- **What** – A description of your buyer persona's primary and secondary goals.
- **Where** – A description of where your buyer persona spends their time both online and offline.
- **Content** – A description of the types of content that your buyer persona prefers.
- **Channels** – A description of the type of social networks and other channels that your buyer persona prefers to access and uses regularly.
- **Trust touchpoints** – Identify where your content and the preferred channels of your buyer persona can intersect and create trust in your brand.
- **Pain touchpoints** – Identify the objections that your buyer persona may have to your brand, your content or the channels that you use.
- **Customer, Consumer or Influencer** – Identify the role of your buyer persona as a customer, a consumer, an influencer or a combination of all three.
- **'They say'** – Use quotes from your buyer persona to make them come alive.
- **'We say'** – Use sample quotes of the messages that you might send to your buyer persona.
- **Keywords** – What are the keywords and phrases that you will associate with your buyer persona?

In the Buyer Persona Spring, there is an emphasis on identifying the roles that your buyer persona plays in relation to your organisation and your products and services. There is a complex interaction between being a consumer, a buyer or customer and an influencer for your products and services. Your buyer persona is a user of the Internet, with all of the competing opportunities that this access brings, as well as the potential for being an influencer to other consumers and customers for your brand. This complexity of personal circumstances is what you are navigating in creating a comprehensive description of your buyer persona (Figure 3.1). It may appear sensible to shape the story of a single buyer persona who is located right at the centre of this complexity (Figure 3.2). However, this obvious target for your attention is not always possible and does not always bring the best return on your investment. However, this is a conclusion that can only be reached by undertaking an iterative approach within your marketing strategy and activities. Your organisation may, over time, recognise the need for two or more buyer personas that specifically speak to different combinations of this intersecting complexity (Figure 3.3). Our representation of the buyer persona places the individual customer and consumer within the broader category of customers and consumers. This separation reiterates the need for your buyer persona to speak of an individual as a single, discrete person.

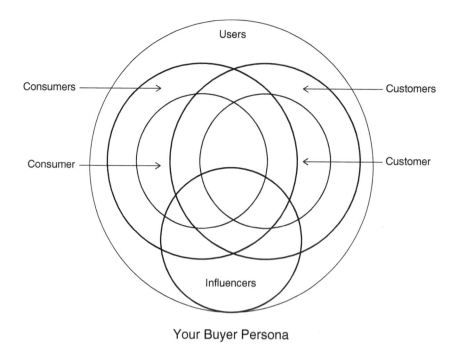

Your Buyer Persona

Figure 3.1 The buyer persona

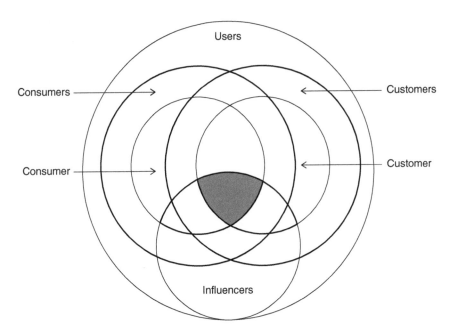

Figure 3.2 The single cover-all buyer persona focusing on the intersection of users, influencers, consumers and customers

Case Study 3.1 *Help Scout* gets to know its buyer personas

Software company *Help Scout* has two different customer personas it caters to. This is how it describes one of them:

1 Growth Graham

Background: Graham is the founder of a small business and he signs up for *Help Scout* because he's curious. He cares most about scale, price and providing outstanding, personalised support for customers. Company size is 30 or fewer but growing.

　Role in purchase process: founder or decision maker.

　Goals and challenges: growth, deliver excellent customer service. Graham is utilising a free product but he is facing a challenge – he doesn't want to give up the personal touch of email, but his team is overstretched by their current workflow.

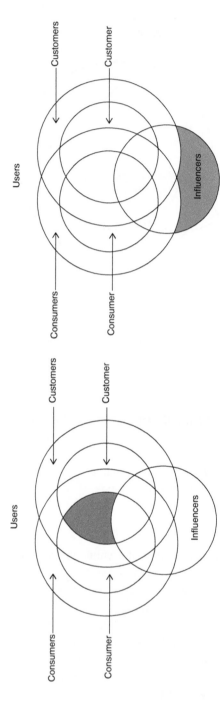

Figure 3.3 Multiple buyer personas addressing different roles (representing a customer who is also a consumer but not an influencer, and one influencer who is neither a consumer nor a customer)

Figure 3.4 Growth Graham vision

Main sources of information and preferred content medium: Graham gets what it means to love customers. He's held on to using email (Gmail, usually) for a long time because he loves how personal it is, but his business is growing fast and he needs something that scales better.

Quotes: 'Great customer service is everything to us, so we need a tool that is personalised, yet scales to meet the needs of our business.'

In the process of identifying user goals for the buyer persona, *Help Scout* identified three key questions that need to be answered:

1   What language would this customer use to identify their current problem?
2   What is their greatest hesitation in trying out our offering?
3   What is the best way to engage with this customer?

Understanding the buyer persona's goals, current problems and the language they use to describe them will provide you with insights into how to write and communicate in a relevant and persuasive manner. For example, *Help Scout* knows that Growth Graham is concerned about emails slipping through the cracks in his overcrowded Gmail account.

Figure 3.5 Growth Graham strategy

In response to this, the copy on its 'Our email page' is written specifically to address those issues.

Figure 3.6 Growth Graham tips

An organisation will sometimes require more than one buyer persona.
This is an example of another buyer persona developed by *Help Scout.*

2. Help Desk Heidi – Heidi is the lead customer support manager for
a larger company, and she has been given the task of finding a new company help desk. She wants a product that makes her a better manager,
so she is most concerned about agent productivity, reporting and team
collaboration.

Figure 3.7 Help Desk Heidi example

Source: www.convinceandconvert.com/social-media-strategy/how-to-
create-customer-profiles-to-reach-your-target-audience/

Case Study 3.1 shows the ways that two different buyer personas can benefit
from the organisation's offering, even though each buyer persona has quite different motives. Heidi, for example, needs in–depth, data–driven customer service resources, whereas Graham's interests focus on what integration solutions

are available. Understanding the needs and motivations of your buyer personas is important because:

- a customer's needs define the interest they will show in you;
- a customer's motivations define how they respond to your goods and services;
- a customer's perception of your offerings and brand will shape their opinions of your organisation.

In website design, this principle would be applied to the 'About' section, where a description of what you offer must fit the buyer persona's needs and motivations. The buyer persona drives you to create content that is sufficiently relevant, useful and persuasive to create customers and brand advocates.

Factual information that will help to develop your buyer persona can be found through analysing *Google* Analytics Audience data, CRM data and social platforms such as *FollowerWonk*. This factual information that is gathered will help to define the more measurable aspects of your buyer persona including age, gender and geographic location. By conducting market research such as focus groups and interviews with your existing customers more subjective details can also be added to the story of your buyer persona, including aspects of their behaviour and psychology. Development of your buyer persona is an iterative process, as each new detail that is added to the story invokes new questions, and the need for further detail and to ensure that the overall story remains coherent and consistent. As you bring the elements of the story of your buyer persona together it may also become necessary to bridge the gaps in your current knowledge. Linking the details together will help everyone in your organisation understand and recognise the buyer persona, but even if these linkages must contain elements of fiction they should be based on a 'best guess' of your buyer persona that comes from knowledge of your existing customers and not be built on an unrealistic 'fantasy customer'. A range of techniques exists that utilise the skills of fiction writing to construct meaningful workable prototypes. For example, science fiction prototyping (SFP) and micro science fiction prototyping (µSFP) specifically use the futurist perspective of science fiction writers to describe new products and services. Within the field of literature, the classic work of Propp in identifying common repeating characters in traditional fairytales provides useful guidance to define the types of character roles that individuals assume in different situations. Propp's work is also usefully extended further in the area of media character theory, where archetypical roles are described in relation to contemporary situations, including participation in online forums and groups (Campbell et al., 2009).

With a workable buyer persona developed, your complex organisation can now consistently address and engage with a specific target for your attention. However, this process is not at an end. Your buyer persona should also be part of a continuous process of refinement and evolution.

3.3 Characteristics of ethical, moral and green consumer behaviour within digital environments

Increasingly, your organisation will have to cater to a new dimension of the online consumer: the ethical online consumer. This consumer has a moral conscience for issues ranging from the environment, animal welfare, working conditions, local origins, organic ingredients and eco-friendly materials to the political affiliations of brands. These consumers make their voices heard by buying products that reflect their ethical position. You may or may not choose to cater directly to these consumers, but you cannot ignore their presence, as ethical consumers are also influencers. In terms of developing a buyer persona, the ethical consumer may represent a core feature or necessitate the development of an additional buyer persona (Figure 3.3). Some organisations have been quick to capitalise on the ethical consumer movement by offering easy-to-find local products and by providing the ability to sell second-hand products, as the consumer demand for both is rising.

There are now numerous blogs, websites and ethical community groups that rate or discuss which brands are acting ethically and which ones are not, making consumer choice incredibly straightforward. For example, ethicalconsumer. org ranks brands in a table, based on the sustainability of their products and how they affect the environment, animals, people and politics, so that consumers can see where their favourite brands rank and whether they should continue buying from them. This requires brands to become more transparent in how they operate and what they produce.

With the ethical consumer movement even brands generally regarded as ethical can come under scrutiny when their ethical standards are seen to slip. This was the case when ethically prized brand Stella McCartney started to collaborate with brands like Target and Adidas, both of which have poor environmental standards and manufacture in under-developed economies (Ethical Fashion, 2012). This confirms the need for your organisation to do-as-you-say in a world where all our actions are visible and where consumers will actively communicate when anyone acts unethically.

You can harmonise with ethical consumers through a series of actions (Banaji and Buckingham, 2009):

- maintain strong visuals;
- support these with descriptive ethical texts that are based on credible facts;
- use clear navigation;
- address your buyers in a way that informs and does not just sell;
- encourage representation so that your buyers also become advocates;
- legitimise your efforts with the transparency of your ethical efforts, use authentic ethical labelling, display third-party ethical certifications, provide ethical leadership and training for your employees and create an ethical code of conduct (Delmas and Burbano, 2011).

Case Study 3.2 *Estelle & Thild* emphasise 'natural' in their branding

Consumers globally have become more and more inclined towards ethical considerations when purchasing products, which also extends to the online world. Women's cosmetics and skincare brands in particularly are adapting to this shift in consumer behaviour. Northern European countries are notorious for very dry weather, hence they are renowned for their skin care innovations. Sweden's SME *Estelle & Thild*, for example, has incorporated an ethical dimension into their product offering, using organic and eco-friendly materials, both in packaging and in the actual products themselves. This has given them a more niche market, as they can advertise to clientele that have particularly sensitive skin (i.e. women during pregnancy, as well as younger and older women).

In order to bolster this sense of 'natural' in their brand, *Estelle & Thild* have paid special attention to how they present their website. On their home page the brand displays bright and beautiful imagery of their product alongside brightly coloured flowers, so the consumer immediately receives an impression of just how natural their products are. This imagery is also accompanied by relevant language, with the brand using phrases such as 'pure extracts' and 'hand-selected innovative ingredients'. Most importantly, ethical consumers will look to see third-party certification to ensure the brand's claims. *Estelle & Thild* have an easily findable section concerning their certification. It is important to note that they have not just presented their certification but have also explained it (i.e. Eco Cert means over 95 per cent of ingredients must be certified organic and of natural origin).

There are instances when consumers might be sceptical about natural products and their actual effectiveness, so it is crucial for ethical brands to portray their products' effectiveness as well as how ethical they are. This brand shows consumers pictures of popular ethical celebrities who have used the brand, as well as awards that have been given based on the products' effectiveness. Finally, in order for consumers to truly grasp the ethical values of the brand, the website contains a section on how to have a healthy and ethical lifestyle, containing, for example, ingredients for fun and healthy smoothies and featuring regular updates from the CEO herself.

Source: www.estellethild.com

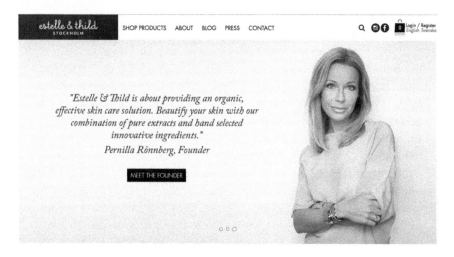

Figure 3.8 Estelle & Thild example

3.4 The buying journey

Once your buyer persona is defined it is important to describe a buying journey that will lead the buyer persona to a fully completed action. This exercise needs to be kept simple, it should be done from the buyer persona point-of-view and, where possible, it should use actual customer feedback to define the path. The ultimate aim for your organisation is to identify areas for improvement and where to influence the journey. You are attempting to capture your buyer persona's journey from, for example, seeking information through to their decision to buy and onwards to the actual purchasing process. In building the buying journey and thinking about the Buyer Persona Spring, consider the three sub-strategies that link your organisation with the buyer persona, namely content, channels and data.

Mapping the journey allows you to visualise current and planned buying journeys and to document the touchpoints across multiple channels. Each of your touchpoints is a single point of contact, the interface between people and products, services or brands before, during and after an individual interaction. Your buying journey should map all the relevant touchpoints.

Roberts (2014) suggests four steps to mapping buying journeys:

1. *Understanding the customer touchpoints and channels*

Identify the core purchase channels. Depending on your type of organisation it could cover the store, website or call centre, and can be expanded to your marketing channels (email, postal, *Facebook*), order fulfilment (delivery and payment) and research channels (website customer services). Direct and indirect contacts such as social sites and customer reviews should also be considered as touchpoints (Figure 3.9).

2. Buyer journey activities/actions

The touchpoints, actions and activities of your buyer persona will differ according to which industry you operate in, but overall the activities of your journey can be grouped into awareness, discover, purchase, use and bonding with the product.

3. Mapping the journey

Once the touchpoints and activities are listed, they can be plotted as a table (Figure 3.10).

Figure 3.9 Direct and indirect channel touchpoints with the buyer persona (adapted from Roberts, 2014), www.mycustomer.com/feature/experience/mapping-your-customer-journeys-across-touchpoints-examples-and-techniques/168259

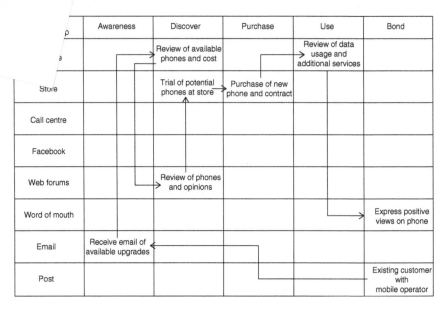

	Awareness	Discover	Purchase	Use	Bond
ρ		Review of available phones and cost		Review of data usage and additional services	
Store		Trial of potential phones at store	Purchase of new phone and contract		
Call centre					
Facebook					
Web forums		Review of phones and opinions			
Word of mouth					Express positive views on phone
Email	Receive email of available upgrades				
Post					Existing customer with mobile operator

Figure 3.10 Mapping your touchpoints

4. *Using the buyer journey*

Having built an understanding of your buyers' journey, you can now set about improving it. More buyers can be retained by understanding their steps through their individual journeys. Your task is to optimise the interactions your organisation has with the buyer persona on their buying journey. You will also be able to identify communications gaps, where conflicting messages are being sent or where replies are not being received.

Pain touchpoints can be identified across different areas of your website, as well as blockages or delay points that may impede the customer journey. Once these are identified, a solution can be developed with an optimisation strategy for improving the buyer's experience. For example, an online classified ad site wanted to encourage visitors to sign up for email alerts when they were exhibiting behaviour indicating that they were about to leave the site. Using the buyer journey map and optimisation techniques, the company identified that a prompt at 1 minute after entering the website gave visibility, but it was a prompt at 6 minutes that led to the highest completion rates and the greatest level of returns to the site.

3.5 From the buying journey to online purchases

Google analyses millions of consumer interactions through *Google* Analytics and identifies how different channels affect online buying decisions. This work enables *Google* to provide a free benchmarking tool (the 'Customer Journey to Online Purchase') that your organisation can use to understand the roles that different channels play, including which channels work better together and when to use them. Although the tool is not available for all European countries, the information is still valid for all SMEs that want to grow sales beyond Europe and understand the generic trends in their industry. By using this tool, you can choose an industry, organisation size and country to explore how different combinations of digital channels influence a typical buyer before the completion of a sale. Figure 3.11 shows how marketing channels for medium-sized businesses in the UK's industrial sector influence the purchasing decision.

Channels to the left of the diagram (Figure 3.11) – in this case generic paid search and organic search – tend to play an early and assisting role in the typical sale. The channels positioned to the right are more likely to be the last interaction before a purchase.

The tool allows flexibility to explore how the channel's position on the path is likely to influence a purchase and helps in choosing the right channels for different campaign objectives. For example, channels on the left are more appropriate for branding campaigns whereas channels further to the right are best for conversion-focused campaign objectives. The Buyer Persona Spring identifies channels as one of the three essential sub-strategies for digital business success. Understanding and using channels appropriately and with increasing

Figure 3.11 *Google*'s customer journey to online purchase (reproduced with kind permission from *Google*), www.thinkwithgoogle.com/tools/customer-journey-to-online-purchase.html#!/the-uk/business-and-industrial/medium/organic-search

sophistication will draw the buyer persona closer to your organisation and represent measures of success.

A clearly defined buyer persona, in conjunction with a well-developed buyer journey and use of the 'Customer Journey to Online Purchase' tool, allow your organisation to deliver engaging experiences and effective positive touchpoints. These provide an environment in which your organisation is delivering clear value for your buyer persona and converting them into repeat buyers who trust and advocate your goods, services and brands.

3.6 'Trust touchpoints' for buyers

Your buyer persona is constantly 'in touch' with all types of brands through their own individual touchpoints. Each of these touchpoints can increase, not affect or decrease, a consumer's trust in a brand. Building trust with buyers is paramount as an incentive to purchase a product or service and create brand loyalty. Some organisations are more sensitive to trust issues, such as banking, but any business that incorporates a financial transaction with their buyers shares aspects of this sensitivity. As a consequence, it is important for you to understand the digital trust touchpoints that engage your buyers. Buyers legitimately worry that brands may misuse personal and financial information, or, indeed, that a website might be entirely fraudulent.

The positive insight is that buyers trust branded websites more than traditional touchpoints such as ads in newspapers and on TV or brand sponsorships (Nielsen, 2013). The bad news is that consumers generally greatly distrust ads on websites (8–10 per cent), branded social network posts (10–15 per cent), branded emails (11–18 per cent) or sponsored search engine results (24–27 per cent) (Wasserman, 2013). This reinforces the fifth of the five rules for social media success described in Chapter 1: 'The buyer persona will resist the most blatant advertising messages on social media.'

Touchpoints are moving targets. You must constantly evaluate at which touchpoints your buyers find the most trust and which touchpoints are regarded as completely untrustworthy or significantly lacking in trust. Even the most trustworthy touchpoint will still compare unfavourably with the trust that is built through personal recommendations and reviews or testimonials. Anderson (2014) cites these independent third-party touchpoints as being trusted by 88 per cent of buyers.

3.7 'Pain touchpoints' for buyers

Touchpoints that are not optimised successfully for your buyer can rapidly become 'pain touchpoints'. Your task is to discover where these potential pain touchpoints are located. Use 'blog patrols' to periodically peruse blogs that deal with similar products or services that you are connected with, and update your pain touchpoints based on what users are saying about your service, reliability and quality. You then have a core set of issues that can be addressed. Take this examination further and analyse the reviews of your competitors to identify sector-wide sets of pain touchpoints and speak to those people who deal directly with your buyers for more details about other potential pain touchpoints. *Google* Analytics can also assist by identifying how and if your products and services are being searched for and how readily customers are able to find you. Finally, constantly review and track the journey that your buyers take and recognise the points at which they turn away from completing a purchase. Inward emails, online surveys and live chats will all point you towards those touchpoints that create the most pain.

After having identified the main pain touchpoints for your buyers, you must act to reduce that pain. For some buyers, the main source of pain is the need to pay large amounts of money up front. One solution to this is to offer different payment options. Another common source of pain focuses on the buyer's concerns about being charged for returning an item. A solution for this particular problem might be to integrate services within your offering to minimise this pain. Options for integration include providing prepaid return pickup and allowing the buyer to organise a return through different channels including phone, email and live chat. Other buyers worry about not being able to track their purchases. This concern can be eased by providing an order number and confirmation email with meaningful information, including a tracking number. Buyers can then check on the progress of their package at any time.

Out-of-stock items also create pain touchpoints, but this can be mitigated by letting your potential buyer leave their email so that they can be contacted when their item is back in stock. Similarly, not being able to try on clothing items that are bought online is a common source of pain for buyers. Offering third-party reviews, comprehensive details of the product (measurements, materials used, product origin and distinctive features) and free returns could resolve this pain touchpoint. Some brands take pain touchpoints and – by applying the theory of constraints – turn these into a feature of the buying process. For example, personalising a shoe would traditionally have been regarded as a source of pain, but Nike I.D. now makes personalisation a feature with minimal steps and an easy-to-follow customisation process.

In the Buyer Persona Spring knowing both trust and pain touchpoints is an integral consideration in assessing the success of campaigns and how well the application of specific tactics for each campaign has achieved the planned outcomes. Pain touchpoints push the buyer persona away from your organisation, while trust touchpoints draw the buyer persona closer to you and your organisation (Figure 3.12).

Each of the three sub-strategies within the Buyer Persona Spring interacts with touchpoints in different ways (Table 3.2). Your goal is to maximise the positive consequences through these strategies without at the same time increasing the negative consequences.

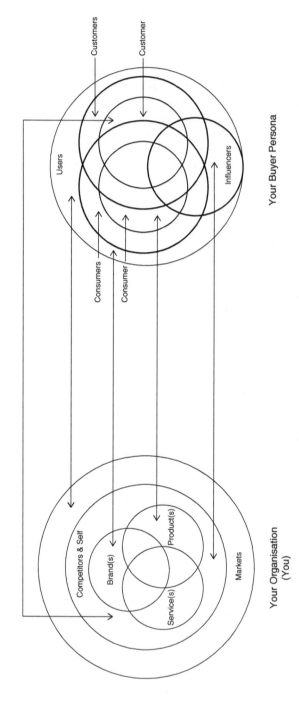

Figure 3.12 Mapping potential trust and pain touchpoints within the Buyer Persona Spring

Table 3.2 Using the sub-strategies of the Buyer Persona Spring to increase trust and reduce pain touchpoints

The Channels sub-strategy	Trust	Pain
Increase	Utilise channels that are respected by the buyer persona Genuine engagement with a specialist channel for the buyer persona (positive consequences)	Require a sign-in or the use of an unfamiliar or unattractive channel for the buyer persona Introduce the use of a new channel into the buyer journey (negative consequences)
Decrease	Use material from individual users on a respected channel without attribution or recognition (negative consequences)	Offer options that allows the buyer persona to choose the channel they prefer – e.g. *Google*, *Twitter* and *Facebook* sign-in options (positive consequences)

The Content sub-strategy	Trust	Pain
Increase	Users rather than copywriters produce brand content (positive consequences)	Vague, onerous or overly long conditions and disclaimers attached to content Media mismatch, e.g. text when video is expected or vice versa (negative consequences)
Decrease	Veiled editorial content, blatantly copywritten items or content that is inappropriate for the buyer persona (negative consequences)	Reduction of content repetition, e.g. the online catalogue is also the shopping cart (positive consequences)

The Data sub-strategy	Trust	Pain
Increase	Transparent matching of the buyer persona with further relevant content and goods and services (positive consequences)	Sign-in systems that mistrust all users rather than helping legitimate users to verify their identity (negative consequences)
Decrease	Poor algorithmic matching of keywords in content with the intent of the buyer persona, e.g. Private Eye's *Malgorithms* column regularly documents these failures (negative consequences)	Checkout systems that remember preferences Systems that respond 'naturally' to the expected actions of the buyer persona (positive consequences)

3.8 Strategies to gain trust and minimise pain

A key risk in the development of your buyer persona is that the perspective is developed in isolation. A buyer persona developed in this way is then in danger of becoming an artefact solely of your organisation's imagination. This can never be a realistic view of the buyer persona for your organisation to adopt. Extending this thinking to a logical conclusion, any buyer persona that has an exclusive interest in your organisation represents the pinnacle of success for your marketing activities and is equally an impossible situation to maintain. Realistic internal SWOT analysis in conjunction with an external PESTLE analysis should ensure that your buyer persona is connected to both your organisation as well as the rest of the world. The Channels, Content and Data sub-strategies of the Buyer Persona Spring can then be designed to gain trust, reduce pain and engage with your buyer persona in ways that make your organisation become part of their wider everyday life.

Your Channels sub-strategy

Your buyer persona will respond to the pain touchpoints with your organisation by considering alternative organisations and workarounds. When an entire market has common pain touchpoints the increasingly common response by that market's intended consumers is to look for new solutions that can be generated within digital environments. Hallmark examples of this collective response include the rapid shift to digital distribution for music, news, television series and films. The shift to entirely digital business models also changes consumer expectations regarding the price of goods and services. The most extreme example of this type of shift is found with the sustained pressure that has been placed on the traditional newspaper publishing model. The success of the printed newspaper relies almost entirely upon control of the production and distribution of a specific form of cheap media – newsprint. The value added to newspapers by quality journalism is a largely unappreciated aspect of the model that has increasingly been eschewed for free news delivered by social media and other digital channels.

Depending on your organisation, you may see yourself as interacting with your buyer persona 'through' a channel or you may actually 'be' a channel. In the world of digital business, irrespective of your sector you should see yourself as being both. A dual channel approach enables you to work with your buyer persona in multiple ways by offering a range of services that fit their requirements.

E-commerce is a business model that has been challenged by consumer workarounds that respond to existing poor service and unattractive price points that are based on traditional business models. As e-commerce has primarily been regarded in marketing terms as a business-to-consumer (B2C) or B2B activity, there is a tendency to regard e-commerce as a channel through which you engage your buyer persona. In these two models, businesses either sell directly to individual consumers or to other businesses. However, alongside these approaches, there has been a quiet revolution in the form of consumer-to-consumer (C2C) selling. We would prefer to use the term buyer-to-buyer, but the abbreviation B2B is already taken. The idea of C2C is best recognised through platforms that let consumers sell directly to other consumers, with *eBay* and *Etsy* being the most well known. The two main forms of C2C platforms are classified ads and auctions. This form of transaction substitutes the traditional third-party 'middleman' with a platform that enables C2C interaction in exchange for a small percentage of the transaction price (or, in some cases, a fee charged for listing the item, or based on the type of listing, such as using pictures and bold headings). If your organisation experiences pain touchpoints through conventional e-commerce models that narrow your channels, there is potential leverage in using C2C platforms to reduce pain and engage your buyer persona in spaces that are already familiar to them.

C2C transactions can also be completed face-to-face through platforms such as *Craigslist* (where the platform itself generates income through traffic and advertising), while other customers can meet the seller and purchase the product directly (local C2C). On platforms such as *eBay*, there is an option to sell products internationally (although this requires consideration of shipping and duty charges), within their country's region (which avoids worries about additional hidden charges) or for local pickup only (such as by car). The flexibility and range of options that have been developed through C2C platforms present opportunities for your organisation to reduce pain touchpoints and increase trust by utilising your physical premises in new ways, including becoming the place for third-party face-to-face transactions for your buyer persona in addition to the interactions you already have directly with them. In this way your organisation 'is' a channel for enabling C2C commerce.

Your Data sub-strategy

Trust is a central issue when consumers buy from someone who lacks brand reputation or trust. The potential for fraud or the misrepresentation of items is much more common in C2C than in other forms of e-commerce. But, just as in any other form of commerce, ratings or the accumulation of reviews regarding the seller help assure a buyer that the seller is more likely to be trustworthy. You can potentially support your buyer persona and increase your own trust touchpoints by supporting their interactions with others. Your data sub-strategy can set out to enable your buyer persona to offer feedback about an entire relevant sector of business, including qualitative information (with a word limit) to express what was good or bad about the transaction and quantitative measurements such as rating the speed of delivery, accuracy of the described item or communication. Long-term and successful engagement with your buyer persona in this type of way could even create new opportunities for your organisation. If your buyer persona incorporates new or first-time users, you can build trust with them by providing them with a safe environment in which to undertake their first C2C transactions.

With a fully developed data sub-strategy your organisation controls a much wider dataset regarding your buyer persona than was previously possible. This collection of data enables the extraction of additional insights for your own organisation and – if you so choose and when suitably anonymised – for your consumers and your sector too. The priority within your data sub-strategy should be your awareness that your organisation *will* become a digital business, and that in becoming entirely digital it is data that becomes your primary asset. Your data sub-strategy should set out to make data out of all interactions with your buyer persona.

Your Content sub-strategy

The increased use of social media has produced an increased interest in understanding effective content and, by extension, viral content. As a result of limited budget and resources, many small businesses are increasingly interested in the reach and buzz that can be generated by viral content for little or low cost. Libert and Tynski (2013) highlight the advantages of your content 'going viral':

- Break through the noise.
- Create significant brand exposure and free press.
- Generate high levels of social engagement through sharing and brand interaction.
- Expand the rates of brand advocacy.
- Dramatically improve organic search rankings.
- Increase brand engagement.

There is no exact threshold which determines that content is viral. Kevin Nalts, a *YouTube* celebrity known for his viral videos, stated that a video hitting a million views was viral. More recently, a video is considered as having gone viral when it reaches 5 million views. Some researchers using epidemiological models focus on a reproduction rate that is higher than 1, meaning that each person who receives the message should pass it to at least one more person (Watts et al., 2007). Irrespective of the precise definitions of virality, your organisation should be aiming to create content that people, especially your buyer persona, want to share.

Research about why people share content online suggests the priority of emotions. Berger and Milkman (2012) examined *New York Times* articles published over a three-month period to establish the characteristics that made content go viral. They identified that positive content is more viral than negative content and that virality is partially driven by physiological arousal. Content that evokes high-arousal positive (awe) or negative (anger or anxiety) emotions is more viral. Content that evokes low-arousal or deactivating emotions (e.g. sadness) is less viral. These experimental results demonstrate the causal impact of specific emotions on an individual's preparedness to share, and illustrates that sharing is driven by the level of emotion that the content induces.

Botha and Reyneke (2013) researched the role of content and emotion in viral marketing, particularly in viral videos. They identified that, in specific video content, the first determinant for people to share is the relevance of the content and the second is the emotion it evokes. Feelings depended on content familiarity. When a viewer was familiar with the content, they had a stronger emotional connection and were more likely to share. If the viewer was not familiar with the content and had little (if any) emotional reaction, they were not likely to share (Figure 3.13).

Shifman (2012) identified six common features found in the most popular meme videos – a focus on ordinary people, flawed masculinity, humour, simplicity, repetitiveness and whimsical content. Each of these attributes marks the video as incomplete or flawed, and effectively invites further creative dialogue. A combination of circumstances and qualities reflects the significant increase in popularity for mimicry in contemporary digital culture. This suggests a complex interaction of circumstances that contribute to the creation of viral material that incorporates, among other things, content, presentation, cultural references and channel.

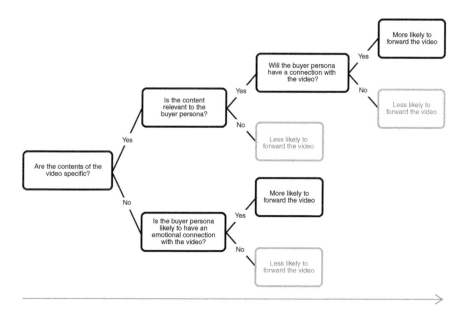

Figure 3.13 Decision tree aiding marketers to plan a viral campaign (adapted from Botha and Reyneke, 2013)

Libert and Tynski (2013) suggest the following steps for creating viral content:

1. Have a compelling title. Good titles attract the attention of new viewers.
2. Use strong emotional drivers to make people care and share. Capture your audience's attention in the first four seconds, but don't go for longer than two minutes.
3. Create content that strikes the correct emotional chords. Successful content that uses negative emotions is less common in highly viral content than content using positive emotions. However, evoking anticipation or surprise can also work.

Creating content and your content sub-strategy should not be a random or haphazard process. Your organisation must consciously address your buyer persona with the conscious purpose of positively evoking their emotions. Sharing should not be the primary goal of your content but rather, a natural response and outcome of your buyer persona's engagement with your content.

3.9 Summary

In this chapter, we have seen how creating your buyer persona and mapping their buying journey is vital to understanding the touchpoints that build trust and offer a positive brand experience. Likewise, determining your customer's trust and pain touchpoints ensures that the buyer persona feels connected and can enjoy the experience of engaging with your organisation.

Utilising sub-strategies for channels, content and data within the Buyer Persona Spring will ensure that your buyer persona trusts your organisation as part of their everyday life. Data will increasingly become the central asset of your organisation and you should maximise the amount of data that you gather from your buyer persona. A successful data sub-strategy may eventually open up and create new business opportunities. Your content should engage your buyer persona with positive emotions that encourages them to share with like-minded buyers. Content should be consciously created systematically and with a consistent perspective. Your organisation should simultaneously aim to use a variety of channels, as well as becoming a channel for your buyer persona.

3.10 References

Anderson, M. (2014) *88% of consumers trust online reviews as much as personal recommendations.* http://searchengineland.com/88-consumers-trust-online-reviews-much-personal-recommendations-195803

Banaji, S. and Buckingham, D. (2009) The civic sell: Young people, the internet, and ethical consumption. *Information, Communication & Society, 12*(8), 1197–223.

Berger, J. and Milkman, K.L. (2012) What makes online content viral? *Journal of Marketing Research, 49*(2), 192–205.

Botha, E. and Reyneke, M. (2013) To share or not to share: The role of content and emotion in viral marketing. *Journal of Public Affairs*, *13*(2), 160–71.

Campbell, J., Fletcher, G. and Greenhill, A. (2009) Conflict and identity shape shifting in an online financial community. *Information Systems Journal*, *19*(5), 461–78.

Delmas, M.A. and Burbano, V.C. (2011) The drivers of greenwashing. *California Management Review*, *54*(1): 64–87.

Ethical Fashion (2012) *Behind the label: Is Stella McCartney a sustainable brand?* https://stellamccartneyethicalfashion.wordpress.com/2012/11/16/behind-the-label-is-stella-mccartney-a-sustainable-brand/

Libert, K. and Tynski, K. (2013) *Research: The emotions that make marketing campaigns go viral.* https://hbr.org/2013/10/research-the-emotions-that-make-marketing-campaigns-go-viral/

Nielsen (2013) *Under the influence: Consumer trust in advertising.* www.nielsen.com/us/en/insights/news/2013/under-the-influence-consumer-trust-in-advertising.html

Roberts, J. (2014) *Mapping your customer journeys across touchpoints: Examples and techniques*, 27 October. www.mycustomer.com/experience/engagement/mapping-your-customer-journeys-across-touchpoints-examples-and-techniques

Shifman, L. (2012) An anatomy of a YouTube meme. *New Media & Society*, *14*(2), 187–203.

Solomon, M.R., Bamossy, G., Askegaard, S. and Hogg, M.K. (2013) *Consumer behaviour: A European perspective*, 5th edition. Prentice Hall Financial Times.

Wasserman, T. (2013) *Report: 70% of consumers trust brand recommendations from friends.* http://mashable.com/2013/03/21/70-percent-brand-recommendations-friends/

Watts, D.J., Peretti, J. and Frumin, M. (2007). *Viral marketing for the real world.* Harvard Business School Publishing.

4 Digital and Social Media Marketing strategy

Ivan Stoychev, University of National and World Economy (UNWE), Bulgaria

4.0 Learning objectives

In this chapter you will learn how to:

- create a marketing strategy and use a strategy development cycle;
- align your strategy with your buyer persona;
- set appropriate goals;
- monitor and update your strategy.

4.1 What is digital marketing strategy?

Whatever your organisation, you need to adopt a long-term strategic perspective. A strategy will emphasise the most advantageous direction for your organisation over a defined period of time. A strategy will then help to guide you towards the most suitable tactics and activities that should be used to execute your chosen direction. Before moving forward with digital marketing, your organisation should first determine what it wants to accomplish.

Characteristics of Digital and Social Media Marketing strategy

A digital strategy can be seen as a roadmap that helps you to maximise the impact you get from channels, content and data in order to support your organisation's mission, vision and goals. Your digital strategy should build awareness and promote your organisation, your brands and your products and services. This is an interactive and iterative process. Since the Internet allows for immediate feedback on your actions and the ability for significant and focused data gathering, you will be constantly optimising and improving your marketing efforts.

Digital marketing focuses on the use of specific content delivered through specific channels. The range of channels and opportunities includes possibilities for email, online video advertising, banner advertisements, product placement and search engine activities. The rising importance of digital channels and the direct feedback available through these channels also means that increasingly digital organisations are using their digital marketing activities to influence and shape their presence in offline channels including TV and radio.

For the Buyer Persona Spring your starting point is to know your buyer persona. The details you should consider in order to define your buyer persona can be categorised systematically (Table 4.1). The buyer persona will be based on your knowledge and research of your consumers, customers and influencers, drawing upon qualitative and quantitative data blended together with a mix of reporting and storytelling. In conjunction with the discussion in Chapter 3, Table 4.1 can also act as a template for developing your own buyer persona.

Within the Buyer Persona Spring, three key sub-strategies are identified to draw the buyer persona closer to your organisation. The three sub-strategies focus on content, channel and data. Each sub-strategy is closely interrelated with the other, but each represents a different level of engagement with the buyer persona. The content sub-strategy focuses on the specific conversations that you initiate and engage with your buyer persona. A separate content sub-strategy enables you to focus on producing a consistent message. The channel sub-strategy focuses on where this content is positioned (or not positioned) and relates directly to the 'usual' locations of your buyer persona. The data sub-strategy represents the most generalised strategy in that it employs the data that your organisation collects from the buyer persona, other consumers and open sources to inform your further planning and to develop and extend your organisation's activities.

Your channel sub-strategy will change over time as you draw in new channels and retire less effective channels (including more traditional channels). The channel sub-strategy will be influenced heavily by technology developments

Table 4.1 Defining your buyer persona

Element	Content
Who	A short biography of your ideal customer, including where they work, their responsibilities and their commitments to family and friends
What	A description of your buyer persona's primary and secondary goals
Where	A description of where your buyer persona spends their time both online and offline
Content	A description of the types of content that your buyer persona prefers
Channels	A description of the type of social networks and other channels that your buyer persona prefers to access and uses regularly
Trust touchpoints	Identify where your content and the preferred channels of your buyer persona can intersect and create trust in your brand
Pain touchpoints	Identify the objections that your buyer persona may have to your brand, your content or the channels that you use
Customer, consumer or influencer	Identify the role of your buyer persona as a customer, a consumer, an influencer or a combination of all three
'They say'	Use quotes from your buyer persona to make them come alive
'We say'	Use sample quotes of the messages that you might send to your buyer persona
Keywords	What are the keywords and phrases that you will associate with your buyer persona?

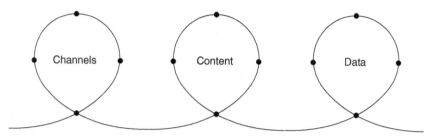

Figure 4.1 Strategy within the Buyer Persona Spring

that offer alternatives to existing traditional and digital channels. Your choice of channels will also be influenced by the reporting and analytics capability available through each channel. This aspect of your choice of channels will be determined in part by your data sub-strategy. Your channel sub-strategy will also move at a different pace to your evolving content sub-strategy, which is more influenced by the changing external environment and internal organisational developments.

By planning and thinking strategically, whilst leaving room to be flexible and dynamic, you will be able to take advantage of new technology, resist purely reactive responses to the actions of competitors and achieve your overall goals as an organisation.

Digital marketing planning cycle

Experienced marketers constantly monitor the progress of their strategies by monitoring the outcomes of and responses to specific marketing activities; they will test alternative approaches and adjust their plans based on the evidence of their observations. The Buyer Persona Spring references the four-step action learning cycle (Figure 4.2), a well-tested model found especially in the context of education. The action learning cycle is significant for its iterative perspective and the degree to which it advocates continuous improvements.

The Buyer Persona Spring adapts the action learning cycle to a strategic marketing perspective. The cycle within the Buyer Persona Spring takes you from the broadest strategy and planning through to a specific campaign that then implements appropriate tactics. As these tactics are undertaken they are constantly assessed using the evidence that is drawn from available analytics. The tactics may be adjusted as a result (by taking a step backwards in the activity loop) or, if the response is failing to address the buyer persona effectively, then the campaign may need to be significantly modified or completely suspended (and necessitate the initiation of a new loop of activity). Assessment will initially encourage small revisions in the current cycle of activity but will ultimately reach a point at which it informs further refinement of your strategy, which, in turn, commences a new loop of activity that will more effectively reach your buyer persona.

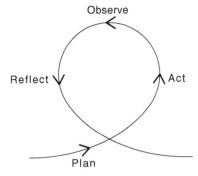

Figure 4.2 The action learning cycle

Figure 4.3 The action learning cycle within the Buyer Persona Spring

A **situation analysis** and background research is the first step in creating your strategy. From Chapter 3 you have learned that, in order to do this, the best way is to start by understanding your current customers and your ideal customer. Listening to what the customers, consumers, influencers and users of your buyer persona are saying enables your organisation to comparatively assess the situation in relation to competitors and the industry in general. Both the SWOT analysis and PESTLE analysis provide frameworks that guide and structure your strategic thinking. The insight gained from this research can then shape the setting of objectives and the key performance indicators (KPIs) that will indicate the success of your strategy.

It is critical for your organisation to discover what people are talking about before becoming part of the conversation. This lets you gauge the tone and activities of the communities that your buyer persona is part of.

Result of stage 1 – Identify the main current issues and key competitor activities, and define your buyer persona.

Objective setting is done by considering the location, behaviour, tastes and needs of your buyer persona and is informed by your external and internal

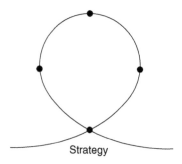

Figure 4.4 Strategy stage

analyses. You can then set objectives that set out to satisfy the needs and desires of your buyer persona in ways that capitalise on the unique strengths of your organisation while mitigating your organisational weaknesses and external threats. Your objectives should be Specific, Measurable, Attainable, Realistic and Timely (or SMART).

Result of stage 2 – SMART objectives are set.

Campaigns turn strategy into a plan of action so that you can create a dialogue with your buyer persona that aims to hit your SMART objectives and supports the overall mission of your organisation. Campaign planning includes the practicalities of budgeting and planning the deployment of people within your organisation. Your plans should separately consider the content you will utilise, the channels that you will focus upon and the data you will collect and analyse as part of the campaigns. While content, channels and data interrelate, they should all be considered as separate parts of your overall strategy and are the key mechanisms for connecting your organisation with your buyer persona.

Result of stage 3 – Timelines, resource allocation, external support and agencies, content, channel and data plans.

Tactics turn the overall plan of action within your campaign into specific actions. Your tactics include selecting the tools to target your buyer persona and focusing the available resources in your organisation towards implementation of the campaign (Table 4.2).

Result of stage 4 – Concrete list of activities to implement with specific tools.

Assessing allows you to optimise your campaigns, objectives and strategy. The feedback provided by assessing enables you to maintain **control** that optimises objectives, campaigns and tactics. Monitoring is the process of tracking, measuring and evaluating an organisation's social media marketing initiatives. Your buyer persona will comment on, react to and interact with your campaigns. Your purpose in assessing is to ensure that the two-way conversation is in place and that it is producing positive responses that reflect your defined objectives.

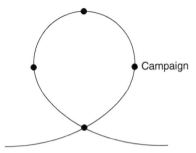

Figure 4.5 Campaign stage

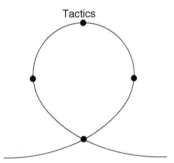

Figure 4.6 Tactics stage

Table 4.2 Tools to convert your campaign into specific activities

	Tools
Content	Curating, Workflow Management, Editing, Graphics, Crisis Management
Channels	Posting, Monitoring, Interaction, Mobile Control, Access Control
Data	Measurement, Tracking, Analytics, Demographics, Location, Collecting

Result of stage 5 – Measurement through web analytics, conversion optimisation and other techniques that allow assessment in relation to your strategic objectives.

Updating is the constant and continuous process of adjusting and improving the elements of the plan to maximise the chances of success. Fine-tune your strategy until the results not just meet, but exceed your objectives. The Buyer Persona Spring is centred on a fluid cycle of activities. Your organisation should keep its action flexible and adaptive in order to be in constant conversation with your buyer persona.

Result of stage 6 – After assessing your results, your strategy will evolve and initiate a new cycle of activity (and learning).

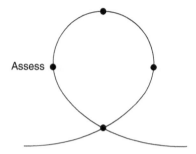

Figure 4.7 Assess stage

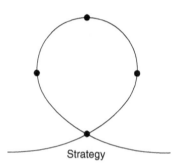

Figure 4.8 Updating (Evolving Strategy) stage

4.2 Aligning your strategy with your buyer persona

Analysis of your existing audiences will drive an understanding of the behaviours of your customers. From this understanding you can recognise a range of characteristics that can be represented within your buyer persona. Your buyer persona enables your organisation to focus its marketing strategy on effectively reaching those who are most receptive and most likely to become customers, influencers and even brand advocates. By addressing your buyer persona you are effectively speaking to a range of individuals who share and recognise the values, sentiments, opinions and lifestyle of your buyer persona.

By creating an insightful buyer persona you create for your organisation a decision tool that will shape your strategies first and then inform your campaigns and tactics. Your buyer persona will tell you what your core customers and consumers do, how they do it, why they do it and how they think. Speaking to your buyer persona aligns your organisation's brands, products and services through consciously created content that is delivered on relevant channels, with a suitable feedback loop to ensure that you collect data. The collected data will let you know the response to your actions and over time will drive your organisation towards becoming a fully digital business.

Table 4.3 The benefits of content, channels and data strategies to your buyer persona

	Benefits to the buyer persona
Content sub-strategy	Relevant and meaningful in ways that encourage sharing
Channel sub-strategy	Familiar spaces, and the site of communities for like-minded individuals includes channels to drive your buyer persona to (discovery) channels where they already congregate (centrality)
Data sub-strategy	Offers value back to the buyer persona in the form of summary and aggregation of actions, personalisation based on data insights and recommendations based on prior actions

Your buyer persona turns the complexity of qualitative and quantitative data into insight and understanding of your customers and consumers within the external environment. By endeavouring to connect your organisation to your buyer persona through the Buyer Persona Spring, your content, channel and data sub-strategies should return clear benefits directly back to the buyer persona – and all your customers, consumers and influencers (Table 4.3). If the benefits for your buyer persona of your marketing actions are not evident to the buyer persona themselves, then your conversation is obviously one-sided and unsustainable.

Case Study 4.1 *Famish'd Salad Bar*: knowing your customer brings results

Georgia Samuel used to work as a corporate lawyer, but now, she is the sole owner of a very successful *Famish'd Salad Bar*, serving soups, gourmet salads and spuds to up to 800 of downtown's business crowd each day. Georgia credits much of her success to her previous corporate role. 'The customer I'm targeting is who I was for six years – the corporate customer. I know how precious time is and how long they are prepared to wait and I know how easy it is for them to go somewhere else if the quality and customer service isn't there.'

Georgia opened the business with a very clear marketing strategy in mind – she would not engage in paid advertising, which she felt would devalue her brand. Instead, Georgia relied upon cost-effective social media networks such as *Twitter* and *Facebook* to grow the business.

'Marketing that works for hospitality and food is generally word-of-mouth style marketing. If a business is offering a quality product, it will get people talking, so naturally this is the best form of marketing.'

Georgia has stuck to her plan, using social media platforms to engage with the various different audiences who are interested in her food. She uses *Facebook* and *Twitter* to promote the daily menu to her followers, which include industry professionals.

'Social networking is all about generating talk,' says Georgia. Last winter, interest on *Twitter* led to a double-page write-up in the *Herald Sun* about *Famish'd*'s soups. Since then, *Famish'd* has been voted best for soups and salads in town on a number of different blogs.

Recently, Georgia has had the *Facebook* and *Twitter* logos printed on all *Famish'd* packaging. 'Since we added the logos, we've noticed a marked increase in the number of followers on both *Twitter* and *Facebook*.'

Famish'd has never limited its social media engagement through a rigid strategy and in some respects that is a strategy in itself. Georgia is, however, very aware of her own personal boundaries around tweeting and posting under the company's profiles. 'We are pretty liberal in what we post; that said, we rarely post anything about our private lives. I make sure that I reply to most tweets we receive.'

According to Georgia, it's also very important to try to make your posts creative and fun to read. 'We often post photos because they generate greater interest from our followers and we try to be creative; we only post what we as customers would like to read.' Georgia and the team at *Famish'd* are careful to remember, too, that social media isn't just a marketing tool; it's a way of engaging the public with the business and its staff.

'I see *Twitter* as a way of creating a personality for the business; it's about letting the customer see behind the scenes.'

Georgia's top tip: be transparent and don't be afraid to let people know about your muck-ups; it helps to give them a realistic insight into your business. 'Around 80% of our new followers on *Facebook* and *Twitter* are generated from the new social media logos on our packaging.'

Unlike some innovations, it's difficult to measure the level of return generated from social media engagement. 'We do know we're generating talk,' says Georgia, 'which can only be generating sales.' Georgia only spends around five minutes a day updating the company's *Facebook* profile or sending tweets. 'We only post as many tweets as we would like to see as customers; sometimes it's only one or two a day and sometimes we don't do any.'

Following the marketing success *Famish'd* has experienced with its online presence, Georgia has vowed to continue investing the business resources and increasing its social media activity in the future.

Aligning your content, channels and data with your buyer persona

The buying journey is the sequence of steps and decisions that your buyer persona takes from first contact through to the first and subsequent purchases. The channels you use should align with your buyer persona and the experiences they enjoy on their journey. The data analytics provided by most channels – or through third-party tools – allow you to build a solid picture of how people behave on your website and other channels you have decided to use before converting to customers and completed sales. Tying this together, your content must be appropriate for the channels you are using.

Listening to and viewing channels should be a key aspect of your assessment of tactics and campaigns, but this listening should also incorporate a range of channels that reach beyond the ones you or your buyer persona regularly use. This approach can eventually become horizon scanning and prospecting in each new iteration of your strategy informing your choice of channels, the forms of content that you use and how you gather data. Time spent listening and observing will benefit your strategy and enable it to dynamically respond to changes in the market as well as the behaviours of your buyer persona. Balancing the best choices of content, channels and data use will draw your brands, products and services into closer communication with your buyer persona (Table 4.4).

A strong strategy starts with the development of your buyer persona. Then you can figure out your big idea, define your objectives and set the timeline. Reaching people effectively is achieved if the channel supports the content and vice versa. Social media, email marketing, mobile marketing and video

Table 4.4 Channels, content and data advice for maximising engagement with your buyer persona (adapted from Corliss, 2012)

---

1 **Create content that answers your buyer persona's biggest questions.** If you can answer those questions you will attract potential customers and you'll also make some seriously loyal fans.

2 **Use formats for your content that fit your buyer persona's preferences.** Ensure your content is easily digested and enjoyed. Ensure that your content is in a format that is widely shareable.

3 **Use channels that your buyer persona prefers to use.** Promote your best content through your best channels.

4 **Measure** how much traffic and leads are generated by each channel.

5 **Learn to speak the language of your buyer persona.** Use this language appropriately in the content directed at your buyer persona.

6 **Post content on the right channels at times when your buyer persona is most engaged.** There will be times when your buyer persona uses specific channels. Identify the schedule and continuously adapt your tactics to meet these patterns.

7 **Present your content through the channels that your buyer persona respects the most.** Where possible, build closer relationships with the channels that most appeal to your buyer persona.

8 **As much as possible customise content to conclude with clear calls-to-action that are based on your buyer persona's needs and goals.** This approach is especially helpful if your organisation has multiple buyer personas.

---

marketing are just some disciplines that will form part of your marketing strategy creation arsenal.

4.3 Setting objectives

The key to defining strategic objectives is to link the overall mission of your organisation with the practicalities of completing sales actions. Your objectives should include but not be limited to:

- **Build Brand:** One of the most important tasks for marketing is to establish your brand. You want your buyer persona to be talking about your brand and to be sharing their enthusiasm for your brand with others.
- **Create New Products:** By opening up a conversation with your buyer persona you can draw together your data-driven understanding with their creativity to co-create new products.
- **Drive Customer Satisfaction:** Continuously talking to your buyer persona enables nagging concerns to be addressed immediately and before they become complaints. Small concerns can be turned around and potentially become the basis for product improvement or evolving your content sub-strategy.
- **Increase Word-of-Mouth Recommendations:** Encouraging your buyer persona to share their positive comments and reviews will increase the range of your products and services through genuine enthusiasm for what you offer.
- **Generate Leads:** Increasing the range of types of content can produce wider interest at varying points in the buying journey. By enabling a new conversation with your buyer persona you can acquire new data from them, including email addresses and mobile numbers. Each new piece of data from your buyer persona is a new opportunity for conversation that drives them towards completion of a sale.
- **Managing Reputation:** Your marketing strategy should include provision for crisis communication management. Your content should be able to respond to crisis with targeted messages through appropriate channels and be customised based on the data you have that connects the crisis with your buyer persona.
- **Integrated Marketing, Public Relations and Advertising:** Your strategy should not artificially distinguish between these categories of activity. Good content that is well placed on the right channels and customised based on the data you have gathered from your buyer persona will work equally well as marketing, public relations or advertising.

Your strategy can incorporate a range of objectives. Regardless of how many are chosen, having a SMART objective (Table 4.5) is important in the development of your strategy.

Table 4.5 All your objectives must be SMART

Specific	Clear and detailed, rather than vague and general
Measurable	So that you can gauge whether you are attaining the desired outcome
Attainable	Something that is possible for your brand to achieve, based on available resources
Realistic	Sensible and based on data and trends; don't exaggerate or overestimate what can be achieved
Timely	Linked to a specific timeframe

Examples of SMART objectives could include:

- Increase unique visitors to our website by 5x from social networking sites (based on evidence from *Google* Analytics) over the next five months.
- Increase blog subscriptions signups by X per cent in six months by adding two new social media channels.
- Increase *Facebook* fans by X in eight weeks.
- Increase *Twitter* mentions by 300 per cent in six months.
- Increase the number of interactions on *Facebook* page by five each week for the next five weeks.

Measuring objectives through key performance indicators (KPIs)

KPIs are the specific metrics that you will consider to determine whether your strategy is performing well and meeting your objectives. For example, you might look at a range of data points to determine whether a chosen tactic is working. KPIs are determined per tactic, with an overall eye on your objectives.

Targets are the specific values that are set for each KPI that are to be reached within a specific time period. They may include customer acquisition and retention targets, customer satisfaction targets, added value measures (the wow factor), level of customer engagement or quantifiable efficiency gains (WOW Blog, 2014).

If you meet or exceed a target, you are succeeding; if you don't reach it, you're falling behind on your objectives and you need to reconsider your approach (or revisit the values you have set for your target).

From 2010 to 2014 there was a clear shift towards KPIs that are referral and text measures rather than financial metrics. These metrics also offer indicative examples of KPIs that you can use within your own strategy (Table 4.6).

4.4 Creating campaigns and reaching your objectives

Once you know your overall strategic direction and have clear objectives you need to determine the specifics of your campaigns. Your strategy will be unique

Table 4.6 Digital marketing KPIs used by companies (%)

Metrics	August 2010	August 2014
Hits/visits/page views	47.6%	60.7%
Number of followers or friends	24.0%	45.0%
Repeat visits	34.7%	38.7%
Conversion rates (from visitor to buyer)	25.4%	31.3%
Buzz indicators (web mentions)	15.7%	24.2%
Sales levels	17.9%	16.8%
Online product/service ratings	8.2%	14.0%
Customer acquisition costs	11.8%	13.7%
Net promoter score	7.5%	12.8%
Revenue per customer	17.2%	12.5%
Other text analysis ratings	6.6%	11.7%
Customer retention costs	7.7%	6.3%
Abandoned shopping carts	3.8%	6.0%
Profits per customer	9.4%	6.0%

Source: World Market Watch, 2014

and consequently, what you do to achieve your objectives must be done on a case-by-case basis. The eight **Cs** (Table 4.7) assist in shaping your campaigns and ensuring that they are built on the unique strengths, weaknesses, opportunities and threats of your organisation.

Campaigns to acquire and retain customers

In the Buyer Persona Spring, the key to acquiring and retaining customers is to maintain a conversation with them. This does not mean you are committing to a daily email or even weekly messaging but rather, a paced and sensible exchange that takes place over time and feels natural to your customers. This is where the content, channel and data sub-strategies must work together and develop iteratively (Tables 4.8 and 4.9).

Customer acquisition and retention is important. As you collect more and more data about your customers you may consider a Customer Relationship Management (CRM) system to help you navigate the volume of data that you have collected and to extract maximum intelligence from this data.

Branding campaigns

Digital marketing focuses heavily on developing conversations in order to build trust with your customers. Your brand is a powerful symbol for this trust and represents the unique qualities and values of your products and services.

Your brand building is part of the development of your content, channel and data sub-strategies (Table 4.10).

Table 4.7 Guidelines for digital and social media strategy development (8Cs Model)

1 **Categorise**. Focus on the channels where you are most likely to find your buyer persona. This focus will produce the greatest chances of success.
2 **Comprehend** the rules of the channel by observing. Adhere to the policies and guidelines of the channel so that you conform to its expected norms. Your buyer persona will be more likely to do business with you if you know, like and respect their favourite channels.
3 **Converse** with, acknowledge and respond to other users of the channel. Always be a contributor and never a promoter. Display your knowledge of a product area and show genuine concern towards the key issues of the channel to build trust for yourself and your brand.
4 **Collaborate** to build mutually beneficial relationships. Co-create and co-consume your products. Your buyer persona will personally connect with and trust a brand or product that they have invested their time in.
5 **Contribute** content to build reputation and improve the community. Position yourself as a thought leader by showcasing your unique knowledge. Knowledge about the subject equates with a product that will most likely be of higher quality.
6 **Connect** with the influencers to help shape opinions about your product or service. Provide everyone with outstanding service. This combination of efforts will attract the attention of the influencers and give them ample reason to praise and promote you.
7 **Community** participation (and creation) can elicit valuable suggestions for improving products and innovative suggestions for new products or services. Encourage two-way conversations that lead to feedback and new product ideas from customers.
8 **Convert** your overall strategy into campaigns and tactics that will raise awareness, gain attention and create loyalty for your brand.

Source: Adapted from Barker et al., 2013

Table 4.8 Acquiring customers

Sub-strategy	*Steps to customer acquisition*
Data	1) Research the current market and assess the external situation. Use internal data that you may already have to direct this research.
Data	2) Create a buyer persona from your acquired knowledge so you know who you are looking for.
Data	3) Identify what products and services your buyer persona needs and desires.
Channels	4) Identify the channels where your buyer persona is regularly found.
Channels	5) Identify which channels you will utilise in your strategy. Which channels are appropriate and which are not?
Content	6) What value do your products and services bring to your buyer persona? Describe these benefits.
Content	7) Present content that engages your buyer persona, exudes the value of your organisation and is highly shareable.
Content	8) Create incentives for existing customers to become brand advocates, reviewers and influencers about your brand, products and services
Channels / Content	9) Keep encouraging the conversation. Encourage likes, tweets and sharing of content.

Table 4.9 Retaining customers

Sub-strategy	Steps to retaining customers
Data	You've acquired a new customer. Engage them in conversation to learn about them.
Content	Give your new customer a personalised space for feedback and comments.
Data / Content	Respond to comments and feedback. Celebrate positives and address the negatives. Attempt to exceed expectations.
Data	Collect additional data from your customers. Use additional methods including surveys. Incentivise completion if necessary.
Content	Develop loyalty programmes as part of your content sub-strategy.
Data	When a customer leaves, try to capture their reasons for leaving. If possible, use this data to encourage them to return.

Source: Adapted from MailerMailer, 2011

Table 4.10 Actions to build your brand

Action	Activity	Content	Channels	Data
Increase Brand Awareness	For a new product or service, build awareness of its existence	Emphasis 'newness', highlight the values and benefits of your offering over the competitor	Inhabit the channels of your buyer persona. Choose to contrast their positioning or compete head to head with competitors	Identify the activities of competitors, the preferred channels and current value propositions
Improve Brand Perception	Positively influence the perception of yourself by aligning with leaders in the industry	Share positive testimonials, reviews and discussions	Use the channels of industry leaders and influencers	Curate the positive perceptions within the industry and what they look like
Position your Brand	Even popular brands can create a more positive impression with their buyer persona	Differentiate your content from competitors. Be distinctive	Take your buyer persona on a journey to discover new, 'better' channels	Collect the responses to positioning. Are you bringing your buyer persona with you or turning them away?
Expand Brand Loyalty	A loyal buyer persona can market your brand indirectly by telling friends and family about you	Enable your buyer persona to share good content with others	Bridge your current channels to those used by the family and friends of your buyer persona	Where are the messages going? Are there new channels for you to inhabit?

Case Study 4.2   *ao.com*: setting an example with social media campaigns

Electrical appliances company *ao.com* (formerly known as *Appliances Online*) knows more than most about the power of social media. A pure-play online retailer, it has created its brand from scratch since launching in 2000, relying extensively on platforms such as *Facebook* and *Twitter* to gain a share in the ultra-competitive white goods market.

'Fun and engaging content' is key to the brand's success online, says Andrew Kirkcaldy, marketing director at *ao.com*. 'We have to think a little out of the box because white goods aren't the sexiest of things to create content around,' he admits.

Examples of recent content, which is all created in-house, includes filming a man who is in the Guinness World Records for balancing a washing machine on his head for the longest time, and sponsorship of 'Tony the Fridge' (@tony_the_fridge), who runs marathons for cancer charities with a 42kg fridge strapped to his back.

To get this content seen, *ao.com* has invested heavily in *Facebook* advertising to get the necessary reach. Consequently, *ao.com* now has nearly 1.6 million *Facebook* likes and is also active on *Twitter*, *Pinterest* and *YouTube*.

ao.com's *YouTube* channel regularly hosts live competitions to win white goods, as well as providing recipes and what it calls 'AO hacks' – tips such as how to keep your clothes fresh or how to put two plates in the microwave at the same time.

What *ao.com* has constantly found is that there is a direct correlation between its social media activity and the number of people coming to the website through search. Mobile traffic is particularly important to *ao.com*, with the brand's recognisable smiley face logo having to work across all devices.

Of course, with engagement online also comes the potential risk of negative as well as positive feedback from customers. For *ao.com*'s Kirkcaldy, the key is to respond quickly and honestly if someone has an enquiry or isn't satisfied.

'We have a customer service team of eight people who are on the sites managing the comments. They will usually reply to customers on social media within two minutes, ten minutes max,' he says. Adds Kirkcaldy: 'If we've made a mistake, we admit it and tell the customer that we will sort it out as quickly as possible.'

Importantly, the same customer service agent will deal with the problem until it's resolved so the customer isn't passed around. Most of the time *ao.com* will deal with the problem publicly, but it may be in private if the customer wishes to take the complaint offline. *ao.com* also regularly checks comments on Trust Pilot, an independent online community where people leave reviews of retailers.

Finally, one important aspect of customer service for *ao.com* is the '*Facebook* Feedback' booklet that all delivery drivers see and which contains positive as well as negative comments from previous deliveries. 'The drivers are the only people who meet our customers, so the impact they can have is massive. It makes them realise how important it is to make a good impression.'

4.6 Tactics

Many tools enable you to implement the specific tactics of a campaign once you have defined your digital marketing objectives and strategy. Each tactic brings specific benefits, for example, customer acquisition may best be driven by search advertising, while email is one of the most effective tools for selling more products to existing customers.

Table 4.11 expands on some of the most popular tactics available to you and their desired outcomes.

Choosing which platform to invest your energy and resources in is important. Determine who your audience is and how they interact with your brand before establishing a presence. Remember that in order to make an impact you must post regularly and consistently.

Actions and control

In order to measure success you need to define a clear and measurable call-to-action. A call-to-action is simply the action that you want your buyer persona to engage in at a specific point in the buyer journey. Many different calls-to-action exist (Table 4.12).

Getting to the sale (conversion) is the final step in a chain of actions. For example, one chain of actions leading to a sale may be:

1. Click on a blog post link from *Twitter* or *Facebook*.
2. Sign up for an email newsletter at the end of a blog post.
3. Sign up for a webinar announced in a newsletter.
4. Have a representative call as a result of this signup.
5. Purchase.

In each small incremental step of this chain of actions, the goal is to increase the level of interaction and engagement. Although the final desired action is

Table 4.11 Marketing tactics, relevant campaigns and their desired outcomes

Tactics	Relevant campaign	Desired outcomes
Search engine optimisation (SEO) involves creating content that search engines index and serve when people enter a relevant search term.	Customer retention or acquisition	SEO has a key role to play in acquisition. It ensures your offering will be well ranked in search results and allows you to reach new customers. Optimised websites are also by definition clear, relevant and well designed. These elements ensure a strong user experience, meaning that SEO also plays a role in retention.
Affiliate and partner marketing are lead generation systems where referrers are paid a 'finder's fee' for every referral.	Sales and return on investment	Promotion of e-commerce websites. Return on investment (ROI) is central to this tactic, as the commission that is paid is within the ROI parameters.
Search advertising (PPC) means the advertiser pays only when someone clicks on their ad. The ads appear on search engine results pages.	Sales, customer retention and acquisition	Pay-per-click (PPC) is keyword based, which means an ad will appear on a results page in response to a search term. It allows an advertiser to reach people who are already in the buying cycle. It offers immediate search engine presence in contrast to SEO tactics, especially for new markets.
Online advertising including emails, ads on social networks and mobile devices, and display ads on websites.	Branding and acquisition	Online advertising raises brand awareness. This form of advertising can generally be targeted to physical locations, subject areas or past behaviours.
Video marketing	Branding, customer retention and value creation	An interactive and engaging format for capturing and retaining customer attention. A video can provide information, entertainment and inspiration – potentially all at the same time.
Email marketing	Customer retention and value creation	Build relationships with potential and existing customers by sharing valuable content and other messages. Targeted and segmented emailing means that a brand can direct messages to specific categories of customer to maximise results.

Source: Adapted from Stokes, 2013

Table 4.12 Examples of calls-to-action

Click Here	The classic web-based call-to-action. This call will conclude motivational copy.
Download Now	Content that is delivered immediately satisfies immediate interest and encourages a conversation.
Click Here For Details	Your reader likes what they've seen so far. Now they can take the next step.
Join Now	If you have gained sufficient reader interest the next step is offered as a chance to belong, affiliate or associate more closely.

probably to generate a sale, the best way to get there involves intermediate steps. The call-to-action is the important 'glue' that links each of these steps in a structured way.

4.7 Summary

Strategy is the first step in positioning your brand. A strategic perspective lets you create a roadmap to reach your organisational goals.

In this chapter you have stepped through the development of strategy. Strategy is connected to the widest context of your organisation, including the sector in which you operate and the pressures that currently exist in the sector. However, strategy also connects this big view to the details of specific tactics you might employ to, for example, attract new customers.

In this chapter we have emphasised the importance of planning campaigns that will bring your buyer persona into close connection with your organisation. Of particular importance is the need to constantly consider the three key sub-strategies of digital marketing: content, channels and data. All three sub-strategies interact closely and are equally important to achieving the objectives of your digital marketing strategy.

4.8 References

Barker, M., Barker, D., Boermann, N. and Neher, K. (2013) *Social Media Marketing: A Strategic Approach.* South-Western, Cengage Learning, pp. 26–35.

Corliss, R. (2012) *7 Ways to Master Buyer Personas within Your Marketing.* https://blog.shareaholic.com/use-buyer-personas-within-marketing/

MailerMailer (2011) *Develop Customer Acquisition and Customer Retention Strategies.* http://blog.mailermailer.com/tips-resources/develop-customer-acquisition-customer-retention-strategies

Stokes, Rob (ed.) (2013) *E-Marketing: The Essential Guide to Marketing in a Digital Marketing World.* Quirk Education.

World Market Watch LLC (2014) *Highlights and Insights Report, CMOsurvey.* www.cmosurvey.org/results/

WOW Blog (2014) *Digital Marketing Strategy Case Study.* http://blog.wowconsulting.co.uk/blog/digital-marketing-strategy-case-study

Section III

Operational planning

5 Campaign planning and project management

Anna Tarabasz, University of Łódź, Poland

5.0 Learning objectives

In this chapter you will learn how to:

- understand the stages of the campaign planning cycle;
- translate your strategic goals into SMART campaign objectives;
- estimate, budget and use evidence-based decision-making processes to select and evaluate the performance of your digital marketing actions;
- communicate and document your project management processes using Gantt charts;
- apply appropriate risk management techniques.

5.1 The importance of planning

Successful digital and social media marketing campaigns do not just happen. They are the result of good campaign project management actions, which are closely related to your digital and social media strategy implementation. The adage 'failing to plan is planning to fail' is true for many digital marketing campaigns. This chapter outlines how each digital marketing campaign is essentially a project and therefore, good project management skills are needed to control digital marketing activities.

The 24/7 culture of online activities compounds the potential gravity of issues that an organisation can face by opening up digital channels of communications. Some of the major brands have digital customer service teams who communicate with customers around the clock. Other organisations make their online 'customer service times' public to reduce disappointment amongst their customers.

Staff burnout and high staff turnover rates are common in digital marketing agencies. Speed is a characteristic of the fast-paced digital industry and can have negative side effects on organisational structures if not managed well. Organisations and their digital teams have expanded rapidly and many are using the same management methods that worked in a small team environment – which do not work well in a larger team setting. Likewise, for a one-person organisation – owner manager – it is essential to be well organised, manage one's time and have

Marketing	People	Finance	Production	Operation

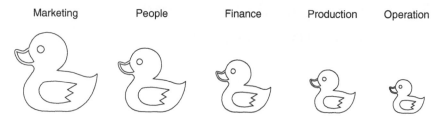

Figure 5.1 The implication of marketing actions across an organisation

good project management skills. Spending a whole day just on social media might not be an option for those in a busy organisation, but using tools to schedule and automate some of the engagement activity can be an option. For example, automatic subscription to mailing lists does not require any human intervention, but setting it up does take time and planning ahead helps in this respect.

On the positive side, the Buyer Persona Spring (see Chapter 0 for more detail) highlights how an organisation can engage around the clock and this offers the possibility of ongoing interaction, especially if multiple aspects of this can be automated. Internal stakeholders have to be managed too. Considerations of how the marketing campaign impacts your people, finances, production and operations need to be made. In this way, having a common strategy used for aligning the processes and procedures of an organisation, in line with marketing activities, helps to focus and lead an organisation to success. Likewise, operational constraints have to be taken into account to make sure marketing does not over-generate demand for products and services, which could have a negative effect of not being able to satisfy demands.

If you plan to use digital channels for creating and curating content to engage your buyer persona, you will need to consider various factors such as product and services life cycles and seasonality. From this point of view, each campaign is essentially a project which has to be managed. Therefore, this chapter focuses on key project management practices related to stages of Planning, Acting, Observing and Reflecting.

This chapter stresses the importance of integrated activities across multiple digital channels within marketing campaigns, activities of which are prioritised by referring to your overall strategic business objectives. Understanding digital marketing campaign project management and its key planning tools and stages offers insight into repeatable success patterns, which can be re-created and integrated into an organisation's culture.

5.2 Project management in the context of digital marketing campaigns

Project management of digital marketing campaigns is a combination of processes, tools and techniques used for intelligently organising resources in order to successfully meet the set digital marketing objectives.

Processes include communication protocols such as update meetings with relevant stakeholders, both internal and external. Tools include spreadsheets for tracking campaign activities and analytics packages for measuring success. Some of the tools are channel specific, but others, like SproutSocial, Pardot, Hubspot and Net Results, offer integrated channel management options. Techniques include the use of Gantt charts and identification of critical paths and risk management.

There is no single approach to project management that fits all organisations. For example, detailed project management methodologies such as PRINCE2 (**PR**ojects **IN** **C**ontrolled **E**nvironments) are popular in the UK, and the Das V-Modell is preferred for digital projects in Germany. Digital marketing activities do rely, to a large extent, on the development of digital artefacts (e.g. e-commerce website application and mobile apps) and therefore, for large campaigns, these methodologies can offer more detailed guidance. Both of these methodologies broadly fit into the four steps of Planning, Acting, Observing and Reflecting.

Objectives and key performance indicators leading to success

One of the key differences between managing a digital marketing campaign and a 'non-digital' marketing campaign is the availability of tools for the management, automation, capturing and reporting of data. Many of these tools have a free entry-level version (e.g. *MailChimp*, *Google* Analytics and *TweetDeck*). These tools allow the measurement and capturing of data even at the smallest interaction along the Buyer Persona Spring. Therefore, using data to set SMART objectives and track these through related key performance indicators (KPIs) and optimising resources intelligently is one of the most important skills of a digital marketing campaign manager.

Each channel, such as search engine optimisation (SEO) or social media platforms, offers its own set of KPIs, which can be measured and tracked automatically (subsequent chapters highlight the potential KPIs which can be tracked for each channel). Whilst this information is usually available for free, one of the first activities that a project manager, and the team if relevant, would have to agree on is which tools will be used for tracking this data. Sometimes it is useful to use more than one source of data for tracking your KPIs, since no one dataset is 100 per cent reliable.

Creating and setting up KPIs for tracking SMART objectives helps to define and agree what 'success' looks like. To measure campaign impact it is therefore useful for a campaign manager to be familiar with tools such as *Google* Analytics and *Google* Search Console for website traffic measurement (see Chapter 12 on web analytics). For example, tools such as *Google* URL Builder can be used for creating campaign-specific URLs for sharing with a specific campaign. Campaign impact can therefore be better tracked through *Google* Analytics. Capturing this data using one tool allows cross-campaign comparisons as well as measurement of factors, which might have not been the original intention. For example, noticing an increase in brand awareness through a higher volume of website visitors, for a campaign that was aimed at increasing sales and identifying user interface difficulties, is a secondary benefit of getting insight from your customer interaction.

For campaigns that are repeated seasonally, use of consistent tools is also useful to ensure comparability of results. For example, a florist can compare the volume of website visitors and sales data in the run-up to Valentine's Day over previous years. Understanding what the individual KPIs measure is also important. For example, for a social media KPI, simply using the number of followers or likes on your organisation's digital profile is not really helpful, especially where campaigns are outsourced and it is unclear how results are being achieved. Therefore, more qualitative measures could be used, such as the sentiment of comments and the number of meaningful interactions. For example, social media listening tools such as *Sprout Social* and *Radian 6* offer a qualitative analysis perspective on your data and provide KPI reporting for your social media. Many social media platforms such as *Facebook* and *Twitter* offer their own reach and engagement metrics beyond the likes of the page and the number of followers on your *Twitter* account. Even customer complaints and negative reviews have value for your organisation – those that pinpoint a weakness help you to refine and improve your offering, and customers who see the improvement are more likely to trust you in the future.

Having set strategic business and marketing objectives for the next three to five years, very often organisations cannot wait this long to see if these have been met in order to determine if the digital marketing activities were effective. Therefore, digital marketing strategy implementation involves breaking down the long-term objectives into distinctive transient campaigns (e.g. building brand awareness could be split into different viral marketing actions and sponsored articles, appearing every two months or scheduled to coincide with events relevant to your buyer persona). Not only are shorter campaigns easier to budget for, but they also reflect seasonality and the buying cycles of your buyer persona. Seasonality can be seen online using tools such as *Google* Trends or *Google* AdWords Keyword Planner, or if you have an existing website, *Google* Analytics. Enabling e-commerce tracking from past purchase history can help here, so that you can export your data into external data analysis and manipulation tools such as spreadsheets to make more detailed and customised reports.

These campaigns or digital marketing projects are distinctive from other day-to-day operations (such as everyday maintenance of the website or new blog entries) in two main areas: first, because they are time-bound and so they do not go on indefinitely; and second, they are focusing on releasing defined outcomes (e.g. brand awareness or conversions) and outputs (e.g. campaign-related collateral material such as web pages, video and images). For these particular reasons the digital marketing campaigns, as well as digital presence seen from a broader, long-term perspective, offer three important points:

- an opportunity for sense checking – if the mix of channels and content is generating the desired outcomes;

- reflecting on this campaign performance compared to other campaigns by your brand, as well as your competitors;
- points for refining the digital marketing strategy implementation tactics chosen to achieve long-term ambitions.

The success of a digital marketing campaign is usually defined in the 'non-digital world' through the judgement of interrelated aspects – the so-called triple constraint or the iron triangle, creating the Project Triangle (Figure 5.2). Each side of the Project Triangle cannot be changed without affecting at least one of the other sides. For example, through increasing the campaign scope (e.g. target audience), it is inevitable that other factors will be engaged – for example, more time would be required, and the budget will likely increase. A further refinement of three previously mentioned variables (Scope, Time and Cost) is 'Quality'. Quality is closely linked with Scope and in fact, some notations replace it altogether. Quality in digital campaigns encapsulates KPIs in the project. Defining quantitative and qualitative measures for quality assessment helps to define what 'success' looks like and the key priority areas for campaign activities.

These four aspects set out the constraints for each project and have to be clearly defined and agreed amongst the relevant stakeholders at the outset of a digital marketing campaign. However, in a digital marketing campaign, cost does not apply in all scenarios. Some resources might have incurred costs in previous campaigns, but they would not have a direct cost for the current campaign. For example, an organisation might have a very strong brand advocate who creates content and leads an online community on their own because of their own self-interest and brand advocacy. The Internet culture is full of 'unboxing videos' – where individuals film themselves opening up a box containing a product and sharing the excitement with others by posting the content on video-sharing sites such as *YouTube*. If this benefits the brand, such campaigns may not really involve financial cost. This applies to a number of sectors that rely on volunteers

Figure 5.2 The Project Triangle

Figure 5.3 The Digital Project Triangle

and the community to help in developing a service or a product, and they use the resource of social capital. Social capital is essentially the likelihood of someone helping you because they know you and you have helped them in the past. Social capital cannot be quantified in conventional ways such as money, but if it is present, it offers a competitive advantage to an organisation (Heinze et al., 2013). Some basic indicators of social capital that a brand can have are the number of interactions it receives from its buyer persona representative when it asks them for feedback (read more on social capital in Chapter 8). For example, the 'My Starbucks Idea' website is dedicated to customers of *Starbucks* to share their ideas on how to make *Starbucks* better – the volume and the quality of the recommendations are an indicator of how much social capital *Starbucks* has.

Therefore, the four variables that constrain the project of digital campaign assessment and planning criteria as represented in Figure 5.3 are:

- **Scope** – specific objectives of each individual digital marketing channel.
- **Time** – start and end dates of the campaign.
- **Resources** – financial resources, in-house human resources, social capital.
- **Quality** – KPIs and data used for measuring the digital campaign impact (e.g. clicks, traffic, sales and shares).

The implementation cycles and importance of nine steps

Digital marketing strategy implementation does tend to go through a number of iterative cycles. By drawing conclusions from the lessons learned, you act on continuous improvement, constituting the basis for the development of the next iteration. This iterative nature is also characteristic of digital activities, since so many variables keep changing all the time – for example, when search engines release their ranking algorithm updates and refreshes, when social media platforms come and go, as well as the impacts of competitor activity on your campaigns.

The four phases of the action learning cycle (Plan, Act, Observe and Reflect) (Figure 5.4) will constitute the main themes in this chapter. Although their role will be described in the following sections, these stages can be defined as:

- **Plan** – refers to the setting of project triangle-related activities (resources, times, scope and quality).
- **Act** – indicates operational stages (message building, allocating and curating campaign content).
- **Observe** – involves results monitoring (KPIs), optimisation and risk management.
- **Reflect** – constitutes a basis for the next cycle of promotional activities.

A more detailed example of a digital marketing campaign approach is illustrated in Figure 5.5.

Planning (cycle steps 1–5) – a digital marketing campaign starts with identifying your strategic aims. Such an approach requires you to define where you want to be in three to five years and predict what your organisation will achieve in this time horizon.

In the second step, based on the seasonality of your industry and key related events for your buyer persona, the scopes and aims should be set for individual campaigns. A florist preparing for Valentine's Day could have campaigns that are targeting the search term 'Valentine's Day flowers'. Based on past performance, tools such as *Google* Keyword Research offer insight into when your buyer persona will start their research journey. The search volume for flowers slightly increases in December, has a high increase in January and is at its highest in February (Figure 5.6). The data clearly points to the need for your organisational planning to focus on the four months from December to March for your Valentine's Day flowers campaign.

The third step of planning is translating a campaign into shorter-term Specific, Measurable, Attainable, Realistic and Timely (SMART) campaign

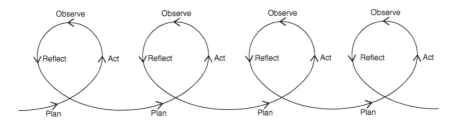

Figure 5.4 The digital marketing implementation cycles

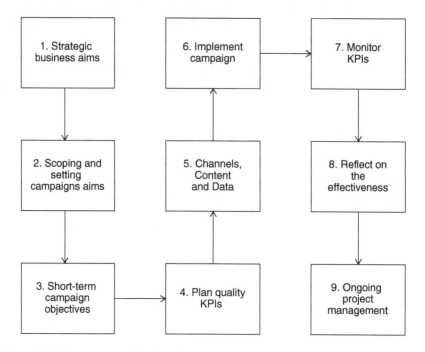

Figure 5.5 The nine steps of the digital marketing campaign implementation cycle

Figure 5.6 Keyword research tool data showing seasonality (*Google* AdWords)

objectives (see Chapter 4 for an explanation of SMART). This involves indi-cating the appropriate constraints from the Project Management Triangle, like scope, time and resources for the individual four months.

After defining the quality KPIs to be achieved (fourth step), these can be grouped into monthly, quarterly and annual reports for measurement and reflection. For larger organisations, multiple projects on the same product could be grouped into programmes, and programmes of a particular brand can be grouped into portfolios. Programmes and portfolios show another level of abstraction when it comes to collecting and grouping KPIs. Whilst financial cycles can be broken down into tax timeframes, product and service trends need to take into account seasonality and competitor activity when setting these KPIs.

The **Planning** phase is complete after documenting the communication channels and content (step 5), as well as creating a Gantt chart, which lists all the main activities and identifies critical paths to the success of the project. Risk assessment is completed and the main risks are documented with management; mitigation of these is also identified. Whilst communication with all relevant stakeholders is important at each stage, before acting commences it is essential to get buy-in and agreement from all primary stakeholders. Face-to-face meetings are usually best for presenting and clarifying the plan for a campaign, but other forms such as written documents and virtual presentations are important. Organisations such as the Association of Project Management produce templates for project plans, which can guide you in thinking through an individual campaign cycle. These can be adapted to your own needs.

Even though the **Acting** phase (step 6) of the cycle consists of only one step, it is certainly no less important. The majority of project manager time is spent in preparing and briefing all parties at the planning stage. The acting stage is mainly driven by implementing activities specified within the Gantt chart and managing project-related risks. The planned activities are now being implemented. However, things don't always go to plan. The actual campaign implementation might need to be adjusted due to unforeseen circumstances. The already agreed list of project priorities offers a supporting guide for making minor adjustments.

The **Observing** phase (step 7) focuses on monitoring your current activity and its progress in relation to the planned Gantt chart and the risk table. The tracking Gantt chart is produced to monitor the actual time and tasks undertaken to complete the project. The difference between the Gantt chart and the Tracking Gantt chart is that the former is produced ahead of the project implementation and is based on estimation, whilst the latter is a documentation of actual time, resources and scope delivered. Any problems that occur throughout a campaign are also added to the Tracking Gantt chart and Risk Management table, and documented. The mistakes and errors of a campaign as well as all successes have to be documented so that future campaigns can use this insight to improve.

The last steps of the digital campaign implementation cycle are based on the **Reflecting** stage (steps 8 and 9). This stage is used for reviewing the campaign results and effectiveness and the likelihood of achieving the annual and strategic aims. The Tracking Gantt chart is compared to the estimated Gantt chart and risks are reviewed. Reflecting on past campaign management and reviewing against set objectives and KPIs helps to better estimate KPIs for future campaigns. Stakeholder correspondence and feedback are also taken into account when writing the campaign report. At this stage your analysis should focus on determining which activities to continue and which to stop. The reflecting phase closes the cycle and, due to the approach of continuous improvement, constitutes the basis for the development of the next iteration.

5.3 Planning – starting a new project

The planning stage plays an important role in digital marketing campaign project management. Often, organisations focus on the short-term campaigns, not taking into account strategic priority areas. However, this kind of thinking does have its challenges, in particular when considering justifications of major investments in people or in tools such as a customer relationship management systems or an extensively customised e-commerce application. Such investments are needed to facilitate long-term organisational growth, hence longer-term planning is needed to see a return on investment (ROI). For example, an email database needs to be used regularly and needs to be up to date in order to be useful for many years to come; spending a lot of energy on a one-off email campaign and finding that it did not work the first time because most of the addresses were out of date is not a reason to never use email marketing again.

On the other hand, *emergent strategy* allows for flexibility and gives freedom for individual short-term activities, which, with time, can translate into a repeatable pattern and become documented in a formal strategy document. The emergent strategy starts with **action** and is contrasted with *prescriptive strategy*, where the process starts with **planning**. Emergent strategy is more appropriate for dynamic industries and fast-changing activities such as digital marketing. The prescriptive strategy translates a long-term organisational vision into strategy and through tactics to programmes.

Defining aim and objectives

Based on an understanding of the strategic priorities, the short-term digital marketing campaign aim and objectives are set. These can be broadly grouped into two types – brand awareness and conversion-driven campaigns.

Brand awareness objectives

The aim of brand awareness is to generate positive publicity for the brand and its products or services. Some of the objectives could be focused on increasing brand mentions, engagement with the buyer persona, generating high-quality incoming links to the website or footfall to physical premises where relevant.

Digital content produced and optimised for this activity could be based on broad keyword search phrases (as discussed in more detail in Chapter 7). These campaigns assume no or limited awareness of brand, its product and services names.

Conversion-driven objectives

Conversion-driven aims can be focused on achieving any specific calls-to-action. For example, objectives could be to measure enrolments to an event, mailing list subscriptions, visits to physical premises, if relevant, and most importantly, number of sales in volume and value. The type of content used for these tends to be more products and services specific.

Content should be produced and focused on more specific keyword search phrases that include both organic and paid search terms (discussed further in Chapter 7). This content would be focused on longer search terms bringing the buyer persona closer to the final decision-making process.

Example Box 5.1   Florists

Two florists, A and B, plan their digital marketing campaigns. A aims to increase brand awareness and B aims to increase the number of bookings. Both florists are aware that January is the time of year when most buyer personas tend to research and arrange details of their wedding flowers.

Basing their activity on the SMART objectives principle, both have to specify the precise and unique outcome (Specific), that will refer to quantitative values (Measurable), and be possible to attain (Attainable), based on estimations from previous campaign experience where possible (Realistic) and defined within a specific period of time (Timely).

Because A aims to increase brand awareness, it defines its objective as:

'To develop and launch three-month-long campaign for January 2020 comprising 1 minute long YouTube video and four related blog posts and related social media networks amplification targeting subject of "wedding flowers ideas" and reaching 1,000 new company website visitors.'

B aims to increase bookings and so defines its objective as:

'Double the number of wedding flowers related bookings in January 2020 compared to the year before by creating a four-month-long campaign targeting "wedding florist in Chorley UK", comprising a 1 minute long YouTube video, four blog posts, PPC and offering a bottle of champagne for every non-refundable booking deposit in January 2020.'

The selection of channels for individual campaigns will depend on understanding the channel mix as proposed by 'the Customer Journey to Online Purchase' (see Chapter 3 for more details). All campaigns should prioritise the strategically committed channels of communication based on the understanding of the buyer persona to ensure that the right channels and messages are used.

Budget setting

In general, there are four main methods of planning the digital marketing budget (Table 5.1).

The percentage of sales and the affordability methods of budgeting emphasise that the marketing budget can be almost unlimited. This unlimited budget idea does not work for all industries; for example, a hotel with a fixed number of rooms cannot sell more rooms for the same period of time. But the concept works well in digital content consumption, e.g. watching an online video or listening to a song.

Table 5.1 Main methods of marketing budget planning

Budgeting method	Description	Advantages/Disadvantages
Affordable method	Budget is estimated as the remainder of funds once all operational expenses have been deducted from overall revenues.	*Advantages*: spending will never exceed financial capabilities. Supports organic growth of an organisation. *Disadvantages*: usually results in under-spending on marketing, which leads to uncertain annual promotion budget and ignores the effect of promotion on sales. Accessing external funds and investments for growth are not advocated.
Percentage-of-sales method	The budget is set at a certain percentage of current or forecasted sales per unit.	*Advantages*: very simple, emphasises the relationship between marketing spending, selling price and profit per unit. *Disadvantages*: leads to false impression of sales affecting marketing instead of resulting from them. No basis for choosing specific percentage ranges.
Objective-and-task method	The budget is set by defining specific objectives and determining the marketing tasks required to achieve these objectives. The budget is set to cover the costs of these tasks.	*Advantages*: forces managers to link the level of spending to expected results. Accessing of external funds where necessary to facilitate growth and transformational thinking is encouraged. *Disadvantages*: it is difficult to guarantee results without having past performance data. Large-scale investments that rely on borrowed capital create a risk for those organisations that expect activities to deliver sales to repay the borrowed capital.

Source: Adapted from Kotler and Armstrong, 2012

Your budget will also depend on your digital channels mix selection. For example, while using social media networks such as *Facebook* and *Twitter* is free of charge, the human resources for monitoring and engaging in these networks takes time.

Ultimately, deciding what to spend should be based on what is sensible for the size of your organisation, your strategic ambitions and your available resources. As consumers increasingly use digital channels, your marketing channels need to follow them. Whether you establish a modest or robust budget, it is important to learn what will work for your organisation today and in the future (Association for Project Management, 2015). As your awareness of the Buyer Persona Spring grows, you will also learn what works, so that you can set more realistic objectives for the next campaign.

5.4 Acting – executing your project

From a project management perspective, acting is an ongoing process, and focuses on keeping the Digital Project Triangle under control. This role is mainly focusing on leading activities such as stakeholder expectations management, team management, roles assignment, scheduling and workflow planning and amending Gantt charts. From a campaign operational perspective, acting involves researching and developing content and digital engagement tools, as well as implementing these in practice. In larger organisations a project leader can be assigned, who oversees the activities of others. In smaller organisations it could be one person who is responsible for all activities – in this case, it is particularly important to allocate time to reflect on the campaign process (how things are done) and not just on campaign operation (what is being done). This chapter focuses on the project management perspective, and subsequent chapters will review channel-specific actions such as conducting SEO and implementing social media optimisation.

Campaign documentation

Documentation of all project-related information is placed in a single file – Project Documentation. This document is continuously updated as the project progresses so that it can be used for future project estimations and as a template. Dependent on the scale of your project, the Project Documentation could range from a single spreadsheet to a host of files that help to define the project based on the following five W-questions: Why? What? Who? Where? When?

- Why is this project being done?
- What will be done as part of this project?
- Who will do what and how?
- Where will content be created and published?
- When will activities take place?

Perceiving a digital campaign as a short-term project, the Project Documentation principally justifies and clearly defines your project as well as indicates its scope. If necessary, it also secures funds for the project from a previously established budget. Moreover, it assigns the roles and defines the responsibilities of project participants and it can be referred to as a source of information for other team members.

For larger organisations, introducing a digital campaign project requires contributions from appropriate team members inside your organisation as well as external actors. Contributions could be knowledge of past similar projects, or implications of the current project on their activities. For this purpose a project initiation meeting with them is a must – this outlines the project and makes clear the communication protocols and timeline of activities. Ongoing stakeholder management would be agreed and involves communicating with the wider organisation as necessary, e.g. as outlined in Figure 5.1.

The Project Documentation could have the following sections:

- Campaign name – name campaigns to make them distinct from one another.
- Aim and objectives – setting the direction and scope of the campaign.
- Business case – the reasons that rationalise the campaign activities as being worthy.
- Project team – outline of project sponsor, manager and other team members.
- Communications plan – how the project team will communicate, how frequent these communications will be and the contact details of these individuals.
- Quality plan – how quality will be assured and assessed during and at the end of the project.
- Deliverables – the expected tangible artefacts produced as a result of the project.
- Scope – detail of how objectives will be achieved, e.g. which channels, what content and what activities would be part of this campaign.
- Resources – what financial and non-financial resources are available to the project.
- KPIs – for tracking and assessing what a successful campaign looks like.
- Risk register – what activities can go wrong and how risks will be managed and mitigated.
- Work schedule – including the project Gantt chart and critical path analysis.

Project team

Team management techniques are a response to the 'What? Who? Where? When? and Why?' questions from the 5Ws approach. While describing the initial roles in a project team (Mind Tools, 2016), you need to define:

- Project sponsor – the individual with ultimate authority and control over the project and its implementation.

- Project manager – the team leader, responsible for implementing the project, assigning roles and clearly defining responsibilities of other members. Person responsible for delivery of project on time, on budget, within scope and to the defined quality benchmarks.
- Team members – individuals with specific roles and responsibilities in a specific project.

By assigning roles to your remaining key members of your project team you define their job descriptions. A team membership diagram showing the lines of authority and reporting for each project team member can help in complex projects.

The project manager is central to communications between team members and the project sponsor. It is often a difficult position, balancing operational reality with strategic priorities (Table 5.2).

Communication plan

Managing projects requires formal and informal communications between all the stakeholders, and agreeing when these communications take place and their purpose is important. Regular communications as illustrated in Figure 5.7 can be done at different frequencies with different team members – these could be to review and reflect on campaign progress and seek solutions to emerging problems. Problem-specific communications can also be set up to facilitate

Table 5.2 The responsibilities of project management

Do	Don't
• Keep a holistic overview of the project • Take into account integration between tasks • Delegate tasks to team members • Schedule and communicate activities for yourself and others • Manage and motivate the project team and act as a leader, and be prepared to be flexible • Engage all relevant stakeholders and project team members with relevant information • Control quality of project-related tasks and deliverables • Manage project costs • Assess and review risks related to the project • Overcome obstacles arising in the course of the project – cooperation facilitating	• Get involved in micro management – you can't control every single task of the project • Get carried away with operations, forgetting the aim and objectives of the project • Ignore poor-performing KPIs – if the project is not working, don't worry about stopping the whole project • Leave questions from your team members unanswered • Create authority based on negative team members' emotions (fear, bullying) • Rely on a single point of information – where possible, always consult multiple sources to make your decisions • Rely on informal communications with all your stakeholders • Prioritise urgent over the important • Assume you know it all

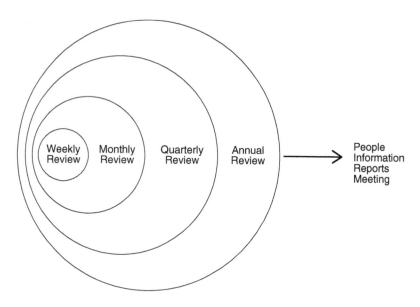

Figure 5.7 Communications plan

Management by Exception when intervention is required. Management by Exception is based on the assumption that the team implementing the project can make deviations from the project plan as long as these are not significantly different. The project manager is only consulted when these go beyond certain agreed boundaries. Communication agreement is also needed on tools for documents sharing, contact details for video conferencing, and the phone numbers and email contact details of all relevant stakeholders.

Work schedule

To complete a project successfully, you must control a large number of activities and ensure that they are completed on schedule. A delay of one activity or task may lead to negative consequences for the entire project, while prolonging another activity can have no impact on the overall project. For this reason, the idea of 'divide and conquer' works for projects, which is based upon the assumption that controlling smaller parts of the project helps to control the overall project.

Gantt charts are a common technique in project management, and present a project in a visually accessible way. A basic Gantt chart lists project tasks, the individuals responsible for those tasks and when the tasks have to be undertaken (see Figure 5.8). In its simplest form it uses bars on a horizontal timescale to show the start, duration and finish of activities.

Project task	Name and % responsible			Project Months					
	Aleksej	*Tahir*	*Gordon*	1	2	3	4	5	6
Identify target market	50	30	20	X					
Client meetings	30	30	40	X	X	X	X	X	
...									

Figure 5.8 An example of a basic project management Gantt chart

Work schedule management is the process of developing, maintaining and communicating schedules for available resources. The Gantt chart must show all the work related to the delivery of the project according to the assigned time. An additional benefit that a detailed Gantt chart offers is the ability to log activity precedence. By calculating the duration of each activity and which activities rely on the completion of others, it is possible to estimate the project's longest time for completion. In project management, this longest sequence of activities is called the 'critical path'. On a Gantt chart the critical path could be a line connecting the bar charts for the critical interdependent activities. Interdependent activities could be creating a web page before a pay-per-click (PPC) campaign is launched, or driving traffic to that page. More sophisticated variations of Gantt charts can convey other project-related information such as cost per task, resource over-allocations and percentages of completed tasks.

Knowing the activities on the critical path allows you to allocate the best resources in your team and therefore increase the chances of your project being successful. Also, knowing the critical path activities offers you the ability to prioritise important tasks over those that appear to be urgent (e.g. responding to urgent emails instead of creating content for a video campaign). To create a Gantt chart and the critical path, answer the questions below:

- What are your time/cost constraints?
- What preceding activities need to be completed?
- How do individual activities depend on each other?
- Which activities can be done in parallel?
- What is the estimated duration of each activity?
- Who do you need for each activity?
- What is the skill level of each resource assigned to its task(s)?

To develop a Gantt chart, a number of tools are available, from simple spreadsheets and free online tools such as Trello, to specific tools including commercial tools such as Microsoft Project and free tools such as Gantt Project. Plans change and, therefore, there is a need to re-prioritise activities; in cases where the digital campaign is causing unintended negative consequences, it can be stopped and the project terminated.

5.5 Observing – optimising your efforts

During the acting phase of the campaign, a project might change the activities as the need arises. For example, a *Google* update algorithm is released which requires you to change your approach to your campaign. Factors impacting on the Digital Project Triangle, such as changes in budget, timeframes or illness of team members, result in the need for revision of activities. The knowledge gained from observations of a project has benefits for future campaigns and therefore, documenting lessons learned is a key component in the optimisation of your future efforts.

Continual review of schedule and budget

During the project observation stage, the project manager has to make sure that the project is moving forward as per the Gantt chart schedule. As previously mentioned, online project management software tools are available to allow project managers to track the project schedules, budgets, organisational resources and project-related material in real time. These tools also allow other members of the project team to view and update their contributions to the project, upload related information and inform others about the status of the project. Regardless of the complexity of such tools – whether you use a spreadsheet or an automated digital integrated project management service – you have to have a clear understanding of the costs incurred by the project. Whether working on an in-house digital project or for an external client, the lack of accurate financial information has a negative effect on the sustainability of the project and the overall organisation. To avoid such issues, while preparing a project, relevant finance monitoring systems have to be agreed and put in place, including the relevant software support.

'Re-prioritising' tasks

During the project management process, one has to anticipate risks associated with the project. For example, negative feedback from customers on social media may prompt a project management team to pause their marketing activities or bring in a customer services agent or reputation manager to manage feedback in real time. This exemplary form of unexpected outcome may force organisations to re-prioritise certain activities and introduce new activities into their project. Therefore, project managers must create flexible projects and be ready to re-prioritise their tasks due to unexpected risks from internal or external forces.

Maintaining a risk register

Risk management is a way of anticipating challenges and managing these to reduce their negative effect on a project's success. Risk management involves identifying risks, assessing their impact and probability, prioritising risks and then monitoring and mitigating these. The documentation of Risk Management is logged in a risk register, which in its simple form could be as illustrated in Figure 5.9.

The first column states the name of the risk – Risk Identification. Then the **impact** of the risk is analysed and rated on a scale from 1 to 5 using the following interpretation:

1. Negligible
2. Marginal
3. Important
4. Serious
5. Catastrophic

The estimate of the risk occurring is noted in the **probability** column:

1. Impossible
2. Remote
3. Unlikely
4. Possible
5. Probable

The **assessment** column notes the assessment of individual rows for the risk and is a result of Impact x Probability. The scores for assessment can be colour coded using this notation:

Red: assessment of 15–25
Amber: assessment of 9–14
Green: assessment of 0–8

Risk Identification	Impact	Probability	Assessment	Management and Mitigation
Not being able to gain number 1 position for a secondary keyword 'SK'	2	2	2 x 2 = 4	**Use a range of secondary keywords expectations**

Figure 5.9 Risk register

The final column allows for documenting management and, where possible, mitigation tasks for this risk. The collection of all project-specific risks entered in the register allows the team to make a judgement on whether the overall project is still viable – for example, if all risks are on Red and there is not much that can be done to mitigate these, the team need to consider if the project should be terminated (Figure 5.9).

The project management team should identify possible hindrances and take steps to resolve them if they occur at any stage of the project.

Quality assessment

Quality assessment means that the project is able to meet the objectives of the project team and that it offers the desired quality and functionality. The main objective of quality assessment is to detect and rectify issues as quickly as possible. An early correction of errors tends to result in the reduction of surplus costs and offer overall schedule benefit. The major tools for quality assessment are testing and technical reviews. Technical reviews originate from the software development discipline and are becoming a crucial activity in digital marketing campaigns. They are based on expert peer review, where an expert examines artefacts or content and offers their feedback and overall assessment on the suitability of the artefact for the desired campaign. User experience testing is another commonly used technique for digital artefacts quality assessment. User experience is based on involving representatives of the buyer persona and asking them to use the artefact. Their use of the artefact can be recorded, and users are interviewed about their experience of using the artefacts.

Monitoring results

There is no management without control functions. That is why the role of monitoring and tracking to obtain results is so important within the whole campaign cycle. First, because it closes the whole cycle and thus allows the company to summarise the results obtained in relation to the previously established objectives. Second, and sometimes more importantly, this verification provides a basis to take further actions for future campaigns. Analysis of subsequent campaigns will allow expenditure optimisation and will provide invaluable knowledge for future decision making concerning the most successful digital marketing channels to choose, who should be the target of future campaign messages and which activities will yield the best results for your organisation. Knowing which channels do and do not work for your organisation can save you time and energy in the future. Of course, the digital environment is very fast paced, and new types and forms of digital communication tools are always emerging. Therefore, always scanning for new opportunities is good practice when planning and reviewing a project. Competitors and customers may change and evolve; hence, following their needs and interests is also important, as all knowledge gained from campaigns feeds into an understanding of the buyer persona.

Example Box 5.2   When high click-through rate (CTR) still means a campaign failure

When an electronic retail bank in Poland conducted a digital campaign, users were encouraged to click an advertising form and were transferred to a landing page relevant to the campaign. The campaign resulted in 3 per cent CTR, resulting in website traffic increases; however, the bank quickly found such traffic was not converting into sales and generated no income for the bank.

The bank's previously established banner campaign had given an inferior CTR outcome (around 1 per cent), but a higher rate of customers applied for the advertised online cash loans. So, what went wrong with the new campaign?

Between the two campaigns neither the landing page nor the application form had been changed, and pricing conditions remained constant. It was all about the choice of a new advertising form. The new platform allowed a user to click anywhere on a web page, but only in specific places of the ad image. This resulted in confusion when users who clicked on a space were directed to a link not mentioned in the ad. The new advertising platform gave outstanding CTR results. However, since users were clicking and landing on a non-relevant web page they were confused and did not proceed to apply for the loan. The loan application was a metric as well as the CTR. Despite the high brand awareness due to relatively high CTR of the new campaign platform, the overall campaign did not result in the desired sales.

The example of the Polish bank highlights the importance of measuring the effectiveness of the user experience through continuous observation. Instead of verifying the indicators and metrics you should instead track your most important KPIs.

5.6 Reflecting – closing a project

Reflection at the end of the project allows the project management team to assess its efforts and learn from its experiences. Reflection is not only about looking back; it is also a proactive step taken by the project manager to re-assess their activities regarding the project. Project reflection, in part, allows the project management team the time to identify their strengths and weaknesses throughout the duration of the campaign and to learn from this for the sake of future projects. Key learning can be used to update the Buyer Persona Spring as well as information about the buyer persona itself. For example, by launching a campaign on social media channels and receiving positive feedback from your followers, your organisation receives a positive reinforcement that the strategy is working. This means that maintaining a similar direction for future campaigns is appropriate. On the other hand, as shown in the Polish bank example, with high CTR but low sales, not all high numbers inevitably show the full story of success. All campaigns require a full set of KPIs that will measure the actual success that you seek.

Preparing for premature closure of a project

Closing a project is a consideration that should be open to the manager and the team. In Management by Exception, the decision of project closure is certainly something that requires careful consideration of the advantages and disadvantages of doing so. Premature closure of a project can be disappointing for any project team, although the experience gathered during the project is always useful. However, you should consider it as a valuable lesson. For instance, closure may become the only way out if the budget for the project is no longer available.

Creating a post-project report (against initial goals and benchmarking)

Developing a post-project report is necessary, since it gives the project management team the opportunity to review the results of the project and determine its success. If the post-project report shows that the project was able to achieve the initial goals and meet the benchmarking required by the project team at the start of the project, this means it was a success. However, even if the original aim and objectives have not been achieved but secondary aim and objectives emerged as the project unfolded and these resulted in a beneficial outcome for the organisation, future projects can use the new aim and objectives as a starting point for new campaign considerations.

Undertaking a project debrief (with relevant stakeholders)

After completion of the project, the project manager should debrief stakeholders who were directly or indirectly involved with the project. The debriefing allows the project manager to understand the viewpoints of the stakeholders regarding the project and learn from others' experiences. The valuable feedback and constructive criticism received from the debriefing permit the project management team to learn from such experiences for future projects.

Making a concerted effort to praise achievements

Whilst the 'Praise Publicly and Correct Privately' rule has some critics, the general thinking is worth noting. It is the responsibility of the project manager to appreciate the project management team when they successfully complete the project. Praising colleagues for the successful completion of the project motivates them to do even better in future projects and makes them feel that they are valued as part of the team.

At the same time, the project manager has to lead the team when they are unable to achieve the desired goals of the project. The project manager must meet privately with the team members concerned and share constructive criticism so they do not repeat the same mistakes in the future.

5.7 Summary

After opening with an explanation of the main stages of the campaign planning cycle, we then explored the first stage of the planning cycle, and considered the campaign setting objectives aligned with the overall digital marketing goals. You have learned how to set a planning budget and how the key message of the campaign needs to be thought through, keeping in mind the buyer persona and the digital media channels selected.

The key digital marketing campaign planning tools for documenting digital campaigns have been discussed. A project Gantt chart and a risk assessment table help you to keep on track of the Project Management Triangle.

The four stages of Planning, Acting, Observing and Reflecting have been given attention from a digital marketing campaign perspective. Whilst project management time is spent mainly on the planning part of the campaign, there are tasks during acting, observing and reflecting that are essential for documenting the actual project and learning from these lessons for future campaigns.

5.8 References

Association for Project Management (2015) What is project management? www.apm.org. uk/WhatIsPM

Heinze, A., Ferneley, E. and Child, P. (2013) Ideal participants in online market research: Lessons from closed communities, *International Journal of Market Research*, 55(6), 769–789.

Kotler, P. and Armstrong, G. (2012) *Principles of marketing*. Pearson Google Publishing.

Mind Tools (2016) *Project initiation documents. Getting your project off to a great start*. www. mindtools.com/pages/article/newPPM_85.htm

6 Developing an effective digital presence

Ana Cruz and Stelios Karatzas, University of Sheffield International Faculty, CITY College, Greece

6.0 Learning objectives

In this chapter you will learn how to:

- recognise what constitutes a digital brand presence;
- differentiate key concepts such as brand equity and social media branding;
- maintain digital presences to create content synergies;
- differentiate media types – owned, earned and paid;
- understand the role of user experience;
- develop information architecture that is based on your buyer persona;
- use key performance indicators (KPIs) to assess your digital presence.

6.1 Defining digital presence

Your digital presence is the sum total of all the online activities managed by your organisation (including websites, blogs and social media profiles) as well as the online activities carried out by your key stakeholders, such as employees and consumers. The interactions that are generated by this presence can make or break brands. Corporate brand managers no longer engineer brands. In a digitally connected world, brands are co-created.

You might see your digital presence as a means to an end but, if managed strategically, it can become an important asset in its own right for your organisation. Your presence is not only for sharing information but also to build credibility (Verisign, 2016), trust, engagement and brand loyalty. These positive responses can all be achieved by influencing attitudes and behaviour.

Influencing behaviour does not solely mean the completion of a purchase. For non-profit organisations, for example, the behaviours that are encouraged may be to support a cause financially, to sign a petition, to donate something or to recycle more and waste less. Of course, influencing and securing purchases remains a vital aspect for most businesses, so having clear calls-to-action (such as buy, like and share) within your digital presence is vital.

6.2 Brand building

Branding is a pivotal aspect of your strategy because it provides a focal point for your buyer persona. Your buyer persona can identify with your brand and will associate it with the value that you deliver. Your brand helps to clearly differentiate the products, services and experiences that you offer from those of your competitors.

The work you have already undertaken that has been described in earlier chapters, for conducting external and internal examinations of the environment, the identification of a strategy and the process of defining and creating your buyer persona, supports the development of a robust market presence.

In the Buyer Persona Spring your brand is an integral part of your organisation, although in small organisations this may currently be an underdeveloped aspect of your digital identity. If you are in this position, then brand building should be an integral aspect of your overall digital strategy and a key consideration for your content, channels and data sub-strategies. A strong brand identity that is well communicated through key content on the right channels will appeal to your buyer persona and tighten the spring to your organisation (Figure 6.1).

Building your brand requires careful consideration of what your brand stands for now and what you want it to stand for in the future (in other words, the brand essence). How does your brand make your customers' lives better, safer, more exciting or more convenient? With popular commentary suggesting that attention spans are shrinking, why should your buyer persona pay attention to you, your product or your website? Why should your buyer persona use your application or read your blog? Consider the message conveyed immediately by brands such as Volvo (=safety), Apple (=simplicity) and Angry Birds (=entertainment). Each of these brand promises is clear, based on fundamental customer needs and consistently delivered by every aspect of the organisation. These messages are delivered by the entire organisation, not just through the products and services that they provide.

Each touchpoint between your organisation and your buyer persona is a moment of truth, where the promise of your brand needs to be consistently delivered. Apple's brand association with simplicity is translated into its product, packaging, web design, apps, interface and usability. Apple promises a life of beautiful simplicity where form follows function, where each interaction is intuitive and the 'I' at the centre (e.g. iPad, iPhone, iTunes) is all of us – individually. Your branding challenge is to develop a meaningful promise of value (the value proposition and unique selling point or USP) that is fully aligned to your organisation. Your organisation must then consistently live up to and deliver this promise of value. Your organisation can develop this alignment by responding to a series of straightforward questions (Figure 6.2).

- 'What do we say?' How do you communicate internally and externally? For example, social media policies for employees are just as important as integrated communications with your buyer persona.

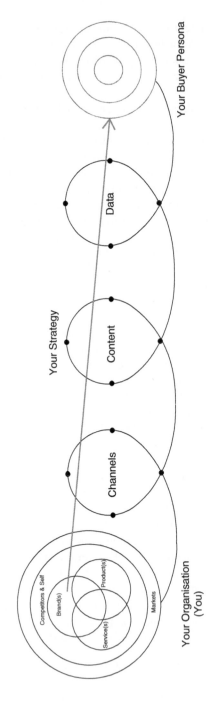

Figure 6.1 Brand building with the Buyer Persona Spring

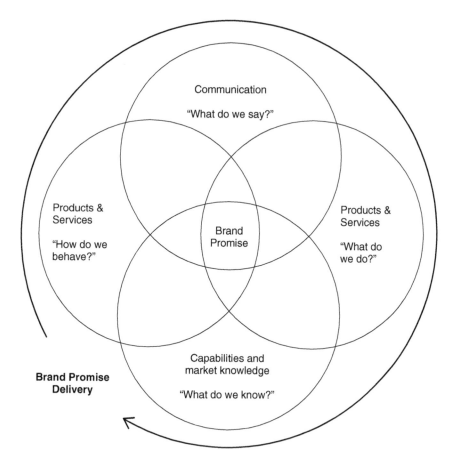

Figure 6.2 Embedding your brand's value within your organisation (adapted from Cruz, 2006)

- 'What do we do?' What are your products, services, experiences and interactions?
- 'How do we behave?' What is your organisation's culture and behaviour? How do you facilitate engagement and conversation with your buyer persona?
- 'What do we know?' What capabilities, and market and customer knowledge can be maximised through market research and social media listening? How much knowledge and understanding does your buyer persona have about your brand?

Brand alignment (or misalignment) can also be recognised in the Buyer Persona Spring (Figure 6.3). Brands that are misaligned will appear to be at odds

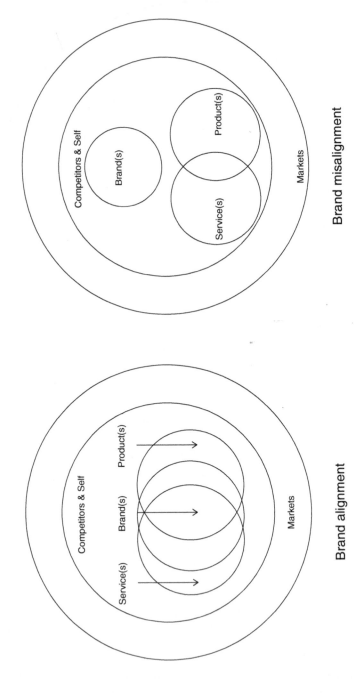

Figure 6.3 Brand alignment or misalignment in the Buyer Persona Spring

with your products and services and will confuse or misdirect your buyer persona. For example, developing a brand that suggests luxury will be misplaced in a retail outlet full of discounted items. In contrast, a brand built on an image of convenience and value for money could be entirely appropriate, particularly if the image distinguishes you from competitors in a unique way.

6.3 Brand equity

Brand equity is 'the extra value customers perceive in a brand that ultimately builds long-term loyalty' (Wood, 2010). Effective digital presence for your organisation requires a focus on building brand equity through brand knowledge, preference and loyalty. Organisations may own a trademark (the name, logo and symbols), but the brand and its equity ultimately lie in the head, heart and actions of your buyer persona, as is the case with the *Newby Trust* (Case Study 6.1).

Case Study 6.1   *Newby Trust* build trust in their brand online

Even when organisations don't rely on online purchases, they still need to build their brand. The same principles of branding apply. The buyer persona must easily recognise what the brand is saying and doing, how it is behaving and what it knows.

For a small charity like the *Newby Trust*, the need to build brand equity is significant, as it acts as a trust for charitable organisations, and most of the public are probably unaware of how these types of organisations function. From its home page, the visitor is immediately drawn to what the organisation has to say (a trust that supports the common good). Scrolling down further we are directly shown what the *Newby Trust* does (makes grants to registered charities and small grants to philanthropic organisations).

The *Newby Trust* successfully communicates its brand behaviour through a concise and informative history section, and in describing how simple it has made the process of applying for grants. In this way, the brand has made an arduous, complicated and time-consuming procedure for receiving funding for charitable endeavours easier. The *Newby Trust* has successfully built its brand online and has enhanced its brand equity.

It has also taken steps to ensure that the basics of brand building are supported by other approaches, to ensure a positive experience for its buyer persona. For example, it repeatedly offers contact details and support for questions and more information. Additionally, the brand reveals its recently audited accounts to ensure transparency, a fundamental position for any trust organisation seeking to gain credibility and legitimacy. This action helps to further build the positive perception of the brand.

   Source: www.newby-trust.org.uk

Brand equity is built as the buyer persona becomes aware of the brand and begins to value its offering, when they know what the brand stands for, when they respond to it and when they want an ongoing relationship with it.

   The Brand Equity Pyramid (Figure 6.4) illustrates these levels.

   The variables that induce positive brand equity in retail include creating an emotional connection, an excellent online experience, responsive service environment, high levels of trust and high-speed fulfilment for orders. In a digital environment, brand equity means getting the hygiene factors right, including findability, speed of download, contemporary site design, intuitive navigation, robust order fulfilment and personalised support (Christodoulides et al., 2006; Cavender and Kincade, 2014). The application of these key factors is discussed later in this chapter.

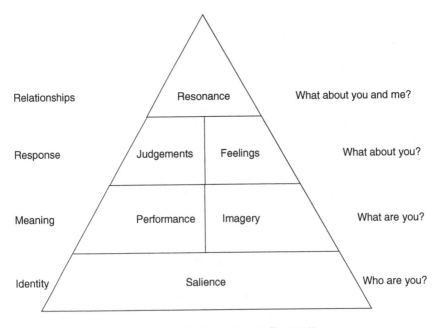

Figure 6.4 The Brand Equity Pyramid (adapted from Keller, 2012)

6.4 The rise of the social media-based brand

The rise of social media, plus advances in technology, mean that consumers are now capable of creating and publishing content themselves. This means that your brand is being co-created right now, whether you are part of that process or not. If we are aware of brand equity, this co-creation includes your organisation. Even if you are not currently creating your brand, your key stakeholders are. Your customers, employees, pressure groups and brand advocates are all working away at presenting your brand through user-generated content (UGC) such as videos, reviews and blogs. Without your participation there are no guarantees that this image of your brand will reflect you accurately or even positively. To build brand equity and achieve resonance with your buyer persona, your brand will need to facilitate relationships, interactions and conversations – to be a social brand that listens and engages. Your conversations should not just be dialogues but forums, with all your stakeholders able to talk to each other – for example, the ability to review products (on multiple channels), comment on blogs and use social media buttons to share, like and tweet (Case Study 6.2).

Case Study 6.2   *Snog* frozen yogurt engages target market in fun conversations

Frozen yogurt is on the rise. In a booming competitive market, two men found a way to stand out from the crowd by creating a cheeky brand name and strapline (Fancy a *Snog*?) and linking it with fun bricks-and-mortar locations and a great product.

In order to complement the fun and excitement of their retail brand, the owners knew they needed a fully functional, engaging website. They first had to ensure that their web page was easily findable, which they successfully achieved. (At the time of writing, a search on *Google* using the key terms 'frozen yoghurt' displayed the *Snog* brand in fifth place just after *Wikipedia*.)

Snog is a vibrant brand, using lots of bright colours and fun flavours, and their presence on social media is essential for communicating with their target audiences. By sharing and posting creative and engaging content, they intrigue their target audiences and create a trialogue (where customers talk to each other). *Snog* achieves this by posting eye-catching and humorous imagery and creating a buzz through likes and comments.

Snog also shares user photos and experiences with their brand on *Twitter*, showing that the brand appreciates and supports its customers.

Snog understands that visuals should greatly outweigh text, particularly for their product and target market. Since their consumers cannot actually buy their product online, their main focus is to entice the user into buying their product through strong visuals that stimulate the senses and through humorous text (showing users fun and interesting ways to mix and match ingredients for their frozen yogurt), showing new products with equally stimulating visuals and text, by telling users where they can find the product with an intuitive map that tells users how far they are from the next *Snog* location, and finally, by sparking users to engage with the brand by displaying their *Snog*blog, *Snog*social and *Snog*mail links with more humorous language like: 'We love to hear from our Snoggers'.

Snog understands its target market well. At the time of writing, the brand is negotiating deals with *Unilever* for the distribution of their brand.

Creating content that facilitates dialogue and sharing is one of the most important activities for delivering an engaging brand experience. The combination of your content, channels and data sub-strategies should enable this brand experience. There are many challenges to this work, and in contrast to traditional approaches to marketing, the digital environment is not necessarily brand-oriented and people want to connect with each other rather than a brand. Brands are not people – usually (Azoulay and Kapferer, 2003) – but the metaphor of a brand personality is one way you can bring your brand to life. If the brand were a person, how would it behave? What are its values? How would it talk? What is its tone? These considerations will clarify the image that you want to project and will set the tone for all your conversations and interactions with your buyer persona.

Building your brand requires you to create and offer content through channels that will get you invited into the conversation, and that get others talking about the brand. Listening – and gathering the data that results from this listening – is a fundamental principle for effective conversation (see Chapter 8 on social media for more details about listening online). Your strategy must include a data sub-strategy that closes the loop and listens to your buyer persona in a way that enables you to respond intelligently and personally.

6.5 Social media presence

In order to build your brand, a social media presence is essential. Almost all social media, including *Facebook*, *Twitter*, *YouTube* and *LinkedIn*, allow customisation features for brands as well as individuals. The composition of your social media presence will be shaped by the brand you are creating and will be a key consideration for your channels sub-strategy.

A key starting point for a successful social media presence starts with your name (for example, https://twitter.com/EU_Commission). In order for your name to rank well in search engines, your social profile name should appear in the most familiar way that users would search for your organisation.

Most social media channels also allow you to have a profile picture. Larger businesses will use their brand logo and consistent naming of the brand. This approach applies to all organisations. Sometimes your brand name will not be available. If the brand name is already taken, use words like 'official' or the brand's location after the name (for example, UniversalBG for a company based in Bulgaria). Another option is to use your specialism to gain a naming advantage. For example, you could use specialist sector positioning such as 'Sports Financing'.

Some social media channels allow a background picture. This can be used for pictures of new products or services and can be updated regularly. As with usernames, profile pictures should stay consistent through all of your channels to deliver a consistent message and brand personality.

6.6 Developing a network of profiles

It is very important that each of your social media channels as well as your primary website are well interlinked. This consistency makes it clear to your buyer persona that your brand wants to engage. Consistency also enables better data collection to track which channels produce results – whether this is sales, engagements or actions. On the channels that allow a biography there is an opportunity to share your brand philosophy, brand personality and USP. Keep it short. All your channels should also be linked from your organisation's website, making them consistently visible as well as through email signatures, business cards and forum signatures.

There are different types of social media buttons for web pages – most importantly, 'Follow' and 'Share'. The 'Follow' button links a social media profile and allows a visitor to follow your brand through multiple channels. The 'Share' buttons allow the user to share content across social media channels, and can also incorporate a counter that allows some basic activity data to be gathered. A higher number of shares for a particular piece of content is also a proxy measure for the trust that is being placed in your brand by your buyer persona. Measures of trust are particularly important for e-commerce web pages. Writing a review can be an onerous task, but a like or a share is a quick way for a visitor to endorse one of your products or services. However, there is a risk in publicly displaying sharing counts, as low numbers all too clearly reflect low popularity.

Organisations use social media channels to connect with their buyer persona. One of the most effective channels for doing this is a blog. Developing a blog and then amplifying the content of the posts through other channels contributes to the longevity of your content (Figure 6.5). The nature of social networks is such that they are constantly changing, so it is a risk to invest a lot of energy into a social media network that might become less popular in two years. If you have a blog, your customers can access your content without

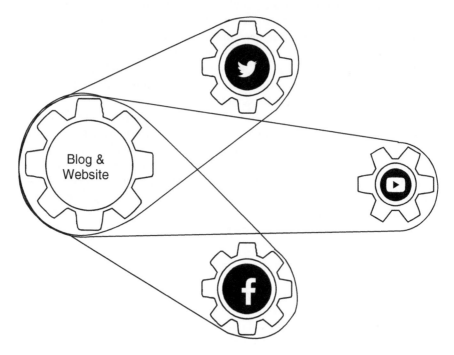

Figure 6.5 The centrality of a blog in your brand development

signing up to a particular network, and the content will always be available through a search engine, offering a safer longer-term social media presence. Also, all social network profiles can be used to amplify blog content that is based on the main website – driving traffic and engagement to the main digital profile of your brand.

6.7 Owned, earned and paid content

One of the most crucial ways for a brand to stand out is through engaging content which makes users want to comment on and share it, and which sparks conversations. There are three different channels where content can be placed: these are described as owned, earned and paid.

Owned channels and content include corporate, product and brand websites, blogs, campaign sites, social media profiles and mobile applications. This category also includes bricks-and-mortar stores and offices which connect your buyer persona with your digital activities.

In contrast to your owned content and channels, both paid and earned content are external endorsements of your brand which can be earned through genuine positive word-of-mouth or paid advertising. Paid-for content has lower levels of credibility when compared to earned content, but it can still be a powerful tool. For example, online and offline advertising and retargeting (where

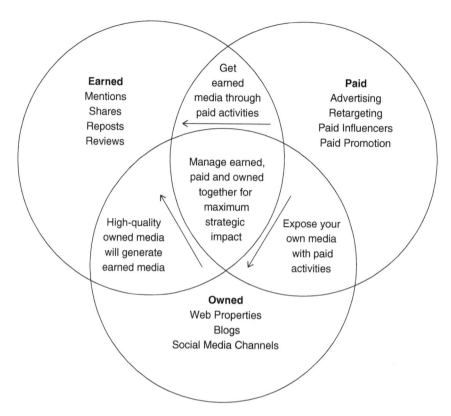

Figure 6.6 Owned, paid and earned content and channels (adapted from www.titan-seo. com/newsarticles/trifecta.html)

an ad follows a website visitor who left your website without a purchase) can be effective ways to generate brand awareness and drive traffic to your website (one of your owned channels).

Organisations also pay influencers to share or endorse content. Paid endorsements, both online and offline, must be clearly labelled as advertising to comply with good practice guidelines for advertising and codes of ethics. This form of paid content introduces specific ethical considerations when it is unclear if the endorsement is genuine positive word-of-mouth – earned content – or just a paid-for promotion.

Earned mentions in the form of reviews (UGC) have become the third most trustworthy source of information at a global level (Nielsen, 2013). Thus, product reviews have become an important aspect of earned media due to their potential impact on sales. For example, Ho-Dac et al. (2013) researched the impact of online customer reviews on the sales of the new Blu-ray players and the already mature DVD players. The study's findings indicate that positive or negative online customer reviews increase or decrease the sales volume of the different models belonging to weaker brands, but they have no impact on the sales of strong brands. However, a high number of sales leads to more positive reviews, which in turn can help increase brand equity.

6.8 Building a successful user experience

Your owned channels are the ones that you have the most control over. You can respond most rapidly to external changes through your owned channels, and your owned content is the most malleable to your brand's proposition and positioning. Of all your potential paid channels and content, your website is probably the most central to your entire digital marketing effort and strategy. How easy or difficult it is to use and navigate your website is known as the user experience. A successful user experience translates into positive experiences that can lead to contentment, positive behavioural intentions and even emotional connections with your brand.

Your aim in creating a positive user experience is not merely to satisfy your buyer persona with reliability, convenience and functionality; it is to 'wow' your buyer persona into wanting to return again and again to your website, and to share their experience throughout their network. User experience is a crucial step in converting a user into one of your brand advocates.

Your goal is to improve customer satisfaction and loyalty through the utility, ease of use and pleasure provided by the use of your owned channels. Mahlke and Thüring (2007) describe three user experience factors that assist in evaluating a website experience and to positively influence future user decisions and behaviours.

- *Perceived instrumental qualities*: what users notice as being easily usable and useful (e.g. controllability, effectiveness, learnability). This should include access for every user, regardless of any disability, and should follow W3C (w3.org) guidelines such as always having alternative text for images, or providing transcripts for podcasts and videos.
- *Emotional reactions*: how enjoyable the interaction is and how the content transforms the user's hedonic state of being (subjective feelings).
- *Perceived non-instrumental qualities*: what the user believes to be appealing and attractive (visual aesthetics).

User experience is inherently focused on the user and on where value will be generated through the user's experience of the channel.

6.9 The principles of user experience design

The fundamental objective of user experience design is centred on the end user. The user experience should meet a user's expectations regarding ease of use, while offering a simple process for accomplishing a goal that is obvious to the user. It is important to recognise that search engine robots are among the primary audience for any website, and require easy-to-access information in order to index the website so that it will rank well on search engines and other users can find it more readily (this point is discussed in further detail in Chapter 7).

Slow-loading content on a site is a fundamental *faux pas* of usability. Users are no longer willing to wait for content to appear. Another common mistake is a busy layout that distracts users from clear calls-to-action and inhibits readability. Similarly, when there are no search options or feedback mechanisms, users can get stuck while trying to find what they want and be unable to proceed to a completed action. A clearly visible search option that leads to a truly functional internal search function is an essential feature that allows users to freely look for what they want while also introducing a data-collection opportunity that helps you to identify what users are looking for; the website search data can be captured through a system such as *Google* Analytics and reviewed in regular reports (see the analytics discussion in Chapter 12).

Usability is about being able to make fundamental use of your website, whether it is being accessed from a mobile device like a phone or tablet, or from a variety of web browsers like *Mozilla Firefox* and *Google Chrome*. Anything that prevents efficient task completion, takes someone off course, causes confusion, creates an error, allows the misinterpretation of content or leaves the user unable to understand the navigation are all important considerations when user experience is the focus of your attention.

6.10 Usability guide and testing

According to the US government's online guide to usability (usability.org), there are five steps in creating a usability guide: planning, analysing, designing, testing and refining. These steps are incorporated into the overall user experience design processes, with a specific focus on how easy the website is to use at all times. The easier it is to use, the more a user's attention is directed to all other aspects of the user experience.

Besides simply using a guide and testing, there must also be a process for understanding and identifying usability issues through user testing and observing actual users. Hedegaard and Simonsen (2013) found that usability designs that include emphasis on dimensions of hedonic affect and emotion, pleasure and enjoyment and fun score much better in usability testing. Albert and Tullis (2013) have identified, through in-person studies, that there may be verbal expressions of confusion, indecision or dissatisfaction, and non-verbal facial expressions and eye movements. After issues of this type have been identified, they can be categorised further with severity ratings, for example, from low (annoying but does not result in task failure), to medium (issues that contribute to but don't directly result in task failure), to high (issues directly related to task failure). Issues can then be placed in priority or non-priority categories. Severity issues can also be analysed and reported by frequency per participant or group. It is also constructive to illustrate and collect positive outcomes and possibly focus on them for further development.

6.11 Responsive design

Mobile devices such as tablets, ebook readers and smartphones are growing in popularity. Your digital presence needs to be capable of operating on these platforms too. Building a mobile site demands a responsive design – a web design created for an optimal viewing experience on multiple screen sizes, with easy-to-read content and large navigation buttons that better support small screens and touch-based scrolling navigation. Mobile devices deliver your content on the go, alongside other screens and among a crowd to people who want to access information quickly and easily. Done carefully, your brand and content can be delivered into the heart of a group of like-minded people, alongside that of competitors and at key points in a discussion.

Building a responsive design is a similar task to that of building a great user experience. Simplicity is the key, offering fewer options, using plain language, keeping formatting simple and sticking to conventions. Because mobile devices have smaller screens, content must be organised to include the most pertinent information at the top of a page. Mobile devices rely on touch input, so your functionality should be straightforward. Mobile devices generally also have slower connections, so your web pages should reduce any data transfer to a minimum, and keep content and actions on the same page to save data costs for the user.

There are some specific challenges to responsive design including the complexity of development, and the need to reduce a website to a bare minimum so that it can adapt to all devices and browsers and overcome the inconsistencies of website functions on different devices (especially considering the speed at which new devices are being developed). Some companies have worked around these issues by partnering with other organisations that have mobile capability (Case Study 6.3).

Case Study 6.3   *Sailing Logic* partnered with BookItBee to leverage mobile ticketing

As users increasingly turn to their mobile devices when they want to go online, it is imperative that organisations adapt their content to these shifting consumer preferences.

Sailing Logic is a UK small and medium enterprise (SME) focused on introducing the sport of yacht racing to those who see the sport as being exclusive. The brand offers unique packages that allow individuals who have never met to join together as a team and take part in prestigious sailing races, as well as offering companies the opportunity to team-build with their employees through corporate sailing outings.

Figure 6.7 Sailing Logic logo

In targeting newcomers and those lacking confidence in sailing, *Sailing Logic* built their website's main landing page with bold statements such as: 'Anyone Can Do It!'. Furthermore, the brand ensured that testimonials were highly visible. *Sailing Logic* took particular care to ensure that their previous clients' professions were included in their testimonials to evidence their claims about the accessibility of the sport.

Because *Sailing Logic*'s brand offering was an entirely new experience to most of their prospective clients, and the company expected hesitation, they brought in a trustworthy third-party ticket company for their packages – bookitbee.com. The intention was to facilitate bookings out of office hours, when personal research is often conducted. The site also supports international customers in different time zones. This approach reassures new customers and piggybacks on the trust that exists with the third-party booking organisation.

Sailing Logic's offering requires the dissemination of large amounts of information before a consumer will commit and therefore, they had found it difficult to create a concise and minimal mobile app. Because *Sailing Logic* didn't have a mobile app, they deliberately chose to partner with bookitbee.com – a company that specialises in selling tickets to events via its popular mobile ticketing app.

By partnering with bookitbee.com, *Sailing Logic* allowed their consumers to first research their offering from a desktop and then to book their packages from a mobile device through their partner's utility-based app.

Figure 6.8 Sailing Logic brand

6.12 Website infrastructure

With your owned content and channels defined – based on your strategy and the clear definition of your buyer persona – and your website look and feel and page layouts determined, your next step is web development. The development process will take you from the design phase to an interactive website that will connect you with your buyer persona.

The first step in your development process is choosing and registering your domain name. It is easy to see if your preferred domain name is available – simply type the name into a search engine or web browser and scan the results. Finding a suitable domain name may sound easy, but there are many factors to consider. You might want your domain to be your brand name, if available. However, you may also want to add or subtract from your brand name to make the domain name as catchy and memorable as possible. However, be cautious of being caught up with naming trends, for example, *Flickr* or those offered by the Web 2.0 domain name generator (www.dotomator.com/web20.html).

Depending on where your target audience is, you may choose to use a local domain (such as .gr for Greece or .bg for Bulgaria) if you are primarily serving local markets. But you can also just as readily register a familiar 'global' domain, such as .com, .net or .org, or one of the new global top-level domains (gTLDs) such as .makeup or .watches (http://newgtlds.icann.org/en/program-status/delegated-strings). Another consideration is whether to have multiple domain names to avoid competitors or others registering similar names, while still being able to link those domain names to the main site. Trademarking and intellectual property rights apply online in the same way as they do offline, so there are limits to your choices both legally and ethically. Finally, including keywords in the domain name can help with search engine optimisation (SEO) to make smaller organisations more visible to communicate the purpose of their site.

Another question you will need to answer is whether the website should be static or be based on a content management system (CMS). Static websites have historically been perceived as the cheaper and more secure option (Garner, 2014), since they are hosted without the aid of a database. However, with the maturity of open-source CMSs such as *WordPress*, there are really no technical, design or marketing reasons to use a static website.

Most hosting companies freely offer pre-installed open-source CMSs (such as *WordPress* for information sites or *Magento* for e-commerce sites), which simplify website development for smaller organisations. These systems are easy to use and customise, with many free themes and plugins that make website management easy for those with limited technical knowledge. There are many guides, online courses and help sites for these popular systems, which provide a relatively low-cost form of technical support. There are a number of plugins that allow a CMS to be integrated with other systems such as a customer relationship management (CRM) system or a simple mailing list management system (such as *MailChimp*).

6.13 Information architecture

The best websites are shaped with a strong understanding of their buyer persona's interests, needs and expectations. The content, visual design, organisation and navigation should all work in harmony to enable users to find key information easily and readily complete critical tasks. This arranging and grouping of information can also benefit the website's visibility for search engine spiders to create better SEO results. The term 'information architecture' refers to the organisation and structuring of a website. Better information architecture creates a more coherent, intuitive and satisfying experience for your buyer persona.

With a well-defined buyer persona, a clear understanding of your organisation and a definite digital strategy you should be able to identify the keyword phrases or keyword terms that are of highest relevance to your organisation and your buyer persona. This understanding should produce high specificity (combinations of two or more words), have high search volume (determined by search engine data from *Google*'s Trends or Keyword Planner tools) and should ideally have low levels of competition (indicated by the keyword difficulty tools). These terms should be identified and categorised into themes. The themes will help you determine the pages your website needs, in addition to the more 'standard' content of 'Home', 'About Us' and 'Contact Us' pages.

Having identified the main themes, you will then need to outline the content structure based on these themes. A hierarchy of subcategories should incorporate all of the keywords that you are targeting. The highest levels of your website hierarchy should include the most important but general information, while lower levels of the hierarchy should have less importance overall, with more specific information. Some keyword terms might not fit into the hierarchical structure, but these can still be utilised through blog posts and as part of the overall ecosystem of content that answers all the needs of your buyer persona.

This hierarchical site structuring should then intuitively lead to the creation of a site map (the visual representation of the logical structure of the content). The site map can be translated into a web page that will help to outline the navigational structure for your website in a manner similar to the way a table of contents helps to organise a book.

Good navigation should include menus and submenus similar to the contents page of a textbook. Your buyer persona will be familiar with this system. From a design point of view, it is important that your buyer persona is not presented with more than seven options – simplicity is important for user experience. Your keywords now act as content labels which users will click on, so the words should be meaningful and representative of what users can expect to find on the resultant page. With this increasingly extensive architecture now defined, wireframes can be created as a guide to integrating all of the indispensable page elements in an organised and purposeful manner, and to help you brief and collaborate with designers and developers.

6.14 The AIDA model for creating content

Once your information architecture is well defined, you need to set out the content that will align with the keywords that you have identified and will convey the essential aspects of your brand's message. One formal model for designing content is known as AIDA. This model presents four key stages in converting prospects into customers (Table 6.1).

Brand awareness is increasingly generated through search engine results pages (SERPs). As a result, the more search-engine friendly your website and all your channels are, the easier it is for your brand to build awareness.

As the stages of the buyer journey progress, it can become increasingly difficult to engage the buyer persona. At the interest stage, relevance and usefulness are key. Your engagement must answer why your buyer persona came to the site and what they want to know. This is why a clear USP is of paramount importance for successful marketing. Make your content easily accessible. Use images and video, and write well-formatted text that is designed for online readability and scalability. Use familiar structural elements such as headings and bullet points. Write in short sentences and use short paragraphs.

Develop a desire in the buyer persona by creating an exciting and relevant user experience. It is also about displaying the content necessary to make a purchase decision, either through video, images or text. Other ways of evoking desire include associating your products and services with social causes,

Table 6.1 The AIDA model for content creation

Attention (or Awareness)	Create attention and awareness for your brand, your website and other channels and your products and services. You can measure the success of this stage through the number of visitors, number of impressions, number of pages visited and average duration of a website visit.
Interest	Spark interest in your products and services through engaging content that is created by you for the brand and also by its advocates. Success for this stage can be measured through the number of engagement interactions such as comments and re-shares, as well as how many new conversations are generated that are related to your brand's activity.
Desire	Generate desire to buy your products and services through positive third-party reviews and special offer campaigns. Measures of success include the total number of new mailing list subscribers, new followers on your owned and external channels, and repeat visitors to your website.
Action	Move your buyer persona to complete the desired activity on the website or through social media channels, which has the ultimate business objective of, for example, making a purchase or causing a change in behaviour. Success at this stage looks like the number of sales, the total value of new sales and number of 'earned' positive UGC reviews and comments.

celebrity endorsement and online promotions (free trials, discounts, gifts, competitions and one-time offers). Once desire has been crafted, there should be a clear and logical call-to-action that can be found through directional cues that lead the eye towards it.

During the final action phase, the attention of the user has already been gained, but an obvious call-to-action should be visible, such as a large clickable button saying 'Buy Now', 'Donate Now', 'Sign Me Up' or 'Free Trial'. These buttons usually have contrasting colours, and clearly defined parameters with bold borders for emphasis. Some best practice advice for calls-to-action involves keeping the number of calls-to-action to a minimum and using active language. Any statement that includes words such as buy, call, register, subscribe or donate will use active language. Since a website user can potentially enter your website from any web page, having a call-to-action on every web page is a good way to measure the attractiveness and success of each page. Calls-to-action could be as simple as asking the user to follow you on a social media network or as complex as a full e-commerce interaction.

6.15 Content and website design

Visual content has become imperative for web designers. In a visual culture, 'seeing is believing' is more than a cliché. Humanity is generally drawn to visual information (pictures or videos) more efficiently than text, and this particularly applies to international audiences where written text may be inhibiting their understanding of your content. You can use this knowledge to create a website that wows your buyer persona (Case Study 6.4).

Case Study 6.4   *Audacy* stands out from the crowd with a site designed to wow

Brands are no longer solely about selling products and services; they are selling 'experiences'. Every brand should offer its own unique experience. If you were to search for digital marketing agencies, you might quickly become overwhelmed by the sheer number. This is where the French small business *Audacy* stands out from the crowd.

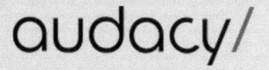

Figure 6.9 *Audacy* logo

From the home page, you are captivated by stunning visuals and interactive displays. The 2016 version of the website uses a CMS – specifically *WordPress*. The moment you scroll over an image, various other images pop out, attracting the user to engage further with the content. A contact number is positioned clearly at the top of the page and an address at the bottom, easing any concerns about legitimacy.

Since most users searching for and eventually contacting *Audacy* will not have a marketing background, it is important that the brand makes the content as easy to understand as possible. The brand has done this by sticking to only four options on the menu bar, presented in a clearly strategic order. They begin the online journey by exhibiting their previous projects in order to 'wow' the user to further engage with their brand. Clicking on the services icon reveals exactly what services are offered. Each of the three services is accompanied by easily comprehended descriptions below each image to clarify the service without overwhelming the user with too many details.

Under the agency icon, *Audacy*'s clear USP portrays the personality of the brand and its uniqueness. Further down the page you are introduced to the company's process, their philosophy, added value, partnerships and testimonials. This is fundamental content for converting their buyer persona, who will quickly see if there is a fit between their business and the agency's brand.

Source: www.audacy.fr

Even though visuals by themselves are good for grabbing attention, pictures and video bring greater value when they are combined with text. The important points in the (concise) text should always be highlighted using bold and italics in combination with headings and subheadings to create visual hierarchies. If more information is required, bulleted or numbered lists and easy step-by-step outlines can be used.

Sparking the senses and enticing curiosity are key. But this must be supported by practical content that is valuable to the user, is conveyed in a professional manner and does not contain typos or grammatical errors. And, just as the principles apply for user experience, language must be easily understood by most readers (unless it is targeted to only a very specific buyer persona). If facts are stated, they should be backed up or referenced to ensure credibility and encourage trust in your brand. All of this content should be presented in a personal tone that adds a human touch to your brand.

6.16 Summary

An effective digital brand presence is the sum of all your digital activities. These include not only content and channels managed by your organisation (websites, blogs and social media channels), but also activities carried out by your key stakeholders when they are engaging with your brand. A robust presence provides a platform to communicate, engage and co-create value for your organisation and your buyer persona. Aligning what the brand and the organisation say and do, how they behave and what they know is vital in order to deliver a unique brand promise and experience.

A robust digital presence begins with an understanding of your own organisation, your buyer persona and the user experience you are setting out to provide. The open ecosystem of social media introduces the prosumer (a person who both consumes and produces media) and UGC. It is vital to listen and to (co-)create value, content and experiences that people would like to share and talk about. This interaction and engagement can be maximised with the use of paid and earned channels to drive traffic to your owned channels and content.

Your website can be optimised by creating an excellent user experience which enables an augmented experience for the user. Your user experience should pay special attention to usability, and should incorporate processes of constant testing of the channel and its content to ensure that it is appealing to your buyer persona. Throughout the processes of building this design, your buyer persona is at its heart, from the creation of content all the way through to the testing stage and thereafter.

Highly usable websites not only increase traffic from consumers, but also optimise the potential to rank higher on SERPs, bring higher social media channel engagement and, ultimately, increase positive brand awareness. Focus on usability must also extend to ease of use for accessing your website from mobile devices. Having a keyword-driven website information architecture is another vital component to satisfy your buyer persona's needs.

6.17 References

Albert, W. and Tullis, T. (2013) *Measuring the user experience: Collecting, analyzing, and presenting usability metrics*. Newnes.

Azoulay, A. and Kapferer, J.N. (2003) Do brand personality scales really measure brand personality? *The Journal of Brand Management, 11*(2), 143–55.

Cavender, R. and Kincade, D.H. (2014) Management of a luxury brand: Dimensions and sub-variables from a case study of LVMH. *Journal of Fashion Marketing and Management, 18*(2), 231–48.

Christodoulides, G., De Chernatony, L., Furrer, O., Shiu, E. and Abimbola, T. (2006) Conceptualising and measuring the equity of online brands. *Journal of Marketing Management, 22*(7–8), 799–825.

Cruz, Ana (2006) *Industrial brand strategy: Mapping a learning journey*. Unpublished M.Ed, dissertation, University of Manchester.

Garner, D. (2014) *A Content Management System (CMS) or static website: Which is right for you?* www.dmgbluegill.com/blog/content-management-system-cms-or-static-website-which-right-you

Hedegaard, S. and Simonsen, J.G. (2013) Extracting usability and user experience information from online user reviews. In *Proceedings of the SIGCHI Conference on Human Factors in Computing Systems* (pp. 2089–98). ACM.

Ho-Dac, N., Carson, S. and Moore, W. (2013) The effects of positive and negative online customer reviews: Do brand strength and category maturity matter? *Journal of Marketing, 77*(6), 37–53.

Keller, K.L. (2012) Understanding the richness of brand relationships: Research dialogue on brands as intentional agents, *Journal of Consumer Psychology, 22*(2), 186–90.

Mahlke, S. and Thüring, M. (2007) Studying antecedents of emotional experiences in interactive contexts. In *Proceedings of the SIGCHI Conference on Human Factors in Computing Systems* (pp. 915–918). ACM.

Nielsen (2013) *Under the influence: Consumer trust in advertising*. www.nielsen.com/us/en/insights/news/2013/under-the-influence-consumer-trust-in-advertising.html

Verisign (2016) Five reasons every small business needs a website. http://blogs.verisign.com/blog/entry/five_reasons_every_small_business

Wood, B.M. (2010) *Essential guide to marketing planning*. Pearson.

7 Search engine optimisation: strategy implementation

Aleksej Heinze, Salford Business School, University of Salford, UK

7.0 Learning objectives

In this chapter you will learn how to:

- create a search engine optimisation (SEO) strategy and implement it;
- research and develop a strategic keyword plan for your buyer persona, including identification of channels to amplify the content;
- understand technical SEO and be able to diagnose potential issues;
- implement the four pillars of SEO.

7.1 The importance of search engines

In countries where Internet penetration is high, using search engines is one of the most frequent online activities. Search engines are popular because they bring a form of order to the Web. Information and resources are immediately available in ways that would be impossible without them.

To harness the power of search engines, your organisation needs to generate high-quality digital content that is interesting to your buyer persona. When this quality content is used with search engine marketing techniques, you can maximise your brand's visibility within search engine results pages (SERPs).

It is generally acknowledged that the vast majority of search engine users do not go beyond the first SERP. This means that if a web presence – a web page, social media profile, app or post – is not found in the top half of the first page of the SERP, your chances of attracting users to your brand's web presence are significantly reduced.

As in traditional marketing, it is important to determine if your buyer persona is actively using the Internet and, presuming that they are, how they use it, e.g. are they mostly using search engines, or mostly using social channels, and which applications and channels do they prefer? Knowing your buyer persona is an essential first step before substantial resources, in terms of your time or money, are allocated to a specific channel. SEO plays a pivotal role in digital marketing as a key link in the chain between your internal resources – but especially your website – and the vast complexity of the Web.

For the Buyer Persona Spring, SEO is an essential part of your strategy. SEO most readily and clearly draws together your three sub-strategies of content, channels and data. The importance of SEO within each of these sub-strategies is equally significant. Leading practice in SEO defines many of the parameters for determining the quality of your content, provides a linkage between all of your preferred channels and gives you the most accessible forms of data for your organisation to make informed decisions.

This chapter will offer insight into the key techniques and tactics that will help to get your organisation's website ranked in organic SERPs.

7.2 The business models of search engines

When you are working with search engines you are communicating with automated computer databases. These databases are constantly collecting, storing, evaluating, sorting, ranking and sharing information. A basis for a search engine's business model is focused upon a fast and positive user experience – ensuring that relevant, high-quality content is returned quickly for any given search query. A successful search engine marketing (SEM) strategy is based on how well you know each specific search engine's standards and requirements. There is no single search engine that is dominant in every country in the world. Although *Google* is a major player in the majority of North America and Europe, *Baidu* dominates the Chinese market and *Yandex* is the leader in Russia. Understanding the search preferences of your buyer persona is the first step in developing your SEM strategy.

SEM traditionally includes a mix of pay-per-click (PPC) and organic search campaigns. PPC is paid advertising, which has an immediate effect on the results at the top of a SERP; in contrast, organic search is a longer-term activity that is achieved through your SEO activity. However, while there are many tactical differences between PPC and organic search, there are also direct strategic synergies that you should plan to recognise. For example, a well-optimised organic SEO web page is likely to have a positive effect on the quality score of a paid campaign if you are targeting similar search terms.

Working with a search engine algorithm

One of the key challenges with SEO is that, unlike other forms of marketing, brands wishing to rank in SERPs are entirely at the mercy of each search engine's algorithm for identifying high-quality content. The initial formula of PageRank (Page et al., 1999), which essentially took the number and importance of incoming web links to a web page to rank its importance, has been substantially revised and the results of this are no longer publicly available. Adding to this complexity, all search engines regularly update and refresh how high-quality content is both defined and recognised. *Google* alone implements around 500 changes to its internal search algorithm each year. Most of these changes are minor with trivial impact, but a handful of these updates each year will require a change on most websites. *Google* have made this situation ever more complex and dynamic, with over 10 per cent of their updates now based on artificial intelligence and machine learning involving no human intervention.

Algorithms are secretive and highly complex mathematical formulas that provide the search engines with instructions on how to rank the importance and relevance of a page. Continual amendments are made to the algorithm, which are rolled out with the aim of improving the quality of both search results and the web pages that are discovered behind the results (further recommended reading are three specific *Google* algorithm updates – 'Hummingbird', which specifies how search queries are handled, 'Penguin', which relates to incoming links to a website, and 'Panda', relating to the quality of content). Clearly, in such a dynamic environment it is important to keep up to date with algorithm changes. This can be done by following SEO-related blog posts and monitoring the MOZ algorithm change calendar (https://moz.com/google-algorithm-change).

To determine if your organisation's website has been affected by a search engine algorithm change, there are a number of tools available, such as *Panguin* (http://barracuda.digital/panguin-tool/). *Panguin* is one of the free tools that maps the known dates of *Google* algorithm updates against the traffic that you are receiving on your website.

Organisations that ignore changes to *Google*'s and other search engines' algorithms risk losing highly ranked positions on their targeted SERPs. In some cases the search engine will apply penalties to pages that contravene what is currently regarded as leading practice. These penalties can be applied manually or automatically, and will depend upon the severity of the violation to a search engine's algorithm. By understanding and adhering to current leading practice, your brand gives itself the best possible chance of achieving high rankings naturally for specific keyword phrases and search queries.

Recent events have shown that sometimes organisations are not operating on an even playing field for SEO when it comes to how large brands fare compared to smaller organisations. For example, a search engine can easily remove a small organisation from its listings if they contravene any of its guidelines, and there is little that the small organisation can do except to rectify their 'error'. However, and in contrast, if a large multinational is found to be spamming, they are likely to receive a much lesser punishment. This reflects an economic reality in that the search engine needs the large organisations for the scale of their advertising revenues and the expectation that search engine users will find these brands through the search engine. This was evident in the case of BMW in 2006 (Malaga, 2008). The brand's website was found to be violating quality guidelines (by creating doorway pages). It was publicly removed from *Google* SERPs but then speedily reinstated once the problem was fixed. A number of other short-lived *Google* penalty examples have been imposed on brands such as *JC Penney*, *Interflora*, *Rap Genius*, *Halifax*, *Thumbtack* and *Expedia*. Controversy has rumbled on over time around search engines giving preferential treatment to large brands, but these brands equally had to respond by fixing their digital presence in order to regain strong SERP performance.

The ethics of search engine optimisation

Some SEO techniques have been described as an active attempt to manipulate or 'game' the search engine ranking algorithms. This approach is also commonly referred to as 'Black Hat SEO'. These are techniques that generally have only short-term impact and risk having a website penalised. This is when your organisation needs to take a clear ethical stance in defining your SEO strategy. The argument that is often used by black hat SEOs to justify their approach is that they are not breaking any laws. They say it is only search engines that set the rules regarding leading practice and as they are solely commercial entities, they have no legal basis for their position.

This chapter solely advocates pursuing ethical 'White Hat SEO' techniques. These are the techniques that adhere to the rules and boundaries of practice set out by search engines. These working practices are often found under webmaster guidelines and can be searched for with the phrase 'webmaster guidelines' in combination with the name of the search engine you are working with. The links should lead you to specific breakdowns of current recommended practice. For example, *Google*'s resources are generally found at www.google.com/webmasters/. Once you are familiar with the additional advice from third-party resources such as MOZ, Search Engine Watch and Search Engine Land you can develop your competitive advantage in SEO.

Search engines are both channels (a platform for communication) and a target audience (the large group who selectively receive your message). Search engines as channels are easier to understand – people go to search engines to find information. Search engines as audiences is a less clear perspective, but just as important. SEO is not the process of putting content on the search engines. PPC can be used to position content in this way. SEO or organic SEO is the process of putting content on the Web and managing this content to ensure that search engines like it. This approach typifies the action learning cycle of Plan, Act, Observe and Reflect and enables the effective marketing of your brand to a large audience. Ultimately, SEO is a balance between satisfying search engine quality guidelines and the expectations of audiences who use search engines. The challenge is to achieve this balance without removing the 'human' element from your brand. Whenever you are in doubt about your SEO decision, the user should be given priority. In *Google*'s 'What we believe' section – 'Ten things we know to be true' – the emphasis is 'focus on the user and all else will follow' (www.google.co.uk/about/company/philosophy/).

7.3 How search engines work

In this section the focus is upon *Google*. The rationale is straightforward – it is currently the most dominant player in the world, with 67 per cent of the global search market share (Netmarketshare, 2016). Where *Google* leads, other search engines usually follow. Although this is not to say that understanding how *Google* works will provide all the answers for other search engines.

In essence, a search engine's spider or a 'bot' finds web page links and then automatically retrieves the online content behind each link, analysing and assigning meaning to what has been found. The meaning that is assigned is based on the algorithmic variables, including the body text, the keywords used and their positions, links, synonyms and word proximity, semantic entities, as well as other variables. There are different types of Googlebots for web content: news, images, video, mobile content, AdSense and AdsBot (Search Console Help, 2016). Each bot gathers relevant variables, such as the links out of a page (these are noted for future crawling by the bot) and the content checksum for the page, which is compared by the indexer (changes are compared at that point with previously stored pages). The frequency of change is also recorded and estimated to schedule future visits. Sorting also occurs at this point, like the creation of a large book index.

After a user types in their query they are presented with a list of content that *Google* believes will satisfy the original intent of the query – these are the SERPs. Typically, the content that is returned in SERPs includes a mix of paid and organic results. Each result includes a link with a short title and a description, as well as optional add-ons such as thumbnail images, videos, site links and knowledge graph data. A relatively recent innovation, the knowledge graph is a short summary answer box, found underneath the search box on the right of the organic search results (Figure 7.1), providing a direct and relevant summary response to the user's query without the need for further clicks through to the source page. For example, if you search in *Google* 'How old is Larry Page?', the knowledge graph gives you a direct answer. The knowledge graph uses a number of reference points, including structured data on source web pages, and can contain images, text descriptions, maps, social media profile links and other related content.

Structured data is an important method for providing additional information to help search engines understand web content, and is discussed later in this chapter.

7.4 Creating a search engine optimisation strategy to engage your buyer persona

In order to reach your buyer persona you need to systematically set out to plan and optimise your website's content. Your strategy should also adopt the action learning cycle that is emphasised throughout this book in order to monitor, assess and respond to the success (or otherwise) of your campaigns and tactics.

A typical SEO strategy is based on four key steps:

1) Strategic keyword research.
2) On-page optimisation.

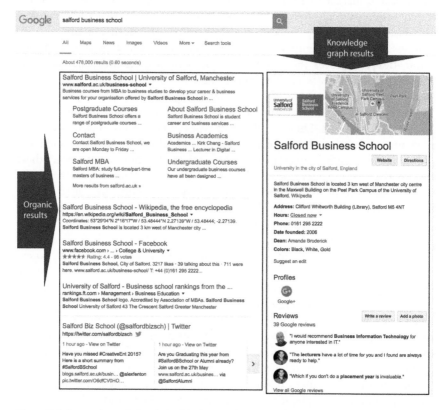

Figure 7.1 Screenshot of *Google* SERP for search term 'Salford Business School', including the knowledge graph on the right-hand side of the page

3) Off-page optimisation.
4) Monitoring of the market.

1) Strategic keyword research – involves identifying the main keywords that are essential to your brand, are likely to be search terms used by your buyer persona and echo the content that is on your website. As your SEO strategy is a long-term commitment, these terms should be generic enough to be valuable to your organisation for years instead of focusing upon individual products or short-lived slang. Three key questions will assist the definition of your keywords:

1 For each term, at what point is your buyer persona in their buyer journey?
2 Why is your buyer persona asking this question at this point?
3 What content is your buyer persona expecting as a result of their query?

Generic intentions can be identified through the specific keywords being used in terms of their stage in the buyer journey and the scale and type of content that your buyer persona is expecting as a response (Table 7.1).

2) On-page optimisation – involves developing or editing your content to reflect your keyword research for a specific service, product or brand. This includes using the words from your research as the basis for developing your website navigation and to shape the hierarchy of your web pages – your website architecture. Thinking about the logical sequence of website navigation for your buyer persona will assist the development of a relevant website architecture. This architecture should also reflect the logic of the changing intention of your buyer persona as they progress through their buyer journey.

Table 7.1 What a keyword reveals about your buyer persona's intention

Type of intention	Intention	Example	Rationale	Content	Assumption (things your buyer persona knows)
Information	Exploratory investigation signalled by plural terms and phrases	'Digital cameras', 'Cameras'	The early research stage in the buyer journey	Your buyer persona is interested in detailed reviews, decision-making guides and comparisons content to inform their decisions	At this stage your buyer persona does not know what they need to know
Navigation	Your buyer persona is seeking a particular website or content	'Panasonic', 'Sony', 'Canon'	Focused-seeking behaviour partway through the buyer journey	Offer rich content product information on your website and social media channels	At this stage your buyer persona tends to know where they want to go
Transaction	Buyer persona wants to actively do something such as buy or download	'Panasonic Lumix DMC-LX100 12.8 MP Compact Digital'	Your buyer persona is looking for the best price for this particular type of camera	Persuade with your price and perhaps current delivery or bundling offers	The camera description itself

3) Off-page optimisation – includes the development of your content and channel sub-strategies that will generate relevant links back to your main 'owned' website. These actions include encouraging (and checking) incoming links generated from social media (e.g. using *Google* Analytics) and from other sites where people are talking about your brand, services and products (e.g. *Talkwalker* Alerts). This work can be done through the amplification available at your owned social media channels. You also want to reach potential industry authorities, industry commentators and bloggers. These earned channels will then ideally engage with and link to your content if they find it relevant and valuable.

4) Monitoring the market – is the final and continuous aspect of your SEO strategy. You should be aware of your competitor's activity as well as key seasonal trends in order to identify any potential strategic opportunities and to evolve your strategy to adapt within a changing environment. Learning about relevant *Moments that matter* (Naughton, 2015) can help you to prepare for and even pre-empt 'moments' in the buyer persona's life. *Google* specifically talks about this aspect of monitoring and responding as micro-moments (www.thinkwithgoogle.com/collections/micromoments.html). This type of monitoring can help you to identify opportunities ahead of time and allow your brand to be there when it matters most to your buyer persona.

The monitoring of competitors is important in SEO, as all SERPs change regularly. In some market sectors these updates occur many times each day; in other sectors the changes may be much less frequent. Being aware of competitor activity and their relative ranking improvements or demotions for specific keywords allows you to anticipate their subsequent actions. A range of freely available tools makes monitoring of your competitors relatively straightforward. *Google* Alerts and *Talkwalker* Alerts can keep track of content changes – and public mentions of your competitors. More detailed SEO analysis is offered by tools such as SEMRush and SimilarWeb, which provide insight into your competitors' action and their visibility on SERPs, traffic overview and the keywords they use. Analysis of the backlink profiles often unveils their off-site SEO strategy by revealing patterns of outreach and site types – see tools such as Open Site Explorer. Likewise, understanding the content types that they are developing – their content 'hubs', for example – may well provide an opportunity to gain advantage by moving more rapidly. The Skyscraper SEO technique is based on the principle of identifying what content works for your competitors and developing similar content but better, and therefore building an even higher presence and engagement with your buyer persona.

The quality of external links coming to your website is regarded as a key factor in off-page optimisation. Opportunities to build up your backlink profile and emulate that of your competitors should be explored at every opportunity.

Personalisation and geo-location are also increasingly coming into play in relation to your page ranking in SERPs. For example, when a person is logged into a *Google* product, their browser history will influence what is shown to them in the organic SERPs.

All of this insight aids your data sub-strategy and will support your expanding knowledge of your own organisation as a digital business.

7.5 Strategic keyword research

Keyword research is pivotal for SEO. Keyword research helps you to focus your energies on generating content that is important to your buyer persona, in their own language, in ways that improve engagement.

Your tactical search engine keyword research informs the wider 'strategic' keywords that apply to your organisation as a whole. For example, a strategic keyword phrase for a florist in Chorley, UK could be 'florist in Chorley', whereas a tactical phrase could be specific to a product or service that is offered for a short period of time, for example, 'Mother's Day roses'. While the specific flower in the phrase might change, the phrase continues to relate to the industry.

Search engines continuously calculate the relevance of the content produced by your organisation in relation to the phrases that users put into search engines. Because search engines base their business model on selling advertising space (see PPC in Chapter 10), they offer potential advertisers information about the keywords that users have entered into their search engines in the past. This information is used to predict the potential volume of individuals interested in that content. Keyword volume and trends data for search engines are accessible through built-in ad management platforms such as *Google* AdWords.

The keyword research process

The overall process of generating keywords is influenced by a number of factors:

- Your marketing objectives.
- How many buyer personas are being targeted and optimised.
- Budgetary constraints.
- National or regional cultures.
- Language, including regional dialect differences.
- The search engine(s) being targeted.

Keyword research needs to be recognised as a combination of art and science; nonetheless, it can be addressed through a methodical three-stage process.

Stage 1 – Keyword brainstorming

Start with an initial brainstorming session, usually in a meeting with your team and, if possible, representatives of your buyer persona. Keywords are inspired by customer needs, as well as your products and services. Additional insight can be gained from focus groups, surveys and social media analysis. Thesaurus lists and other similar sources will help you to find synonyms for words that you have already selected. For example, for someone interested in having their house rewired, they might search for 'house rewiring', 'property rewiring' or 'rewire my home'. Using a semantic keyword search that relies on the meaning of a word or an ontological approach is a good start. For example, list all terms related to a domain or an entity (site topic) – you can also use a range of other 'related' and 'extending' (stemming) terms to enhance topical relevance. For example, it is likely that 'house rewiring', 'property rewiring' and 'rewire my home' may also be semantically found when searching for 'home electricians' or 'house renovations'.

Stage 2 – Keyword refinement

To increase the search volume of keywords in your 'target list' there are a number of online tools available that will suggest additional keywords for you. These tools typically offer relevant data, such as the number of searches conducted each month in specific locations, as well as the term's popularity and competition (others targeting the same term), to help you make an informed decision.

For example, tools that require website access are:

Google Search Console	www.google.com/webmasters/tools/
Google Analytics	www.google.com/analytics/web/

Keyword tools that do not require existing website access are:

Answerthepublic	http://answerthepublic.com
Google Keyword Planner	https://adwords.google.co.uk/KeywordPlanner
Google Trends	www.google.com/trends/
Spyfu	www.spyfu.com
SEMRush	www.semrush.com
MOZ keyword difficulty tool	https://moz.com/tools/keyword–difficulty
Keyword Tool IO	http://keywordtool.io/

Stage 3 – Keywords prioritisation and selection

Now that you have a long list of potential keywords, you need to prioritise the value of your terms with consideration of your buyer persona's preferences, as well as the objectives of your activity. There are four aspects of keyword selection. They are, in order of priority, (Figure 7.2):

1   Relevance
2   Specificity
3   Popularity
4   Competition

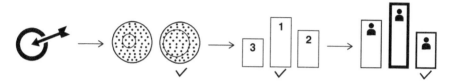

Figure 7.2 Selecting keywords in order of action priority

Selecting keywords benefits from systematic analysis applied to each of these priorities.

1 **Relevance to the business objectives**. Use your judgement and understanding of the buyer persona to define an initial set of keywords. You can use a ranking system, where you rank terms from 0 to 3. Where '0' is irrelevant and '3' is highly relevant. Higher relevance is better.

2 **Specificity of the term**. In general, the longer the keyword phrase, the more specific it will be. If you are scoring your terms, give higher scores to longer phrases. For example, using the 0 to 3 system assign scores ranging from 0 for one word long keywords up to 3 for the longest phrase keywords you have in your list.

There is a continuous trade-off between 'short tail' and 'long tail' terms (Figure 7.3) and this highlights the importance of understanding the user intent behind different types of keywords. In the case of a user completing a search using a single search term with high search volume, e.g. 'Salford', users are unlikely to know what they are looking for and may be at an early exploratory phase of their research. Users arriving at your website through these 'short tail' queries are more likely to quickly 'bounce off' if they do not find the exact information they need and will return to a search engine. Research has shown (Person, 2015) that individuals who are using long search phrases or 'long tail' keywords are more likely to convert into customers, as they are more likely to know exactly what they want from their search. Single-word terms generally indicate that the users are at the start of their buyer journey. The buyer journey is reflected in summary through the evolution of the keywords being used, for example, from 'cameras' to 'second-hand cameras' to 'second-hand digital SLR cameras'. Therefore, the more specific the search term that enables a user to reach your website, the higher the likelihood that you will convert a visitor into a customer.

3 **Popularity of the term**. The average monthly search volume is a good indicator, but it can be significantly affected by seasonality. As a result, your research should consider the annual average search volume in order to even out the seasonality of a term.

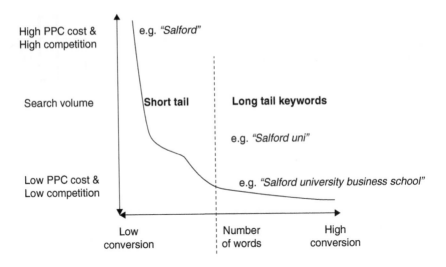

Figure 7.3 Short tail vs long tail keywords

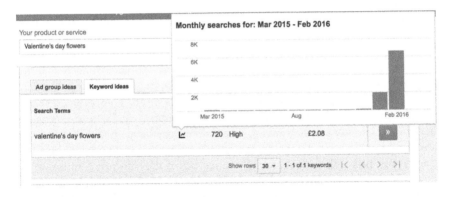

Figure 7.4 *Google* AdWords keyword research data for 'Valentine's Day flowers'

For example, 'Valentine's Day flowers' in the UK has a high search volume in January (1.9K) and February (6.6K), but not much volume in other months (10 to 40 monthly searches) (Figure 7.4). This means that the average figure of about 6,000 searches is a good comparator with other terms where seasonality is not as significant – for example, 'birthday flowers', which attracts an average monthly search volume of about 20,000 searches. Bearing in mind that it can take months to achieve good organic rankings for a competitive term, if a term is relevant and has high seasonal peaks, the highest seasonal peak should be chosen when considering it as a term.

If you are scoring your keywords using the 0 to 3 system, allocate 0 to those terms that have no search volume up to 3 for those terms with the highest search volume.

4. **Competition for the term.** Data regarding competition for individual searches is drawn from paid search results. As a result, it is a less useful indicator of competition for organic SEO; nevertheless, it provides an indication of the competition. In particular, *Google* AdWords provides a good indication of competition by assigning a value between 0 and 1. Other tools, including MOZ and SEMRush, offer similar indications of competition through their keyword difficulty tools.

Your interpretation of these third-party competition scores enables you to apply your own scores. With this priority, the highest competition attracts the lowest score for the keyword phrase – 0. The less difficult a keyword phrase, the higher your chances to rank for it – assign these terms 3.

Having scored all keyword terms based on the four priority criteria, you now add your scores together and use the total of each term as the determinant for a keyword's inclusion. Terms with higher scores will indicate which terms should be chosen primarily for individual pages, while the lower-scored keywords can still be used but as secondary supporting terms.

Using keyword mapping to inform your information architecture

Once all your relevant keywords have been identified and graded, they are grouped into themes. These themes will inform and shape your website's information architecture. Themes are important for capturing the more sophisticated semantic value of the grouped keywords – in other words, themes offer clarity regarding the content that you are optimising. The themes are part of the logic expected by search engine users as well as the search engines themselves (Amerland, 2013). At this stage, you will grade your terms as being of primary or secondary importance for individual web pages. You should aim to have one primary and two or three secondary keywords for each page. Because of the semantic understanding of content generated by a search engine there is no need to include every single variation of your keyword on your website as long as the main themes are clear. Each of your pages should focus on a different primary keyword, otherwise your pages will be competing against each other in SERPs.

The content structure you employ on your web pages should systematically support your themes and keywords. For example, *YouTube* suggests the use of the 'HERO, HUB, HELP' framework. This approach ensures that the site is well structured to accommodate your 'theme'.

- HERO content introduces your brand to your buyer persona as the solution to their problem.

Figure 7.5 The HERO, HUB, HELP framework

- HUB content will address your buyer persona's needs before they are aware of your brand.
- HELP content supports your buyer persona once they have bought your goods and services (Figure 7.5).

Hero content – aims at increasing brand awareness and attracting large audiences to your content. The result of this content is brand awareness and potential for future navigational search results.

Hub content – is based on the main product and services, and offers regular fresh perspectives of interest to your buyer persona. This content would tend to satisfy informational search queries.

Help content – is a must-have for your organisation, and it helps your buyer persona to resolve the transactional and navigational search questions they might have in relation to your brand, products or services.

Keyword-informed website information architecture

When designing and mapping keywords onto pages, one term could be primary on one web page and secondary on another; hence a keyword map (which is usually laid out in a tabular format) that outlines your website information architecture should be developed. This map includes each web page and online profile against its relevant keyword terms.

Once all the pages have been identified, it is important that they are organised in a logical structure, which reveals semantically related themes and sub-themes. Figure 7.6 outlines a website's organisation by themes.

Traditional website structures (Figure 7.7) prioritised products and services at the second level, and then used individual categories to break them into smaller product groupings. Supporting pages such as guides and instructions were then positioned at the next level down. At the bottom level of the structure were the terms and conditions and other information that is not often required.

To show the location of individual pages within its hierarchy, the use of breadcrumbs is advisable (Figure 7.8). Breadcrumbs are good ways to help both

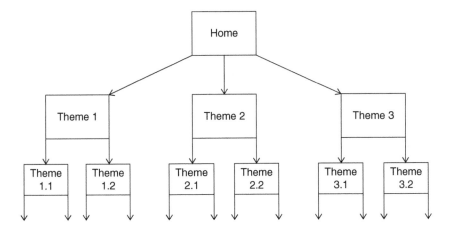

Figure 7.6 Thematically organised website structure

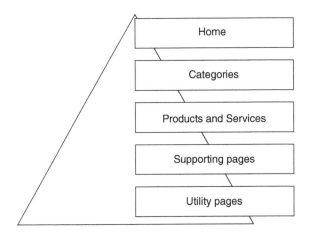

Figure 7.7 Traditional website architecture

the user and the search engine to understand where the page is located in relation to the structure of the overall information architecture and how to navigate towards and away from it.

7.6 Implementing your search engine optimisation strategy

Identifying the most relevant keyword terms allows you to develop a map for a
website and strategic themes for your content, as well as enabling you to refine
the focus for individual web pages and blog posts. But, the implementation of

Figure 7.8 Navigational breadcrumbs

the actual optimisation process comprises four steps in what can be described as the four pillars of SEO.

The four pillars of SEO

The impact of SEO is at its greatest when your strategy brings together all four pillars of SEO. In fact, neglecting any one of the pillars of SEO can leave your website vulnerable to algorithm changes and could even have a negative impact on your long-term SEO performance. If the four SEO pillars are better optimised than your competition, your website has a higher chance of ranking above competitors in organic SERPs.

i) High-quality content

This pillar of SEO is a direct response to the *Google* Panda algorithm update in 2011. High-quality content was always important for web pages, but this is even more so since *Google* penalises websites with low-quality content in their ranking in SERPs. The key attributes of high-quality content have been outlined by *Google*'s Amit Singhal (Singhal, 2011):

- The content must be relevant to your buyer persona.
- The content is unique – it is not duplicated across the rest of the site or copied from somewhere else.
- It is media rich (including images and video), with carefully considered links to other relevant pages within your site.
- Includes a clear call-to-action (e.g. email signup, download, subscribe, call a number, comment or share).

- Do not 'over-optimise' to the point of incomprehensibility and avoid the blatant use of unnatural keyword stuffing.
- Write to engage the user, not just to the benefit of search engines.

Having content that is relevant to the buyer persona and assists them on their buyer journey is arguably the most important factor when it comes to search engine ranking. This is simply because search engines want their users to be satisfied with the SERP they see as a consequence of their queries. For content to be appealing to the buyer persona, it has to be targeted to a specific keyword phrase, as well as being relevant, original, detailed and in accessible formats. Once an individual is engaged with your content – when they arrive via organic search to a web page, video or image – the traditional model of Attention, Interest, Desire and Action (AIDA) applies. This model is explored in more detail in Chapter 6 in relation to content marketing.

ii) On-page optimisation

The second pillar of SEO is on-page optimisation. Once your keyword research is conducted and relevant content topics have been identified to formulate the overall website architecture, a detailed page structure can be developed. This structure is implemented by integrating the keywords in HTML (Hypertext Markup Language) tags on your web pages. These tags are mainly based in the header part of the web page and include title and description tags, as well as tags in the body section of a web page including headings, paragraphs, links and images. Your keywords should appear within page names (URLs), page titles, page descriptions and your top- and second-level headings (also known as H1 and H2 tags). Figure 7.9 compares the code view of a page and the effect of the title tag on what is displayed in a web browser window. In this case, the keyword targeted is 'Salford Business School'.

Figure 7.9 Title tag code and its visual impact

One of the main reasons the meta tags for Title and Description as well as web page URLs are specified at this level is because this information is often used by search engines to describe the page on SERPs.

Although this information is sometimes ignored, as illustrated in Figure 7.10 where *Bing* changes the title from

'Salford Business School | University of Salford, Manchester'
to
'Salford Business School – Official Site'

Google in contrast (Figure 7.11), uses the first line of the text from the title tag, in combination with content of the page description tag, and the page URL shows the web page name. When *Google* is unable to fit in the full description it abbreviates the description with an ellipsis (…), whereas *Bing*'s SERP includes the complete description.

The example of Figure 7.11 and the abbreviated description reveal why titles, descriptions and URLs should not exceed the recommended maximum

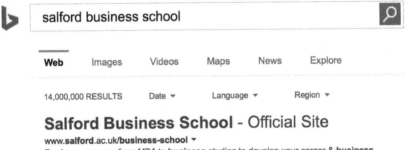

Figure 7.10 *Bing* SERP for 'Salford Business School' search term

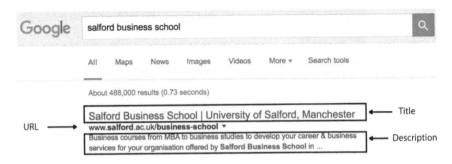

Figure 7.11 *Google* SERP with tags, titles and URL

lengths. Search engines often change the maximum length, but it is also influenced by variables such as the device and screen size, i.e. whether the search is done on a mobile phone, tablet or desktop computer, and the operating system used. The space used in SERPs is calculated in pixels – which means that including a lot of wide characters such as 'm' and 'w' as well as highlighting the keyword by the search engines could push the results off the page. All of these limitations reinforce the need to keep your titles and descriptions tags below the maximum length (see Table 7.2). But, be conscious of the fact that even these recommended variables can change. You can keep up to date with the latest on-page recommendations through SEO tools such as www. ScreamingFrog.co.uk.

In addition, your information architecture should avoid duplication of keywords in your description or title, as this will confuse visitors and potentially be penalised by search engines. A number of content management systems (CMSs) offer different formats for your URL structure. Some contain numbers – effectively counting the content on your site – while others are formatted in text. The textually formatted URL is preferred, since it makes use of natural language and helps the site visitor and the search engine to understand what your content is about.

In some earlier advice and texts about on-page optimisation the keywords meta tag is recommended. However, this tag now has no influence on SERPs, and visual examination of this tag can be used by your competitors on the terms that you have used to optimise your web page. As a result, it is not advisable to use this as part of your on-page optimisation.

TEXT OPTIMISATION

Text refers to the main visible content of your website. It is a cliché that 'content is king' for organic SEO, but it still remains true for search engines as well as readers. Users are people who scan content. It is important to break up pages with headings, images and bullet points. The use of bold text and quotes can also draw attention to the key messages, guiding both readers and search engines.

For search engines, one of the simplest routes to evaluating content is the quality and the semantic relevance of the text. Long form content – for example, an article which explores an issue in detail – tends to be preferred by search engines to content that is shallow and has fewer than 600 words. A number of

Table 7.2 Description and title tag length recommendations

HTML tag	Approximate length
Meta title tag	55 characters (or 482 pixels)
Meta description tag	150 characters (or 757 pixels)

studies have indicated that web pages with over 2,000 words tend to rank better compared to those that have under 500 (Lincoln, 2015). However, it is wholly dependent upon the type of content – for example, blog posts are better if they are longer, whereas product descriptions may not need to be as long. However, including user-generated content (UGC) in the form of, for example, reviews on product pages increases the depth of the text and value to the reader as well as the semantic keyword value. This is where the craft of being able to structure content in an accessible way – using headings, bullet points, images and video – is important to benefit those who want to take a quick look and get the key facts, as well as those who want a more detailed explanation that ultimately increases their trust in your brand.

The key message about good-quality content is that it should not be about selling to people – it should focus on helping your buyer persona to advance their buyer journey towards a purchase decision. A good example of how in-depth descriptive content is structured for e-commerce sales is found in an *Amazon* product description page. The page contains the main information in bullet points and relatively short descriptions – information that is available through every other online retailer. However, *Amazon* also includes user-generated reviews – information that is unique and often goes into considerable detail. This approach provides *Amazon* with almost limitless and free in-depth content, which is also appreciated by potential purchasers. The key lesson from *Amazon* is that content does not always need to be written by the organisation. If your web page allows for comments in combination with your original article, a lively discussion adds value for the reader and is a good strategy for SEO content development.

LOCAL SEARCH ENGINE OPTIMISATION

If your organisation has a physical premises, you can also benefit from location-based optimisation. With the increasingly common use of mobile phones as a substitute for other devices, location-based information is becoming equally important. Effectively your website must be mobile friendly. A reflection of the importance of mobile is *Google*'s release of a mobile-friendly test tool which can guide your appropriate development (www.google.co.uk/webmasters/tools/mobile-friendly/).

As a local organisation you need to claim your *Google My Business* listing and populate it with your own content, which is ideally based upon keyword research around your products and services. The *Google My Business* listing also allows you to invite your customers to review your organisation.

With a physical location you should also ensure that your Name, Address and Phone Number (NAP) are consistently presented on your website – a common approach is to include this in the website template which then appears in either the footer or the header of all your web pages. NAP information can also be presented using schema.org markup, which is described in the technical section later in this chapter.

IMAGES OPTIMISATION

Images should also be an aspect of your SEO strategy. Images play a major role in the description of product and services where individuals want to 'see the product or service in use'. Not only are images offering useful content to your buyer persona, they also offer additional content for image-specific search engines (Figure 7.12). As with text-based SERP, a brand should protect its image results by publishing its own images that present positive reflections of your brand. When selecting images for a web page, they should be relevant to the page and if they are abstract, they should offer some connection rather than simply being used for decoration.

Image optimisation offers three places for the primary keyword to be integrated:

1   The file name. Most images taken with a digital camera tend to be a number by default, e.g. dmc123.jpg. To improve image optimisation, files can be easily renamed to include the primary keyword, e.g. oak-tree.jpg. In this case, oak tree is clearly visible to the search engine and also the user.

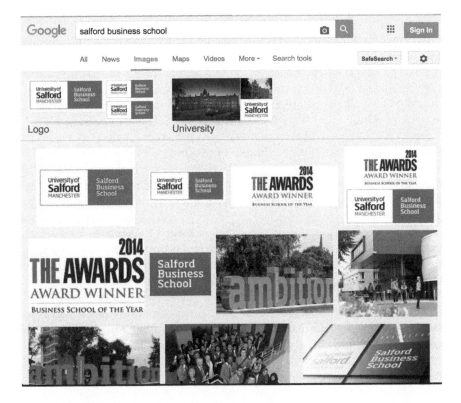

Figure 7.12 Salford Business School image search results

2   The alternative text for the image – or the 'alt' tag attribute. This tag is important for visually impaired users (including search engine bots) – this alternative text attribute offers a text description of the image, and if images are disabled, the alternative text is displayed instead.

3   Caption or description of the image – this information is usually easy to edit in CMSs such as *WordPress*. This text appears next to the image and allows the search engine to associate the meaning of the image with the accompanying text.

The process of integrating images on a web page will depend to some extent on your CMS. It is always good to have a minimum set of requirements for the images that you use, which should include descriptive file names that contain relevant keywords and setting the alternative text.

Images can also be a great source of 'virality' for content. Allowing your image to be used under a Creative Commons attribution licence (https://creativecommons.org/licenses/) increases the likelihood of sharing and re-use, with the inclusion of your name and, ideally, a link to your site if you allow your image to be embedded on other websites.

LINKS

Links are a crucial part of navigation and are the main source of information for *Google*, as they determine which page on a website is important and which is not. The text used for navigation should ideally mirror the keywords that have been identified for a particular page. For example, a page about 'oak trees' should be linked to as '<u>oak trees</u>' – this sends a clear signal to the reader as well as a search engine as to where the link is going.

There is a difference between internal links and inbound links from external sources. Internal links can be (almost) conversational and as keyword-rich as you want, external links not so much. Try to avoid using exact-match keyword links, as this can look spammy, especially when the links come from external pages to your website – if in doubt, use your brand name as the anchor text to your site.

Each external link is classed as an endorsement of your page by a search engine's bot. Therefore, when linking to external pages which you do not wish to endorse, use rel='nofollow' so that the search engine is instructed not to count this link as an endorsement of the page.

Links in images are also followed by search engine bots, and the 'alt' attribute is interpreted as the anchor text. However, search engines are not always consistent in following links that are in images. If you must link to a page through an image, always provide an alternative navigation path using a text link.

Positioning a page's primary keyword links higher in the page content, and inside dense text paragraphs is also likely to achieve better results than simple lists of links or site links positioned at the bottom of every web page.

iii) Off-page factors optimisation

In *Google*, for a number of years, the top result for 'click here' was *Adobe*. Other search engines use different first page rankings, but 'Adobe website with PDF reader software download' is not far down the list (Figure 7.13).

If you examine the *Adobe* page, despite the advice in the previous section, there is not a single mention of the keyword 'click here' in the content, images, title, description or URL. This result is influenced by off-page factors entirely. Specifically, the anchor text is used by all the other web pages that link to this *Adobe* web page when they want their own visitors to download the *Adobe* PDF reader.

This key example highlights the importance of keyword-rich anchor text. This link to anchor text and high SERP ranking was soon identified by the SEO industry and, as a consequence, a number of organisations have over-optimised their websites using spammy link-building techniques. The Penguin update, as well as other *Google* algorithm updates, have targeted poor link-building practices and now penalise websites with over-optimised anchor text linking to the site. High-profile examples of the application of these penalties include *JC Penney* and *Interflora*.

This straightforward example highlights the need for a balanced SEO strategy and sound links ecosystem that connect to your most significant pages. Your off-page optimisation relies upon tactics that build up the links into your web profiles.

A number of tools allow for competitor benchmarking (e.g. www.opensite explorer.org).

These tools compare the number of inward links a website has in comparison to your competitors and suggests the approximate competitive advantage. The assumption made regarding this comparison is that if one website receives

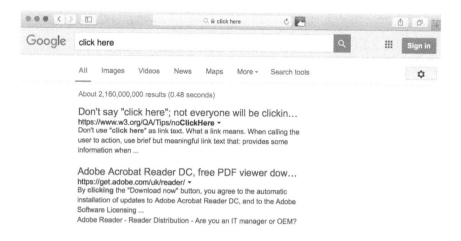

Figure 7.13 'Click here' SERP on *Google*

more quality external links than its competitors, it is then more likely to be better ranked in SERPs.

If you are targeting local visitors, it is helpful to get local directories to list the NAP information in the same format that it is listed on your own other profiles. The links that you build from local relevant websites will also have an overall positive impact on your SERP visibility.

Universal search results that include the specialist search results from *Google* News, Image Search, Videos and Local/Maps are also included on a number of SERPs. Previous studies confirm that seeing a thumbnail or a map on a SERP attracts attention. Your brand can increase its visibility by targeting each of these options.

Different rules apply to these different specialist search engines. For example, for video optimisation on *YouTube*, the title and description are important in the same way that a web page would be optimised, but in this case the tags and keyword should be used extensively. The official *YouTube* Creator Playbook and www.tubebuddy.com offer further guidance on creating engaging and optimised video content. From an SEO perspective all your 'owned' channels should link to your brand's home web page. Individual elements of video and audio content should also have links to the relevant web pages on your site.

iv) Technical optimisation

Technical SEO is the methodical optimisation of on-page technical elements to improve the findability and crawlability of your content by search engines. Having a technically sound site can also improve the overall customer journey by improving elements such as site speed.

On-page and off-page optimisation factors all rely on computers being able to read and understand your content. Technical optimisation brings the additional benefit that it can improve the impact of your other optimisations. There are many technical elements that can be optimised and each brings benefits.

XML SITEMAP

Giving a search engine the location of all your web pages requires indexing. The need for indexing a website has resulted in a common sitemap standard. The sitemap.xml standard provides a concise format that allows a website owner to list a page link, when it was modified, how important it is from 0 (not important) to 1 (very important) and how often it is updated.

The information for a site index is gathered automatically by most CMSs. The URLs included in a sitemap.xml are added to Googlebot's crawler queue and then indexed and made findable by *Google*.

The *Google* Search Console (www.google.com/webmasters/tools/) allows website owners to alert *Google* about a site when a sitemap link is submitted. Once submitted and crawled, any resulting errors will assist you in resolving SEO difficulties. Your sitemap.xml must continue to be accurate in order to have a positive impact on your SEO strategy.

Larger websites maintain index sitemaps to enable the distributed management and administration of different sitemaps. This approach helps search engines, as well as website managers, to manage their energies in maintaining the accuracy of individual sitemaps.

ROBOTS.TXT

Google has the benefit of being linked and reading your sitemap directly, but other search engines require more information. A long-standing common standard is used to allow all website owners to communicate with the many different search engine bots that might visit the site. As part of the standard, the file is consistently called robots.txt.

Robots.txt is examined by a visiting search engine's bot. The consistent format and structure of this file mean that it must be located in the root (top level) of your website – in other words, as part of the standard, robots.txt will always be found at www.your-domain-name.com/robots.txt. The businessculture.org website, for example, has its robots.txt file located at http://businessculture.org/robots.txt (Figure 7.14).

Robots.txt files are openly accessible and visible to any user, as well as web robots. This means that you can look at the robots.txt file of any of your competitors. In the robots.txt file you can specify which search engine bots you want to communicate with and tell them which pages and folders of your website they should not be visiting, as well as the location of your sitemap. Examples of web pages that are often disallowed include any password-protected sections of your website as well as sections that might be used for website development or experimentation. You can keep up to date with the latest guidelines offered by each of the search engines you are optimising for by searching, for example, for 'sitemaps supported by *Google*'. You will be able to use the latest standards for the inclusion of sitemaps for video, images and mobile.

Directing a search engine bot not to crawl a web page using the robots.txt file is not as effective as a password-protected page. If a web page has been visited by a search engine bot and that bot did not access your robots.txt first, it may be ignoring the robots.txt standard. Use the 'robots.txt tester' in the *Google*

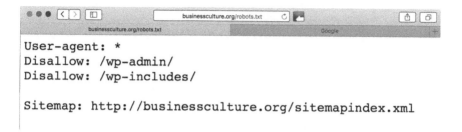

Figure 7.14 Robots.txt example from the www.businessculture.org website

Search Console to check your robots.txt file against what is expected by *Google* (and, by implication, most other search engines).

If your website offers, or will be offering, a common type of information concerning, for example, events, reviews, places or persons, there are recognisable methods of sharing this information and making it available to others through a search engine. A range of advanced markup structures – called schemas – have been defined for common types of information that assist in making your website stand out from competitors in the SERPs.

There are a number of schema types, but the most popular are publicly available and documented at schema.org. These schemas offer a range of options to make your website content as accessible as possible to a search engine as well as including additional data in SERPs to differentiate your organisation from your competitors, for example, star ratings and NAP information that is particularly important for local SEO (Figure 7.15).

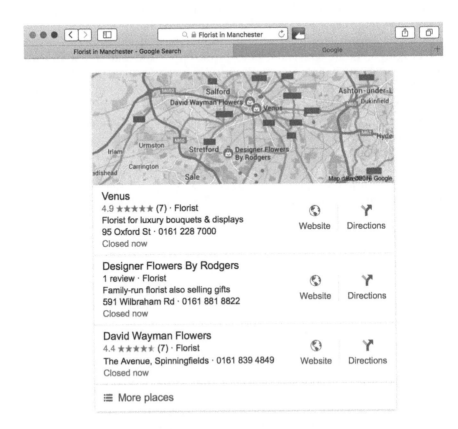

Figure 7.15 'Florist in Manchester' SERP, with star ratings and NAP information

MOVING PAGES

Inevitably over time your website structure will change and individual web pages will change their URL. This may be the result of a new CMS or a redesign. The 301 redirect method allows website owners to define the old and new names of a web page and ensures that all of the accumulated page history and positive ranking is moved too. With '301 redirect' you map all the old URL addresses with the matching new addresses.

If you just remove a web page from its current URL it will produce 404 'Page Not Found' errors. Inevitably any change in information architecture will produce some of these errors. Instead of greeting users and search engine bots with the blank web page that is generated by your website hosting provider or CMS, you can create a custom 404 'Page Not Found' page.

Your custom 404 page can direct visitors back to your home page. This will cover the situation to some extent. Adding a link from your custom 404 page to the human readable version of your sitemap is another alternative that might assist the visitor in finding the right page.

A number of automatic server response codes can assist you in diagnosing reasons for a page not being correctly indexed. A record of the codes that your users received can be retrieved from your web server's logs. Your goal is to maximise the number of '200' responses and reduce the number of failures your visitors are experiencing.

503 – The Web server is not available since it is being worked on at the moment
404 – Page not found
407 – Proxy Authentication Required
410 – Page is gone and *Google* should remove it from its index
412 – Precondition Failed
301 – URL has been permanently redirected to another URL
302 – URL has been temporarily redirected to another URL
200 – OK

More codes are defined at www.w3.org/Protocols/rfc2616/rfc2616-sec10. html. As you become more conscious of the impact of technical optimisation you will also benefit from learning the meaning of individual HTML tags (the markup language that builds web pages).

7.7 Benchmarking search engine optimisation activities

There are a number of key performance indicators (KPIs) that enable you to evaluate your strategy against the four pillars of SEO (Table 7.3).

Some of these current tools are worth closer investigation, as they will positively support your SEO benchmarking efforts.

Found SEO tool – www.found.co.uk/seo-tool/ – is a free technical SEO audit tool that offers a prioritised 'traffic light' system of the required

Table 7.3 KPIs for SEO optimisation

SEO pillar	Examples of key performance indicators	Example tools
Content	Number of comments	*Google* Analytics
	Time spent on page	*Google* Search Console Tool /
	Completion of call-to-action	Webmaster Tools
	Traffic generated	SEMRush
	Keyword visibility in SERPs	MOZ
On-page	Reduction of errors such as duplicate titles, descriptions and headings	Screaming Frog Yoast's *WordPress* SEO plugin
Off-page	Number and quality of links to a page	Open Site Explorer – MOZ
	Number of shares to a page	
Technical	Reduction of technical errors such as w3c validator approval and website speed approval	Found SEO Tools DeepCrawl Webmaster Tools

changes to your site. A more comprehensive, but paid-for, technical SEO auditing tool is DeepCrawl (www.deepcrawl.com). DeepCrawl will crawl a site before it has launched and will recognise thin content, re-directs and many other technical aspects.

Webmaster Tools – e.g. www.google.com/webmasters/tools/ – Most search engines have their own form of 'Webmaster Tools' which allow a website owner to link their website directly to the database of a search engine. It offers a technical view of your website, as it is indexed by a search engine. Any technical indexing issues will be highlighted as well as noting the number of times a web page has been shown in search results and in what position.

***Google* Analytics** – www.google.co.uk/analytics/ – This free analytical platform shows who the audience of your website is, how they arrived at your site and how they engaged with your web pages.

Screaming Frog – www.screamingfrog.co.uk/seo-spider/ – This tool requires download and installation on your computer. It crawls your website as a search engine bot would do, and lets you know which pages are internally linked and which are 'indexable' by search engines.

SEMRush – www.semrush.com – This is a full suite of tools for online marketing covering SEO and PPC as well as social media presence and online video advertising (OVA).

MOZ – https://moz.com – This is a set of tools for SEO analysis. It audits for on-page, off-page and technical issues. The tool is supported by a vibrant community of SEO professionals that you can connect with and collaboratively troubleshoot problems.

7.8 Summary

You should now be aware of the fundamental concepts concerning organic SEO. It is a large topic. Key SEO concepts include the creative aspects of offering relevant content, crafting and refining your keyword selection for each web page, as well as more technical concepts such as the use of primary keywords in the header of the page, indexing your site and considering what happens when something goes wrong for your visitor.

SEO is continuously changing and requires constant monitoring and evaluation. The strategic commitment and expectation of results vary by industry, but these can take from a minimum of three months up to several years, dependent on the resources and the scale of the task at hand. To succeed with your own SEO you need to stay connected to the SEO community and keep up to date with the latest industry trends and tools to ensure that when your buyer persona uses a search engine, it is your organisation that they find.

7.9 References

Amerland, D. (2013) *Google Semantic Search: Search Engine Optimization (SEO) Techniques that Get Your Company More Traffic, Increase Brand Impact, and Amplify Your Online Presence.* Que Publishing.

Lincoln, J.E. (2015) *The SEO and User Science Behind Long-Form Content.* http://searchengineland.com/seo-user-science-behind-long-form-content-230721

Malaga, R.A. (2008) Worst practices in search engine optimization. *Communications of the ACM, 51*(12), 147–50.

Naughton, E. (2015) *Win the Moments that Matter.* www.thinkwithgoogle.com/intl/en-gb/blog/post/win-the-moments-that-matter/

Netmarketshare (2016) *Desktop Search Engine Market Share.* www.netmarketshare.com/search-engine-market-share.aspx?qprid=4&qpcustomd=0

Page, L., Brin, Motwani, R. and Winograd, T. (1999) "The PageRank Citation Ranking: Bringing Order to the Web", Technical Report. Stanford InfoLab, http://ilpubs.stanford.edu:8090/422.

Person, S. (2015) *Off with Your Head Terms: Leveraging Long-Tail Opportunity with Content.* https://moz.com/blog/long-tail-content

Search Console Help (2016) *Google Crawlers: See which Robots Google Uses to Crawl the Web.* https://support.google.com/webmasters/answer/1061943?hl=en

Singhal, A. (2011) *More Guidance on Building High-quality Sites.* https://googlewebmastercentral.blogspot.co.uk/2011/05/more-guidance-on-building-high-quality.html

8 Social media

Alex Fenton and Mostafa Mohamad, Salford Business School, University of Salford, UK

Ashley Jones, Events Director, Social Chain, UK

8.0 Learning outcomes

In this chapter you will learn how to:

- understand the dynamics of social media-based communities, and their composition and behaviours;
- conduct a social media audit including competitor analysis;
- recognise the importance of a blog as a centre of digital presence development;
- use amplification strategies to develop brand presence;
- explore the concept of social capital and its relationship to brand engagement activities;
- develop tactics for measuring the quality and quantity of social media-based engagements.

8.1 The importance of social media

Social media channels are among the most popular channels for online interaction. Organisations are recognising this trend and increasingly telling their story through social channels in ways that show their human side. In countries with high social media adoption rates, including the UK, the majority of users tend to avoid paid advertising material (Davies, 2015). As a result of this avoidance, natural or organic social media optimisation (SMO) is very important to the success of your marketing strategy.

Social media channels connect people and enable them to communicate between themselves and with your organisation. In distinction, the term 'social media platform' emphasises technological infrastructure, such as a website and/or the applications which facilitate interaction.

The *Conversation Prism* developed by Brian Solis and *JESS3* (see conversationprism.com) highlights the range of social media channels that are currently available. These platforms offer a range of options for engagement with your buyer persona, but you do not need to use all of them. You can filter out the irrelevant and marginal channels by understanding the diversity of options and identifying those that best connect with your buyer persona. Once you have identified the channels preferred by your buyer persona you can evaluate if there is an opportunity for opening another avenue of conversation. The decision to engage on a channel is an aspect of your channels sub-strategy within the Buyer Persona Spring (see Chapter 0), and with this decision you are shaping your overall strategic direction.

The *Conversation Prism* emphasises the strategic use of social media beyond marketing functions to include sales, customer service and operations. In this chapter, for the purpose of simplification, we will differentiate between social networks that are primarily for business-to-business (B2B) or business-to-consumer (B2C) interactions. In reality, most platforms can equally play a role in both B2B and B2C settings.

8.2 Social media strategies

Social media interaction broadly falls into four main functions – marketing, sales, operations and customer service (Figure 8.1).

When you open a social media channel of communication you should be conscious of the different applications and techniques expected for each function and the results through key performance indicators (KPIs) for measuring their success (Table 8.1).

| Marketing | Sales | Operations | Customer Service |

Figure 8.1 Main functions for social media use

Table 8.1 Main strategies for social media use in organisations

Marketing

Application	Techniques	KPIs
Use conversation to understand your buyer persona's needs	Survey your buyer persona about their interests	Improved buyer persona understanding
Gather feedback about your brands, products and services	Use competitions to encourage co-creation	Up-to-date contacts
Offer high-quality content about your offering	Amplify and encourage positive feedback	Positive brand mentions
Encourage positive reviews and learn from negative experiences	Identify and support charitable causes that are important to your buyer persona	Engagement numbers
		Social capital acquired

(*Continued*)

Table 8.1 Continued

Sales		
Application	*Techniques*	*KPIs*
Identify influencers and engage them in mutually beneficial ways Involve your influencers in interactions and co-creation as part of your extended 'sales' team	Brand ambassador programmes for endorsing your products and services, including exclusive information, offers and benefits Affiliate marketing agreements giving direct recognition for individual sales	Sales numbers Number of brand ambassadors Number of affiliates Social capital acquired

Customer Service		
Application	*Techniques*	*KPIs*
Customers log their support questions online so that they can be resolved publicly Enable customers to help one another and solve problems related to your products and services on your platforms	Develop support-focused forums on your website or owned social media channels which give the option to moderate Create support-dedicated accounts on networks such as *Twitter* Reward community participation and support with intrinsic motivators	Number of support issues resolved online Volume of publicly available and indexed support topics Number of participants in online support interactions Decreased volumes of support phone calls, emails and other private interactions Social capital acquired

Operations		
Application	*Techniques*	*KPIs*
Internally focused interactions that act as knowledge management tools Help each other find better ways of doing their job Platforms for sharing internal communications	Use private social networks for internal interactions that support your organisation Enable public interactions to show a human side of your organisation	Percentage of organisation participating in maintaining organisational knowledge Volume and accuracy of internally available documents preserving organisational knowledge Decreased volume of email and attachments

Case Study 8.1   *Public Desire*

A number of organisations offer good examples of the four functions being enabled through social media interaction. In marketing and sales, *Public Desire* (Figure 8.2) was created out of social media in 2014. The customer base (16–25-year-old females) spent large amounts of time on *Instagram* and were interested in fashion, music and food. *Public Desire* then posted images, mixing products, inspiration and current content relative to their customers' interests, to drive extremely high rates of engagement. The social following grew from a zero base to 100,000 in less than six months. This interaction is translated into new visitors to the *Public Desire* website and ultimately e-commerce sales.

The reasons for engaging with a brand such as *Public Desire* on social media can be grouped broadly into intrinsic and extrinsic motivation factors. Extrinsic motivation refers to rewards that originate externally to an individual – social media-related examples of this include competition prizes, money, praise and acknowledgements. Intrinsic rewards originate inside an individual – social media-related examples include mastery of a subject, love, curiosity, belonging, learning and autonomy.

While a brand can develop its social media presence using competitions, the motivators being applied should be a balance between extrinsic and intrinsic. Extrinsic competition rewards, in particular those that

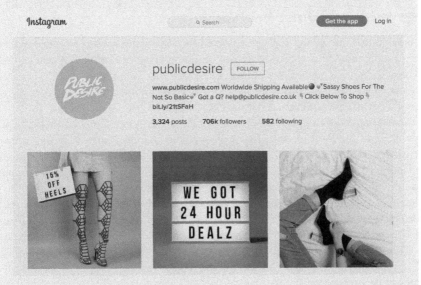

Figure 8.2 Instagram account for Public Desire

have material benefit, should not be used too frequently, as there is a tendency to attract people who have only a superficial connection to a brand (Heinze et al., 2013).

To develop a sustainable online community such as *Public Desire*, the key emphasis should be placed on the intrinsic motivating factors such as pride in belonging to a brand, curiosity and learning. *Public Desire* crowdsource an understanding of what their customers like by offering them the opportunity to share their preferences of shoes. These stated preferences are then translated into products, which the same customers can purchase. The motivation for the followers here is both intrinsic – being able to buy and wear a pair of shoes that they like – as well as extrinsic – being acknowledged by the organisation for the shoes that are designed around their own preference. A key mechanism for fostering intrinsic motivation in your brand is to offer high-quality information that resonates with your audience (Poor Rezaei and Heinze, 2014). The importance of high-quality content for social media connects with the SEO (Chapter 7) and content marketing (Chapter 9) chapters. In the case of *Public Desire*, this high-quality content is represented by reporting the latest news in shoe fashion.

Source: www.publicdesire.com

8.3 Social capital and social media

In Table 8.1, one of the KPIs that is used for measuring success in social media engagement is social capital. There are different types of capital. Physical capital refers to objects such as machines, buildings and computers. Human capital refers to labour, creativity and the knowledge of people. Social media, in contrast, is primarily concerned with social capital.

Social capital is the value of all your social networks, the connections between people and the levels of trust that exist for your brands (Putnam, 2001). As discussed in Chapter 5, social capital is one of the reasons why digital campaign planning does not always have direct costs associated with it, since social capital is difficult to quantify in financial terms. Social capital in the form of social connections and embedded trust is crucial to the functioning of social media. Social capital is the lifeblood of social media channels, and understanding how this form of capital works is critical to the effective use of social media in digital marketing.

There are three different types of social capital (Woolcock, 2001): bonding, bridging and linking. With a social media focus, these three types of social capital can be defined as:

- Bonding social capital includes the closest social connections. These connections are found between you and family members, friends, work colleagues, your employees (if you have any) and perhaps similar types of people from similar backgrounds, locations or those with shared interests. Loyal and happy customers who are also your brand advocates could also be considered part of this group and are the core informants in shaping your buyer persona.

- Bridging social capital includes connections with people from across different groups. These may be acquaintances, friends of friends or secondary connections. An occasional associate, client or customer of your organisation would be part of this category.

- Linking social capital is the broadest and weakest of connections. This type of social capital reaches out to people across the globe. Many of these people will be unfamiliar to your buyer persona and are unlikely to benefit directly from your products and services. However, the aim of engaging with these connections is to find those who would be familiar to your buyer persona and an opportunity for your organisation to create stronger ties with them. This type of social capital also provides the pool from which recommendations and referrals can develop.

Each of these different types of social capital plays a different role in different campaigns. If you are prospecting for your buyer persona, it is wise to reach out as far as possible between groups and use the power of networks to increase your social brand value (Fueller et al., 2011). Having millions of people talking about your brand globally can help your brand awareness KPIs; however, it may not help you to reach your conversion KPIs if you do not successfully connect with your buyer persona.

You should not ignore the value of linking social capital. There is potential power in weak ties amongst a larger volume of people (Widdop et al., 2014). In social media terms, linking social capital provides you with those followers who do not engage, or who may be your buyer persona but are not yet aware of your presence. An overall goal for your marketing strategy is to use the combination of content, channels and data to make those with the weakest social capital connections become more strongly connected with you and your organisation.

8.4 Online communities

Building on the concept of social capital, there are other ways to consider online communities. The 1 per cent rule of Internet culture divides online users into three categories: 1 per cent creators, 9 per cent contributors and 90 per cent lurkers (Figure 8.3).

Observation of this distribution comes from naturally occurring online communities.

- **Creators** – these are approximately 1 per cent of an online community. This 1 per cent consists of the people that visit social media regularly and actively create content (Fueller et al., 2011). They have a strong tie with

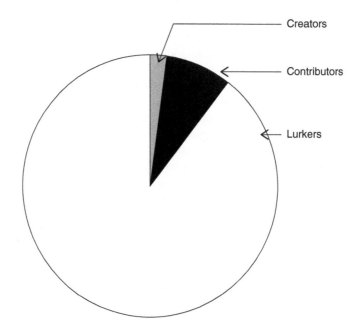

Figure 8.3 The 1 per cent rule of Internet culture

the community and are usually key influencers. Identifying the creators for your brand and building your social capital with them will refine and focus your buyer persona while also influencing your online community.
- **Contributors** – approximately 9 per cent of the community regularly post to social media. This group are not as influential as creators, but they have a good understanding of the digital landscape in relation to your brand. Not all brands will have creators, but you should always be able to find contributors. For example, search for the name of your brand, products and services on a social network and see if anyone has mentioned you. These individuals might be interested in writing a post for your blog, which they can then amplify through their own networks.
- **Lurkers** – the majority of your community, the 90 per cent, will consume your content, but almost never post or contribute to social media (Ferneley et al., 2009). These are the silent listeners and readers. Lurkers are the vast majority of your audience, so it is important to keep them engaged in a way that keeps them comfortable. For example, lurkers can be engaged through low-level interactions such as subscribing to your social media feed, blog feed or mailing list. Monitoring the behaviour of lurkers through analysis of visits lets you learn more about your wider audience. A regular mistake in thinking about social media is to assume that low social media engagement means that nobody is listening. However, this assumption means you might be forgetting about the 90 per cent.

8.5 Cultures

Culture is the way we do things and it is important to recognise that it differs. You are trying to reach people around the world who are enmeshed in different cultures. The global reach of social media is a key reason for organisations rethinking their marketing strategy (Tiago and Veríssimo, 2014). Consider each culture that you are targeting separately. You need to develop knowledge and experience of what type of content is best delivered through which channels, in the right language and tone at the right time, in order to produce positive engagement. Your own research into each culture that you want to connect with will be important to understand individual nuances and preferences. Even if you are simply trying to reach people in your own language and time zone, it is still important to consider more regional cultures.

Culture does not neatly align with national boundaries or equate to a common spoken language. Within a single country, different groups behave differently depending on location, heritage, education, age and experience. Identifying the culture of your buyer persona will shape what social media platforms you will use and how you can best engage with them. Social Media Analytics data can tell you something about the country, city, devices and interests of your buyer persona (Kaushik, 2009). Social Media Analytics will also tell you which social networks are driving traffic to your website – the overall goal of your social media efforts. Becoming knowledgeable about the culture, habits, likes and dislikes of your buyer persona is essential (a cultural awareness of your buyer persona is part of the development process discussed in Chapter 3). This can be done through a combination of digital tools that measure and record – explored later in this chapter – as well as communicate with your buyer persona.

8.6 Sustainability of your social media platform

Social media platforms come and go and there are major geographic differences when it comes to managing and developing social media activities. This presents a challenge for your organisation. For example, *Facebook* is a good network for B2C communications in Europe and North America; however, it is currently blocked in mainland China (see full list maintained on Wikipedia for blocked sites in China and other countries). An alternative and more robust approach is to adopt the tactic of creating a blog that is hosted on your organisation's website and is used as the main hub for engagement with your online community. A blog should be at the centre of your channel sub-strategy implementation (Figure 8.4).

A blog is your key owned channel for creating synergies with other channels and should also be the central hub for your content sub-strategy. Your blog enables amplification across your owned channels and provides content that your buyer persona can share across a wider network of channels.

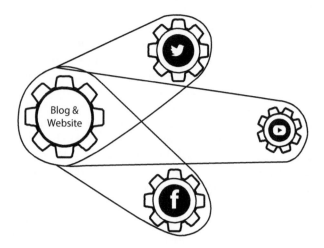

Figure 8.4 A blog and a website are pivotal channels in your social media strategy

8.7 Blogging platforms

A blog provides a good way to combine text, images, video and other media into high-quality content. There are many different blogging platforms – some are free, some can be set up on your own website and some are existing websites where you create an account. Usually, an organisation sets up a blog as an extension to their website (e.g. as www.yourwebsite.com/blog). This sub-folder structure also offers SEO value as well as boosting the social media visibility of your organisation. An alternative sub-domain structure (e.g. www.blog.yourweb site.com) is also an option, but this is considered by search engines as a separate website, which means that you would gain limited SEO benefits for your core website.

There are many different blogging platforms and software. The key to selecting the right platform depends upon your strategic goals and the KPIs you have defined. Some of the most common options for blogging are:

WordPress

WordPress is an open source blogging platform. This means that the software code is free and is developed by many thousands of people around the world. Because of its low cost, powerful features and wealth of themes and plugins, including the look and feel of the interface, it is used on a vast number of websites as both a blogging platform and CMS.

There are two options for *WordPress*:

- WordPress.com is the 'hosted' version of *WordPress*, where you can set up a new blog very quickly. The basic functionality is free, with some 'paid for' additional features. This option is more suitable for individual bloggers.

Blogs on WordPress.com rank well in search engine results pages (SERPs), but there is limited option for more advanced SEO configurations (such as the techniques described in Chapter 7).

• WordPress.org supports the fully featured *WordPress* system. Essentially, *WordPress* can be set up on a web server and this will give you complete access to the look, feel and functionality of the website. Many organisations use this option as a CMS for their own website as well as using it as a blog. Many commercial web-hosting companies offer *WordPress* installation as part of their web package for a reasonably low cost. This is the option used by individuals and organisations to set up websites that require more customisation and functionality. With this version of *WordPress*, SEO plugins such as Yoast are available, and these allow much more control over the search engine friendliness of your pages as well as giving you better data collection and analytics integration.

Blogger

Blogger.com is a *Google*-owned platform specifically set up for blogging. Like WordPress.com it is a freely hosted service, but has an entirely different look and feel. It is also possible to have your own domain name (e.g. www.yourwebsite.com) for free; in comparison, there is a cost for this option at WordPress.com. Although the service is secure, *Google* has not updated *Blogger* for some time. There is some risk in using *Blogger*, as the lack of updates has led to some public speculation that *Google* may eventually close down or move *Blogger* to another service.

8.8 Business-to-consumer platforms

Facebook

Since its inception in 2004, *Facebook* has grown to become the largest social network, with 1.59 billion monthly users globally as of the fourth quarter of 2015. Launched originally at Harvard University, it was then initially made accessible to other US universities. *Facebook* has now become the *de facto* platform for individuals to connect with friends and family. As a result of this focus, *Facebook* has also become an attractive channel for marketing. Organisations can create groups or fan pages as well as having the option to buy *Facebook* advertising to reach customers. *Facebook* is a mechanism for reaching new customers and engaging existing customers with new content. The platform enables easy setup of competitions as well as engaging in real-time interactions.

Twitter

Twitter has been on the rise ever since it was launched in 2006. It is the best-known example of a micro-blogging platform that allows users to communicate in a maximum of 140 characters referred to as 'tweets'. *Twitter* was the driving force behind the hashtag (#) concept, which allows its users to identify a certain topic or conversation with a tagged keyword. *Twitter* boasted more than 320 million users and 1 billion unique monthly visits to sites with embedded tweets (December 2015). However, the *Twitter* system has struggled to capture a large share of the social network market. *Twitter* profiles are usually public by default, but in relatively rare cases they are set to private. Trending topics are a feature of *Twitter* real-time capabilities, which allow users to see the currently most talked about topics. Communities thrive on *Twitter* because it is easy to use, easy to share tweets and works in real time. *Twitter* content, as a result, is highly responsive to current affairs and breaking stories, which, in turn, makes tweets more attractive to share.

Instagram

First released for public use in 2010, *Instagram* is a photo- and video-sharing app and is among the newest of the major social media channels. The platform has enjoyed rapid growth and engagement from users, and there are now 400 million monthly active users on the platform (late 2015). The content that is shared is solely image based. This focus has helped to drive Instagram's success as a result of the increasing image quality available through mobile phones. This image-based focus has enabled individuals, organisations and brands to explore their creativity and to tell visual stories. Brands have especially lauded the platform for its ability to build a visual brand and gain a highly engaged audience. Acquired by *Facebook* in 2012, the platform introduced advertising in 2015.

8.9 Business-to-business platforms

LinkedIn

Founded in 2002, *LinkedIn* is a business-focused social network, allowing users to post their professional work history, education and other professional achievements. *LinkedIn* is aimed at people who want to expand their professional networks as well as develop their career opportunities. The addition of company pages, and closed and open groups, allows conversations around business-related topics. *LinkedIn* is primarily used in the English-speaking world, but is translated into over 20 languages including Arabic and Russian. Known primarily as a B2B social network, the network is used to connect, promote and engage with new customers.

Xing and *Viadeo* are two of the European competitors to *LinkedIn* and offer similar functionality to link professionals together. The key difference between the platforms is language. *Viadeo* was founded in France in 2004 and has a total of about 65 million primarily French-speaking people (as of early 2016). *Xing*, founded in 2003, is popular amongst German-speaking users and has over 10 million users (February 2016) in this core market. *Sina Weibo* is a Chinese solution to *Facebook* and *Twitter* and was launched in 2009. The platform has 222 million active users (September 2015).

YouTube / Vimeo

YouTube and *Vimeo* are video-streaming services. Both are free to use, but place certain limits on the videos that can be uploaded in terms of content and length. The usage figures for these platforms, for *YouTube* in particular, are staggering, with people constantly choosing what they watch from billions of available professional or amateur video clips. Web video continues to be watched and created by a wide audience, with popular content including clips from favourite shows, 'how to' tutorial videos and even interactive or 3D content (which is often tagged as 'SBS', meaning side-by-side). Creating video content that your target audience will engage with and want to share should be a key aspect of your content sub-strategy. Videos hosted on these channels can then be embedded into your own web pages or blog posts and shared on social media platforms.

Google+

Started in 2011, *Google+* ('Google plus') is *Google*'s fourth social network project. The channel was significantly promoted by *Google*. Despite some impressive initial figures and close integration with search engine results, *Google* undertook a redesign and integrated with *Google* Places. *Google+* includes a timeline of events, discussion groups and *Google* Hangouts, which allow video conferencing between multiple people and the ability to record to *YouTube*. Some questions have been raised about the amount of interaction on the platform, but there are other benefits for your organisation to be on *Google+*, particularly if you want to appear in *Google* Local search results (see the local SEO discussion in Chapter 7).

WeChat

Released in China in 2011, the system has evolved from a simple chat app to a multi-functional tool with more than a billion registered accounts (early 2016). Although the majority of accounts are based in China, there is also a growing and significant percentage of users from outside China. *WeChat* enables videos and photos to be shared and altered, as well as video conferencing and collaborative games. The release of an Application Programming Interface (API) has also enabled an ecosystem of new apps to rapidly develop that range from support mechanisms to flight bookings.

8.10 Social media optimisation

The main reason for measuring KPIs in social media is to enable you to look beyond headline figures, such as the number of followers on *Twitter* or the number of likes on *Facebook*, and drill down to your success in engaging with your buyer persona and achieving your strategic aims. In social media terms, you are aiming for engagement with creators and to convert lurkers into contributors. To achieve these aims you need to understand your buyer persona's social media interests and actions.

Understanding your buyer persona using social media data and tools

Your buyer persona uses various channels. They also create large volumes of data. You can also inhabit these environments and use their data to better understand your buyer persona (Atkinson, 2015). Techniques such as social network analysis (SNA) and netnography (Kozinets, 2015) can be used to gain additional insights from market research and better understand social media-based communities.

Netnography

Netnography is defined as a text-based output/result of digital/online environment/field work (Kozinets, 2002). Netnography is derived from the word ethnography (the study of people), but is specifically adapted to study online communities. Netnography has been described as quicker and cheaper than traditional ethnography and is more natural and unobtrusive than offline focus groups or interviews (Kozinets, 2002). The technique has been used for both academic and commercial market research. Listening to what people say online and how they interact is the central focal point of netnography. The careful analysis of conversations online is a vital tool to round out your knowledge and improve the description of your buyer persona. Simple analysis of conversations can be undertaken by constructing a wordle or word map from the text being analysed. In this way, keywords and phrases can be identified in individual interactions as well as across entire communities. More sophisticated tools (e.g. *Radian 6*) can also create a concordance of terms that provide further context for the keywords that have been used.

Social network analysis

The concept of analysing offline social networks with SNA has been part of research for many decades (Groeger and Buttle, 2014) and has been used to identify the structure of networks. These networks can assist in identifying the focus and types of social capital within a network and, ultimately, can map the influence on buyer behaviours. These tools for SNA date back to around 2000 with the release of 'network.S.tools'. SNA has been used to, for example:

- understand e-word of mouth marketing (e-WOM);
- identify key influential people within networks (Groeger and Buttle, 2014);
- discover how people connect with each other over time (Edwards, 2010);
- explore weak ties between people (Granovetter, 1973);

- identify key influencers, who are candidates for further qualitative analysis through netnography or interview (Griffiths and McLean, 2015);
- understand what social capital is (Widdop et al., 2014) and the 'structure' and 'form' of social relations (Jarman et al., 2015).

NodeXL, Gephi and Followerwonk

There are various tools that can be used for SNA, a form of analysis that can be computationally intensive (Butts, 2008), these tools can be used to produce data and visualisations of networks in order to understand the role of an individual in relation to their interactions with an online community (Jarman et al., 2015). *NodeXL* is a popular and low-cost tool for conducting SNA by gathering data from *Twitter* into an *Excel* spreadsheet.

Gephi is not as functional for gathering social media data, but the visualisation tools can be more powerful and clearer than *NodeXL*. It is also possible to import data from *NodeXL* to *Gephi* to take advantage of the strengths of each programme and produce clearer visualisations of social networks and personal interrelationships. Both *NodeXL* and *Gephi* require installation on your computer.

Another tool used to gather social media data is *Followerwonk*. This online tool has the capability to visualise *Twitter* networks geographically and compare different user accounts. This comparison is not possible using *NodeXL* or *Gephi*. *Followerwonk* is used to understand where in the world potential fans are based and identify connections and new contacts based on the contacts of your competitors. It is possible to further look at the content of tweets from particular regions using *Followerwonk*.

In Figure 8.5, a network map of Salford City Football Club @salfordCityFC Twitter followers using NodeXL reveals the number of links and connections that the club account has with one of its owners, Gary Neville @GNev2. The figure also shows the links that exist between the Club's other Twitter followers who are also connected to the Club's official account.

Hashtags (#)

The word 'hashtag' entered the dictionary in 2014. Hashtags are an important part of your social media activities, as they offer a shared designation for all the interactions that happen in relation to a single topic. They take the format of a hash (#) character, followed by a word or words with no separating spaces. A multi-word example is this book's own hashtag '#passion4digital'. Hashtags became popular on *Twitter*, as they allowed users to separate and order their conversations and made it clear which topic they were communicating about. This trend for segmenting topics and conversations has since been picked up by other social media channels including *Facebook*, which now allows users to tag their content to make it more discoverable.

There are no costs associated with hashtags and setting one up is as simple as adding a # to the front of a word, words (with no spaces) or a number. Hashtags

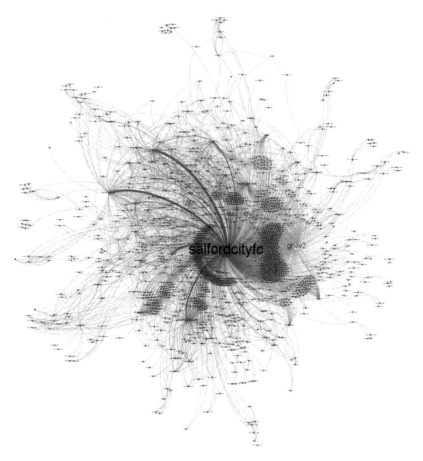

Figure 8.5 A network map of Salford City Football Club *Twitter* followers using NodeXL

work best when they are short and readable. Considering the number of Twitter users and volume of daily tweets it is important to check that nobody else is using your preferred hashtag. For example, #thenewmobilephonecampaign does not make a good hashtag, as it is too long and the words blend into one another, sometimes forming unfortunate new words. Be creative and combine and shorten words into something that is original and distinctive for your organisation and its messages.

When setting up a specific hashtag, make sure you publicise it well and use it in all your communications to encourage its wider use by your buyer persona. You should not try to 'own' your hashtag and keep it constrained, but rather view it as a part of your brand collateral that you want to spread widely. For example, our book uses the hashtag #passion4digital – join in and share your thoughts with others about digital marketing.

Case Study 8.2 *Always*: #LikeAGirl

Always' target audience are female consumers looking for feminine products. In this case, *Always* have identified a challenge faced by their buyer persona – that is, 'being like a girl' has diminutive connotations and is sometimes even seen as an insult. In response, *Always* created an

Figure 8.6 Always #LikeAGirl Google SERP

emotionally charged campaign that challenges the prevailing stereotype of girls as being inferior when it comes to engaging in sporty activities. The campaign is structured around a video that shows an audition for a video shoot where unsuspecting actors are asked to behave 'like a girl'. Both female and male actors are asked to simulate running, throwing and fighting. In the first half of the shoot the individuals are asked to perform the activity and are then asked why they portrayed girls in an inferior way. The actors, once they had a chance to reconsider their actions – which could be interpreted as an insult to girls – are asked to re-shoot the scene again. The campaign used *YouTube* as the primary channel and allowed interaction in the comments. Since it engaged the target audience on an emotional level (see the discussion of what makes content viral in Chapter 9), it reached lurkers as well as creators who were sharing and engaging with that video.

The video generated comments on *YouTube* and on a number of other social networks where the same hashtag #LikeAGirl was used. The hashtag is short and memorable, with every word starting with a capital letter (sometimes called CamelCase) – this makes it easy to read and write. A Google SERP for the term #LikeAGirl (Figure 8.6) is now consumed with *Always*-related content and the results from *Twitter* and *YouTube* all appear at the top.

The SERP is showing images as well as the video thumbnail – the use of images is an important SMO tactic.

A picture is worth a thousand words

Visual material, in particular good-quality images, is crucial for blogging and social media. Studies have consistently demonstrated that blog posts or social media posts that feature good-quality and relevant images resonate with the audience. As a consequence, these posts are more likely to motivate the audience to engage with and share content (Mawhinney, 2016).

Images can be obtained from a variety of sources. It is important that images are original, high quality and relevant. You should check that you have the rights to use an image for your intended specific purpose – this means that you should not use images found elsewhere on the Internet without purchasing or acquiring the image owner's permission. There are several places where you can obtain images:

- Stock libraries – free or paid for. There are many libraries that offer relevant images for purchase or download. Do check the usage rights and fine print for what you are permitted to do with the images even if you have paid a rights fee.

- Take your own photos – using your own camera or working with a photographer, either professional or amateur, produces original material that is customised to your brand.
- Creative Commons was started as a way for people to relax the copyright of the materials that they create. You can search for Creative Commons images on sites like *Google* or *Flickr*. Check the usage rights carefully, as there are different types of creative commons licences, and make sure the original author is always credited.

Working with images is easier with a good image editing package (*Photoshop* or *GIMP*) and a basic working knowledge of image editing. Even learning just how to resize, crop, brighten and fix images in order to improve the quality of your imagery will positively boost your brand.

Customer relationship management systems

A CRM system is a database of real customers' or prospects' contact details such as emails, as well as their social media presences. This is a powerful tool and asset for any organisation and can be very important for digital marketing purposes, since it allows you to segment and target customers with specific messages. One of the key benefits of a CRM system is the opportunity for marketing automation and the subsequent measurement of interactions. Automation also enables the use of regular email communications as well as traditional mail. A well-maintained CRM system will offer clear insight into your buyer persona.

There are a number of CRM systems, ranging from integrated website and email databases such as *HubSpot*, which have a heavy price tag, to systems that will be more relevant for smaller organisations and are free, such as *Really Simple Systems CRM*. Having an email subscription option on your website or blog pages allows you to automatically populate your CRM with new prospects.

8.11 Finding key influencers

By using tools such as a CRM system and SNA, you better know who your audience is, and you can then identify appropriate social networks, key influencers and audiences who fit your brand. You can identify potential influencers using search engines (such as *Google* searches) and SNA, as well as employing straightforward observation. These methods will also identify the locations where the interests you are targeting are being discussed and presented.

For example, if you are researching lifestyle or beauty and fashion, you will need to locate the digital presences of large fashion publishers who make use of guest and celebrity writers. These writers will often have their own blogs, *Instagram* account or *YouTube* content. These are the channels and specific locations where you also want to have visibility and reach out to these audiences and, ultimately, your buyer persona.

Once you have located communities that fit with your own brand's content, you can begin to identify the influencers in each of these communities. Learn the expected behaviours and culture of each community as a lurker before scaling up your activities as a contributor and then a creator. Once you have established your credentials in the community, reach out to the influencers in ways that fit the expected behaviours and culture of the specific community.

Contacting key influencers and building your own social capital is a key step in becoming part of a community. If you are approaching influencers with a reach that numbers in the hundreds of thousands or millions, you are going to have to stand out against a lot of noise. These are busy people who are used to – and largely immune to – a lot of contact requests and communications. Do something that makes you stand out to them in a way that catches their attention – for positive reasons – and starts the conversation off on a good note. A personalised, friendly message delivered through a social media platform such as *LinkedIn*, person to person, is better than a generic message that fills up an influencer's email inbox or *Twitter* timeline. Consider offering something helpful to them or promote a cause that they will be likely to support.

Becoming a key influencer

An influencer is someone who has authority and wide respect for their knowledge, experience or abilities around a topic. An influencer is a driving force in their subject area and will be a thought-leader in some way. If your aim is to become a key influencer you need to consider a number of separate issues.

Content – 'Content is king, but engagement is queen and she rules the house' (Figure 8.7). There are clear synergies between good content and engagement. This synergy is a combination of creating and curating content that will thrive within your community and is the first step in becoming a key influencer. Give the buyer persona what they want (see the SEO and content marketing chapters) and, more importantly, can engage with.

Growth – Being able to grow your account on your platform of choice will boost your efforts to becoming a key influencer. The steps to boosting your efforts are platform dependent, but generally involve you developing content and connecting with others who are positioning themselves as – or already are – key influencers. The basic element in growing your presence on any social platform is to follow those whom you consider to be your audience and to engage with them in relevant conversation. You want to be at the forefront of any emerging trend conversation. Your knowledge and the opportunities to exhibit your knowledge are invaluable opportunities to grow your audience and followers to a size that will have you regarded as an influencer.

Figure 8.7 Tweet by Mari Smith

Building an engaged community

Building a community on a social network can reap significant benefits, if it is done correctly. In recent years, both *UniLad* and *The Lad Bible* have revealed how social media has enabled a new trend in publishing. These communities have effectively killed off the printed 'lads mag' and grown their markets (and their value) to levels that the print magazine could never have imagined. These social media publishers provide content that their audiences want to see, effectively collecting and curating content gathered from across the Internet around a particular topic and placing it in coherent streams on channels where audience interaction is a key element of the experience (*Facebook*). *The Lad Bible* now focuses heavily on delivering video content to *Facebook* – a result of a change in algorithm that positively encourages this form of content. As a result, *The Lad Bible* has reaped the rewards resulting from this change. What once started as a hobby, focusing on providing content, has become a community with millions of followers that can now be monetised for advertising purposes. Building a community online, in the right way, can be a game-changer. Building a community does not involve having to create a new platform, but rather is about building an affiliation with your buyer persona in the right place in ways that fit into their lifestyle preferences and patterns, including, most importantly, their channel preferences.

Building a community utilises the same key principles for becoming an influencer. You need to focus on content and growth. Knowing where to find your buyer persona and working with creators in that space will make your community grow. Building an engaged community involves constantly giving out a high-quality stream of content. *UniLad* and *The Lad Bible* both spent three years building their model of giving before they were in a position to safely ask for something back from their audience. Community building requires a genuine passion for what the community says it is about, a degree of dogged perseverance and the constant building of trust. If you provide the audience with what it wants, you will reap the benefits – but it will take the commitment of time.

Creating a niche

Creating a niche enables you to build a community and deliver content to that community without any impartiality or opinion on the account. A niche begins without a brand sentiment. Lurkers are more likely to follow a niche if they cannot see an ulterior motive connected to it. Contributors and creators will participate if they recognise an opportunity and a USP within the niche.

Examples of successful niches include:

- @Love_Food on *Instagram* – a food page which posts visually appealing content of mouth-watering food and has gained over 6 million followers.
- @BeFitMotivation on *Twitter* – posts motivational quotes, body image goals and gym wear to an audience of over 1.5 million fitness fans.
- @ProblemsAtUni on *Twitter* – is a student humour account revealing the pains of over 300,000 university residence dwellers all over the UK.

These niches thrive off sharing highly engaging content, usually curated from sources discovered all over the Web, and are typically run by people who are personally and passionately interested in the niche. As a result, these niches are regarded as genuine and informative. The pivotal element in creating a niche is to provide your audience with regular, relevant and high-value content.

Creating a hook

Viral content on social platforms thrives by using recurring hooks and concepts that can be applicable to a broad range of topics. When a new trend comes along, the same concept can be applied and the hook refreshed to be relevant. An example of a very successful and effective hook created on UK social media was the use of the 'RT to save a degree' campaign for RefMe, a student referencing mobile app. The campaign was simple but highly effective and targeted towards student communities on *Twitter*. The content was simple. It consisted of three images showing how simple the process of referencing a book is by using the app. Supporting copy for the campaign focused on the theme 'RT to save a degree' and contained a direct link to the App Store. The result of this campaign was many thousands of organic re-tweets and a large volume of app downloads. As a measure of the success of this campaign, RefMe is now positioned as the referencing app of choice among UK students.

Trend awareness

Staying relevant on social media is key to becoming respected in your industry. If you can be aware of trends within your niche you will be at the forefront of conversations. You can go further by taking trend awareness and translating it into engaging content. Trend awareness will also position you as a key influencer. Talking about trend awareness involves drawing in the latest conversations around your interests and not simply being aware of Trending Topics on *Twitter*. Keeping one eye on Trending Topics is useful, as this will highlight the things that the world is talking about in real time. Do not focus on the idea of getting something 'trending', as a trending topic isn't the source of true value. Trending statistics are only a by-product of creating relevant, engaging conversations around a certain topic. If this conversation is done correctly, it will spread organically across the social web, and will eventually become a trending topic as a reward for its engaging nature.

Reputation management

Trust is an essential element of social media and should be embedded in all of your engagement and outreach activities. Trust in your brand is what makes someone confident to complete your calls-to-action, including purchasing. Trust also interacts with social capital in residing between individuals and brands and the individuals that represent brands (Valenzuela et al., 2009). Building brand engagement and increasing your social capital, as well as looking after and rewarding key influencers, all build trust and nurture communities. Trust takes a long time to establish, but is easy to lose.

Based on the conformity concept, widely known in sociology, people tend to follow the lead of others. For example, in a study exploring online purchase decisions it was found that the opinions of peers had a direct impact on the decision being made (Wang et al., 2012) because people wanted to be part of a group and wanted to take an informed decision. If your organisation can work with creators, your community can be encouraged to participate in low-level activities such as sharing feedback. Relevant networks such as *Google Maps* review, *TrustPilot*, *TripAdvisor*, *Feefo* and others dependent on your niche all provide the mechanisms to engage your community and to encourage them to publicly articulate their trust in your organisation, its products and services, and its brands. Once you choose your preferred reviewing system, direct your customers to leave a review, in particular those that are enthusiastically positive about your service. Some of the most successful *TripAdvisor* organisations are not necessarily great in what they do, but they are great in encouraging their happy customers to share their reviews online. With any system that you choose you must regularly monitor and reply to both negative as well as positive comments. Take note of common themes of complaint and genuinely act upon these with real resolutions and personalised comments. Do not be tempted to use websites such as www.fiverr.com, which offer 'genuine reviews'. These are not only unethical, but are also easily identified as false signals. Prioritise encouraging genuine review processes in your organisation, including emailing your customers after a purchase and asking for a review. Consider offering guidelines on how to create and to access review pages. Not all of your users are familiar with these systems.

Monitor your social media profiles regularly and have a team of people who would reply to complaints. It is generally accepted that a complaint is taken offline, since you do not really want to discuss the negative experience of your customers in front of others. Most people are reasonable and are happy to comply with your request to share a phone number for a private discussion of the issues being raised. However, in situations where unhappy customers are unreasonable and you feel that the case cannot be resolved offline, and you have tried reasonable ways of resolving an argument, you can explore the option of answering the complaint publicly as well as offering other community members the option to contribute to the same conversation. Whichever way you resolve complaints it must be one of the entries in your risk register for monitoring and mitigation (see the discussion about project management in Chapter 5).

8.12 Summary

This chapter discusses some of the key principles of social media and its role in digital marketing. Social media is an increasingly important way to engage customers for any organisation that wants a successful digital presence. Strategic commitment to using social media platforms requires the allocation of tools and resources to the four areas of marketing, sales, operations and support.

Social capital is a central way to understand your social media audience and to measure the success of your engagement with your buyer persona. You are also building trust and bonding social capital between your organisation and your buyer persona. This chapter outlines many other reasons for using social media, including the creation of synergies for SEO and the multiple benefits of creating a blog.

The reasons for measuring social media activities will depend on your strategic and operational reasons for using these channels, but irrespective of the strategic aims you have, your organisation should monitor and measure its social media activities. Social media is broadly divided in this chapter into professional networks that are more focused on B2B industries and private networks used more for B2C interactions.

Social media cannot be controlled, but nor should it be ignored. It is a powerful way to communicate with your buyer persona and achieve your strategic goals.

8.13 References

Atkinson, P. (2015) *For ethnography*. Sage. https://uk.sagepub.com/en-gb/eur/for-ethnography/book234711

Butts, C.T. (2008) Social Network Analysis with SNA. *Journal of Statistical Software, 24*(6), 1–51.

Davies, P. (2015) *Digital Trends Winter – UK – December 2015*. http://store.mintel.com/digital-trends-winter-uk-december-2015

Edwards, G. (2010) *Mixed-method approaches to social network analysis*. Discussion Paper. National Centre for Research Methods. http://eprints.ncrm.ac.uk/842/

Ferneley, E., Heinze, A. and Child, P. (2009) Research 2.0: Encouraging engagement in online market research communities.

Fueller, J., Schroll, R., Dennhardt, S. and Hutter, K. (2011) Social brand value and the value enhancing role of social media relationships for brands. In *Proceedings of the Annual Hawaii International Conference on System Sciences*, pp. 3218–27.

Granovetter, M.S. (1973) The strength of weak ties. *American Journal of Sociology*, 78(6), 1360–80.

Griffiths, M. and McLean, R. (2015) Unleashing corporate communications via social media: A UK study of brand management and conversations with customers. *Journal of Customer Behaviour*, 14(2), 147–62.

Groeger, L. and Buttle, F. (2014) Word-of-mouth marketing: Towards an improved understanding of multi-generational campaign reach. *European Journal of Marketing*, 48(7/8), 1186–208.

Heinze, A., Ferneley, E. and Child, P. (2013) Ideal participants in online market research: Lessons from closed communities. *International Journal of Market Research*, 55(6), 769–89.

Jarman, M., Nowak, A., Borkowski, W., Serfass, D., Wong, A. and Vallacher, R. (2015) The critical few: Anticonformists at the crossroads of minority opinion survival and collapse. *Journal of Artificial Societies and Social Simulation*, 18(1), 6.

Kaushik, Avinash (ed.) (2009) *Web Analytics 2.0: The art of online accountability and science of customer centricity*. Wiley.

Kozinets, R.V.R. (2002) The field behind the screen: Using netnography for marketing research in online communities. *Journal of Marketing Research*, 39(1), 61–72.

Kozinets, R.V.R. (2015) *Netnography redefined*. https://uk.sagepub.com/en-gb/eur/netnography/book242765

Mawhinney, J. (2016) *37 Visual content marketing statistics you should know in 2016*. http://blog.hubspot.com/marketing/visual-content-marketing-strategy

Poor Rezaei, S.M. and Heinze, A. (2014) *SME competitiveness through online brand communities: An exploration of brand loyalty*. Institute for Small Business and Entrepreneurship.

Putnam, R. (2001) *Bowling alone: The collapse and revival of American community*. Simon and Schuster.

Tiago, M.T.P.M.B. and Veríssimo, J.M.C. (2014) Digital marketing and social media: Why bother? *Business Horizons*, 57(6), 703–8.

Valenzuela, S., Park, N. and Kee, K. (2009) Is there social capital in a social network site?: Facebook use and college students' life satisfaction, trust, and participation. *Journal of Computer-Mediated Communication*, 14(4).

Wang, X., Yu, C. and Wei, Y. (2012) Social media peer communication and impacts on purchase intentions: A consumer socialization framework. *Journal of Interactive Marketing*, 26(4), 198–208.

Widdop, P., Cutts, D. and Jarvie, G. (2014) Omnivorousness in sport: The importance of social capital and networks. *International Review for the Sociology of Sport*. SAGE Publications.

Woolcock, M. (2001) The place of social capital in understanding social and economic outcomes. *Canadian Journal of Policy Research*, 2(1).

9 Content marketing

Sophie Iredale and Aleksej Heinze, Salford Business School, University of Salford, UK

Martin J Williams, Managing Director, UKcopywriting.com, UK

9.0 Learning objectives

In this chapter you will learn how to:

- create content that will attract relevant and qualified online traffic;
- evaluate a range of strategies for building a positive brand reputation;
- engage with your buyer persona and encourage them to share your brand;
- generate high-quality inbound links;
- encourage positive sentiment surrounding your brand that will generate a positive brand reputation.

9.1 The importance of content marketing

As mentioned in previous chapters, high-quality content is essential for branding and user experience (please refer to Chapter 6), for search engine optimisation (SEO) purposes (Chapter 7) and for pay-per-click (PPC) quality scores (Chapter 10).

Content marketing is the strategic process of creating and amplifying content for the purpose of informing, entertaining and/or building awareness of your brand, products or services within a target audience.

Content marketing is a cyclical process, which incorporates the following four stages informed by campaign management processes (see Chapter 5) for creating consistent content:

1. Plan: Content planning and idea generation.
2. Act: Content creation, development, implementation and amplification.
3. Observe: Content tracking and monitoring.
4. Reflect: Content evaluation.

Content marketing planning

The most crucial stage of a content marketing campaign is the planning process. The planning stage typically encompasses the following phases:

- Goal setting.
- Defining your buyer persona.

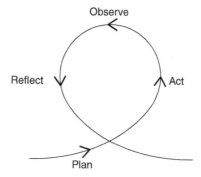

Observe

Reflect

Act

Plan

Figure 9.1 Content marketing cycle

- Resource management.
- Scheduling and editorial calendar creation.

Goal setting

Before any work can begin, it is vital you ask yourself what your content marketing purpose is. For example, is it to raise awareness of a service, an event or a product? Is it to entertain, inform or educate? Is it to increase referral traffic to your site? Is it to build your contact database? Is it being used to supplement marketing and/or PR activity? Without defining this in the early stages of your campaign you will have nothing solid with which to align each stage of the content marketing process. Our recommendation is to think 'SMART' (for further detailed guidance on setting SMART goals, refer to Chapters 4 and 5).

Further explication of appropriate key performance indicators (KPIs) and performance metrics relevant to a content marketing campaign can be found in section 9.5 of this chapter.

Defining your buyer persona

A full breakdown on how to create a buyer persona can be found in Chapter 3. Insight into your unique selling points (USPs) and key messaging, and how to identify the unique values of your brand, services and/or products (that will resonate with your buyer personas), can be found in Chapter 6. Once you have fully defined your USPs and key messages, you can start to build a content story around them.

Segmenting your target audience will allow you to create a composite breakdown of your buyer persona's interests, online behaviour and key demographics relevant to your brand. It will also allow you to think about where your buyer persona is within the buying cycle, so you can shape your content marketing strategy accordingly, assembling ideas, content types, channels and approaches to suit.

Resource management

At this stage it is important to be clear about what budget and time you have allocated to your content marketing campaign.

Content marketing can be incredibly time consuming and, depending upon what content you want to create, expensive to produce. For example, a good blog post can take over a day to create, including time dedicated to researching the content, generating and sourcing unique data and quotes, outreaching the post and monitoring it. Even bigger pieces such as ebooks and videos can take much longer and require a whole host of designer and developer skills. However, if your content marketing campaign is executed correctly, the payoff is worth the investment.

Be sure to keep track of your time and budget in order to determine routes to optimising resources for future campaigns. *Trello* is a free time-management and tracking tool which can be used by multiple members of a content marketing team for full visibility on task lists and work completed. Further details about managing a campaign can be found in Chapter 5.

Scheduling and editorial calendar creation

Once you know who you are targeting and why, another important stage of the planning process is to look at your desired launch plan (see Chapter 5 for more details on operational planning). This is where seasonal trends must be considered to ensure you do not miss your optimum launch time and to give you enough time to strategically plan what resources you require and delegate tasks appropriately.

Supposing your aim is to raise awareness of a new flower shop and your campaign is to promote a bouquet giveaway for Mother's Day, you would need to ensure all relevant content has been created, launched and has given your target audience enough time to enter their personal details before Mother's Day (as well as allowing yourself time to send out the prize giveaway to those that have participated).

Google Trends is a recommended platform for planning your seasonal peaks and drops if your product or service is seasonally driven. For example, retailers selling ski wear would be mindful of peaks around winter and look to plan their promotions in line with winter ski seasons (Figure 9.2).

We also recommend you look at your historical website traffic in *Google* Analytics or other web analytics providers to determine average peaks and drops in activity.

In order to effectively synthesise your activity and allow transparency to all actors and stakeholders involved in the content marketing process, create a shared content marketing calendar (or an editorial calendar) that outlines your weekly, monthly, quarterly, biannual or annual campaign plans. It should ideally contain the following:

- Campaign description, key messages and themes.
- Related objectives.

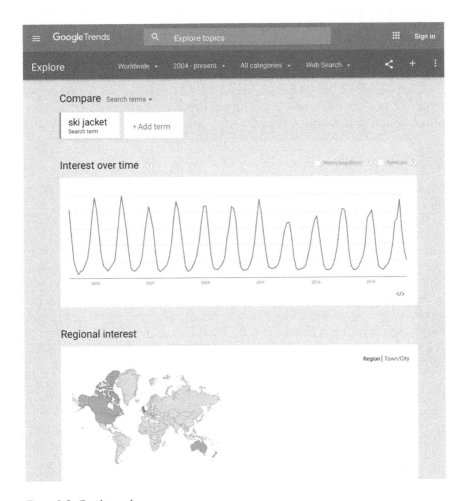

Figure 9.2 Google trends

- Task owners.
- Allocated budgets and time breakdowns.
- Launch dates.

As mentioned in the campaign project management chapter (Chapter 5), this stage of the planning process can take some time but is worth it from a project and resource management perspective.

9.2 The idea generation process

At this stage you should have a good idea about who you want to target, when you want to target them and how much time and budget you have available to create your content. Taking into consideration these key learnings, this is when you can start the idea generation process.

Getting the 'idea' right at the beginning of your content marketing campaign is the most critical stage of the entire process. You want to choose an idea or a series of ideas that resonates with your buyer persona, giving them value whilst not pushing your sales proposition onto them. Contemporary marketing is subtle and not intrusive, and acts as a natural step in the buyer persona's journey to conversion. It is not the end result.

Where to find content inspiration

Sources of inspiration for your content marketing campaign can be found in the following places:

What your target audience is sharing and where – When you have identified your buyer persona you can begin to analyse their online twitter bios and profiles using *Followerwonk*. This can be achieved using your own *Twitter* follower profile or other competitor *Twitter* profiles to cross-compare followers. This will help you to segment profiles by interests as well as identify other similar key influencers they are following. As a result, you open up a whole community of prospects, which allows you to better understand common interests and themes in the most popular content shared.

Other routes to identifying your target audience and segmenting your buyer persona could involve the following:

- Setting up '*Google* Alerts' for terms related to your brand to see who is sharing them and where.
- Scanning other social media profiles such as *LinkedIn* and *Facebook* to look for groups and group members relative to your niche. This can be done using the search bar for related terms to your product or service. Whilst an aim is to identify potential key influencers, you should also be mindful of what topics are being discussed, what type of content is being shared and where they are sharing the content from. This will help you build a picture of your buyer persona's interests and content consumption behaviour.
- You can also use *Facebook* Insights, *YouTube* Insights and *Google* Analytics to give you a deeper understanding of your audience's demographic data, such as geographic location, gender and age.
- Ask them! Supposing you already have a retained customer base, don't be afraid to send out a survey (or an interview, a focus group, etc.) to ask them about their online preferences. This data can then be translated into something with deeper meaning to support the segmentation of your target audience.

Whilst auditing your target audience's preferences be sure to pick up on subtle colloquialisms in their language, as this can help you with your key messaging and storytelling during the idea generation process. Though it is important to stay true to your brand's tone of voice, adopting nuances of your buyer persona can positively impact the engagement rate of your content.

What your competitors are promoting and where – Be sure to analyse competitor content to determine how successful historical creative campaigns have been. Analyse engagement metrics as well as quality links back to site with link analysis software such as Open Site Explorer. This will allow you to determine which pieces of content were the most popular (or not) and will provide a platform from which to develop your own ideas that build upon competitor successes.

Several networks allow you to monitor your competitors' social media profiles. In *Facebook* for example, you can go to the Insights section setup and compare the performance of your page and posts with similar pages on *Facebook*.

At this point it is important to note that it is copyright infringement if you copy the intellectual property of another without their explicit permission, so be careful where you decide to seek inspiration. The default for all content – text, images, video or sound – is that it is 'all rights reserved'. However, content under a Creative Commons licence (Creative Commons, 2016) identified by a CC logo usually offers some exceptions, where authors allow content to be shared without explicit permission as long as the rights of their licence are respected. Several content creators see CC as a way of allowing their message to be amplified and thus reach wider audiences compared to copyrighted content. The use of Creative Commons as a tactic in content marketing is a worthy consideration, particularly if the content is meant to 'go viral'.

Keyword research – Keyword research should not be the only source of inspiration for your content marketing campaign, but it offers a good source of ideas. Understanding what keyword is being targeted in your content allows you to gain maximum SEO value from your content marketing efforts and should be achieved through keyword optimised digital content.

This is where you consider your keyword strategy – keywords related to your product or service that can be incorporated into your content in order to give the content its own ranking capabilities. We recommend that you target semantically driven search terms that answer a specific and relevant question your buyer persona might ask. Free content idea generators such as answerthepublic. com are a good place to start.

Further insight into keyword planning can be found in Chapter 7.

Identifying target publications – Identifying target publications relevant to your brand and to your persona's interests should give you some insight into current topics and popular content ideas.

For example, if you are interested in launching a content marketing campaign aimed at food wholesalers and suppliers, analysing the success of content on well-known fast moving consumer goods (FMCG) publications such as 'The Grocer' might be of value to you. It can also give you an insight into what content topics have already been created to ensure you do not 'reinvent the wheel'.

Pre-campaign prospecting – Pre-campaign prospecting is the process of contacting key influencers, such as website owners, bloggers and journalists, to determine if there are any pieces of topical content they would like to feature on their website.

Sometimes the best ideas are generated with the support of media specialists within your field. Seeking out key prospects for your content requires you to carry out various outreach tactics, which will be explained in section 9.4 of this chapter.

A great way of sourcing content ideas and potential placements is to get in touch with journalists on websites such as *HARO* (Help A Reporter Out), which request specialist insight, personal experience and advice from individuals, groups or organisations across various industries, on a daily basis.

Alternative contact details of niche websites, journalists and bloggers can be sourced on *Twitter* using the hashtag #journorequest, as well as automated content marketing tools such as *Ninja Outreach* and *Buzzstream*.

Content aggregator sites – There are some automated campaign tools available to you, such as *Buzzsumo, Socialmention.com* and *Ahrefs Content Explorer*, which allow you to type in a specific keyword or target phrase/message to determine what content on related topics is being shared, where it is being shared and how successful it has been. This should give you ideas of where the content gaps are, as well as giving you insight into the types of relevant content.

Data sources – Data-driven content is beneficial, as it adds trust, unique value and reliability to your content messages. Data-driven content is especially useful for journalist pieces and press releases, which typically use data to help add gravity to newsworthy topics within the content.

Unique data can be generated through market research and customer relationship marketing (CRM) data. Should you undertake any market research to gain unique data, ensure your sample is of an appropriately large size to certify your results are trustworthy (see Survey System, 2016). Many well-known publications will refuse to take your content if your data sources and sample sizes cannot be certified.

It is recommended that you try not to use statistics that are not your own, as they have likely been seen before and will lose impact. That being said, cross-comparing your data with existing data sources can give rigour to the point you are making. Free data sources such as *Guardian Data* (Guardian, 2016) and *Mintel Reports* (Mintel, 2016), as well as the *Office for National Statistics* (ONS, 2016), can be mined for interesting data insights.

Existing content – Should you have a blog or media section on site, a recommended route to finding content ideas is to analyse historical posts and media to determine what content received a healthy level of traffic and engagement. This data can be found in *Google* Analytics. You can then look at possible routes to repurposing or repackaging content in a different way and relaunching the new content to a wider audience.

User-generated content (UGC) – UGC is any content that is created by contributors that are not employed directly by you or your brand. Content types usually comprise blogs, testimonials, reviews, videos and images – think 'instagrammable' moments – and vlog reviews of your product/service. UGC can empower your users to become part of your campaign, which can build a perception of transparency and trust in your wider target audience. Content ideas can come directly from engaged users and assumes that other similar users will favour your UGC topics too. UGC can also save you production time costs, but it is important that all UGC is proofed and checked for duplicates to ensure that only quality content is added to your site so that it does not violate search engine quality guidelines (please refer to Chapter 7 for more details).

Offline activity – Offline activity such as PR stunts, experiential marketing and offers (in-store/restaurant/bar/supermarket) can be leveraged and amplified through online activity. This would require you to generate a trackable landing page for all related information and traffic generated via the offline PR and marketing activity.

For example, a charity event that is held by your organisation is a perfect opportunity to capture and generate new content. This could entail the following:

- Creation of a landing page with a data capture form to track potential event attendees. Details of who can be used in future outreach initiatives.
- Promotion of the event through your blog, external event promotions sites and your social channels.
- Live streaming of the event via live video transmission (now via *YouTube* and a number of other networks, which allow you this functionality).
- Creation of an event-specific hashtag, which could be used pre-event, during the event and post-event.
- As a way of prolonging the value of your event you could capture high-quality photographs and upload images to your social networks to create a digital footprint of your event to allow your event visitors to engage with your content. As event organiser you could contribute to the discussion, amplify the positive content and reply in real time to your audience.
- Following the event, a press release detailing the amount of money generated through charitable donations could be syndicated across online and offline newspaper publications.

This integrated approach would generate opportunities for brand awareness, reputation building and inbound links.

The psychology behind viral content

When considering virality of content during the idea generation process, it is important to note that the vast majority of Internet users are passive – 'lurkers' – who simply consume content and do not engage with it (see Chapter 8 for more details). As such, whilst a viral campaign is the desired outcome of any content marketing campaign, the term can be considered ideological and there is no one strategy that will guarantee your content goes viral.

However, there is one defining factor that unifies successful viral campaigns and that is emotion, such as empathy, surprise, excitement, sadness, joy and disgust. Generally, we make decisions based on emotion and justify them with logic at a later stage (Carnegie, 2010). Therefore, any content ideas you consider should ideally provoke an emotional response from your buyer persona.

As well as emotion, Berger (2013) observed that there are a number of factors that should be present in order to increase content virality and sharing. Berger's *STEPPS* model can be used as a guiding checkbox for content optimisation, in particular for larger budget content productions such as video.

S – Social currency – based on the assumption that what we talk about and share reflects how we are perceived. For example, does the content that your target buyer persona is sharing make them feel knowledgeable/witty/caring/cool?

T – Trigger – something that connects the audience to the story and how it resonates with your buyer persona. How will the person remember your content? What makes your content remarkable, memorable and mentionable? Is there an easily remembered song, slogan, strapline or hashtag?

E – Emotion – it moves the audience emotionally when we care about something. This is one of the most difficult aspects to achieve in content creation, as the interpretation of emotion is subjective. For example, humour is often used in content, but it is culturally and community dependent and can lead to misunderstanding. As previously discussed in this section, evoking an unexpected emotional response can set your content apart from other noise on the Internet.

Depending on what message you are trying to convey, overly emotive content could be less effective, whereas content that is too practical can be devoid of emotion.

P – Public – information should be publicly available. Keeping your content open in a public forum allows you to engage with a wider audience. Therefore, always consider whether your content really needs to sit behind a data capture form and make sure your content is optimised with social sharing buttons to encourage quick and accessible social sharing.

When putting your content on a public domain always remember people are increasingly aware of crowdsourcing and transparency of content creation. Is it possible to see that a number of other people have consumed your content (e.g. video viewers figures) and shared (e.g. number of shares for a web page)? This public data adds to the logic of persuasion of your content. If the content is placed on a public social networking site, such as *YouTube* or *Twitter*, it is more likely to be amplified by your target audience when compared to a static brand-related web page.

P – Practical value – audiences can apply the lessons they have learned in practice. Informative content that educates and offers practical advice on your product and/or service, as well as offering guidance on topical issues relevant to your buyer persona, makes for highly downloadable and shareable pieces.

'How-to guides' are a common content piece with practical value. As mentioned earlier, tools such as answerthepublic.com offer suggestions for FAQ-style content.

S – Story – subtly and coercively generate a story through your content whilst still communicating your underlying content marketing message. Consumers do not like to be sold to as they peruse content. Too much of a sales pitch can put your target buyer off, and it is important you tread carefully with key messaging within your content.

The content mapping process

Once you have thoroughly researched your ideas and you can confirm they are relevant to your buyer persona, this is when you can start to piece together your content ideas to begin visualising your content story. This is called content mapping or 'storyboarding'.

Ideally this process takes place within a team of marketers and creatives to allow full visibility of ideas, which act as talking points for potential content types and other related ideas that have not yet been addressed. It is recommended that the entire team behind the content mapping process is given a persona brief to ensure that this is at the forefront of everyone's mind when discussing ideas.

Content mapping should be tailored to your buyer persona, as discussed in Chapters 3 and 4. The process should allow you to see the relationships between content ideas, which could then offer potential for a content series or multi-method campaign that can be adapted for various content types and ideas. At this stage you could also consider tying in other online and offline marketing events and activities to make your content marketing efforts more integrated.

Remember to have fun with the idea generation process, as this typically generates the best ideas. It all depends upon the type of content you want to create to fit your persona, whether its purpose is to inform, teach, entertain, trigger an emotional response such as empathy or to grab attention through an unconventional PR stunt.

Be sure to document all ideas and do not throw any away, as they can be used at a later date.

Getting buy-in

A recommended final stage of this process is to ensure that the content ideas have been cross-checked with all relevant stakeholders so that content marketing plans can be achieved on time and within budget and that the idea is in keeping with the brand personality and brand guidelines.

If you have not already carried out pre-prospecting, then we also recommend you pitch your favourite ideas back to journalists and other influencers, including bloggers or vloggers, as well as media contacts, before content is created to ensure that there will be interest in your content before the process begins.

9.3 Content creation and development

Once you are confident in your idea and you have buy-in from all relevant stakeholders, you can commence your content creation.

Be sure to select a content type within budget and of relevance to your persona and content idea. For example, if you are wanting to launch a new and exciting hair product, a video demonstrating possible hairstyles might be better than an ebook or a whitepaper.

We have listed a series of potential content types that you could use to bring your content ideas to life. This is not an exhaustive list, but it contains some of the most commonly used content formats shared on the Internet.

- Blog post

    - What it is – Regular entries on your website that discuss industry updates, news, 'Top 10' lists, how-to guides, case studies, award updates, etc. and can contain multimedia elements such as images, infographics and videos.
    - How to do it – Plan out your editorial content in advance and undertake research to ensure your content is unique and relevant. Good blog posts require high-quality specialist copywriting skills to ensure that copy is written in the style, language and tone relevant to the buyer persona. Try not to write just for search engines, although keyword targeting can be incorporated where applicable. Make sure the heading and URL are optimised, and the page contains social sharing buttons, a comment box and other related links to encourage click-through to the rest of your site. Consider adding a trackable data capture form and ensure that all blog pages are being tracked in *Google* Analytics.
    - When to use it – Aim for weekly posts to keep your community engaged and to have fresh content continually added to the site. Therefore, if you say you will blog once a week you need to stick to it and make sure you always have enough to talk about. However, only write a blog post if there is something of value to write – writing for frequency and not for value will invariably affect quality and turn away readers, though consistency is key to encouraging a retained readership that knows when to expect content. Some of the main objectives of blogging are to position you and/or your brand as a specialist within your industry, as well as generating traffic and related keyword rankings. A blog can also be a strategic hub for all social media engagement activity and offers regular content for amplification on other social media profiles.

- Guest blogging

    - What it is – Guest blogs are typically opinion posts hosted on a website external to yours.
    - How to do it – Guest blogging requires time for sourcing appropriate, high-quality content placements with high engagement and

high levels of traffic. The aim is to drive social engagement and brand awareness, as well as generate quality inbound links and referral traffic back to your website. Good guest posts require quality copywriting from specialists within their field.

- When to use it – Utilise guest blogging only if the host website is relevant and active. A poor-quality guest blogging site will look like 'spam' and you risk a search engine penalty.

- Infographics

  - What it is – Infographics are a visualisation of data or other significant information.
  - How to do it – Good-quality infographics will require design time. Ensure that your content is eye-catching, legible and has a flow to it. Only place content into the infographic if it is meaningful.
  - When to use it – They are typically used in conjunction with blog posts to support and visualise key messages. Do not use infographics too often, as this can look like 'spam', which is not SEO best practice.

- Photographs/images

  - What it is – Taking your own photos or designing/illustrating your own images gives them the potential to be used by other blog writers and websites within content, as memes for example.
  - How to do it – Have a professional photographer at any of your events, or if this is not possible use your own smartphone camera to capture the moments which could be shared. When taking pictures of others, inform them in advance and ask permission to use the image as part of your marketing content. Keeping a bank of your own photos ready and searchable by optimising the images utilising SEO techniques (refer to image optimisation section within Chapter 7 for best practice guidelines) will make your photos easily accessible to others who may then request the use of your photos. Invite them to attribute a link back to your site as the original source of the photo if the host site is of a good quality. Consider sharing photos publicly on photo-sharing social networks such as www.flickr.com and www.instagram. com/ and setting them as a Creative Commons licence, such as Attribution 2.0 Generic (CC BY 2.0). You can also use images of others with permission or well-recognised meme generators such as https:// imgflip.com/memegenerator
  - When to use it – Images have high engagement rates when used as content on social media platforms. Use images when planning *Facebook*, *Twitter*, *Instagram*, *Pinterest* and *Snapchat* campaigns. There is no real limit to producing images, especially now that most smartphones have good photo camera functionality. Most importantly, ensure that your images are legal, unique and not duplicated from any other sources.

- Online video
    - What it is – Audio-visual content that can be streamed live or downloaded to the user's device. Video content includes vlogs, guides, interviews and adverts.
    - How to do it – Producing a good-quality video can be expensive. Ensure you have a good camera, ideally filming in High Definition (HD) – most smartphones film in HD. Use a tripod – this will make sure your shots are steady. Have appropriate lighting so that your subjects are clearly visible and less effort is needed for post-production work. Use video editor software – these are becoming easily available, and even *YouTube* has its own built-in editor and animator if required. Video length will depend on a number of factors, but consider that most online videos will be watched on a mobile device and that data plans are quickly consumed with high-quality long videos. *YouTube* allows you to filter videos under 4 minutes (short) and over 20 minutes (long), so consider keeping it under 4 minutes or, if you are planning to create a long video, meet the search filter criteria. Online attention spans are short, so ideally videos should be under 1.5 minutes long, but it is wholly dependent upon the video purpose itself. Videos typically require storyboarding and a script, which need to resonate with your buyer persona.
    - When to use it – Video and in particular mobile video is one of the fastest growing areas in digital marketing content according to the Internet Advertising Bureau 2015 statistics (IAB, 2015). Younger generations that grew up with constant access to the Internet are more likely to view video online compared to traditional TV (Glennie, 2005). If you can ensure your video content is unique, there is no real limit to posting videos. Just ensure that the content is meaningful and relevant, as you will quickly find viewers will choose not to engage with your content if it has no point.
- Interactive content
    - What it is – Interactive content is any online material that lets the user actively engage with you. It can consist of interactive infographics, long form articles, interactive videos, quizzes, surveys, etc.
    - How to do it – Good-quality interactive content typically requires design time and usually technical developer time to include the interactive functionality and moving elements. For example, a bank can create a mortgage calculator which is useful for providing quick advice to its buyer persona. Consider tracking interactive elements on the interactive content pages through *Google* Analytics or heat mapping software to understand how people are engaging with the content to inform future pieces of content.
    - When to use it – Interactive content is expensive and should be used strategically to maximise budget and make the most out of an expensive activity.

- Free tools

  - What it is – Free tools can consist of downloadable templates, ebooks, whitepapers and software with the intention of helping the end user automate and/or optimise some of their existing work processes. As an example, this could be an *Excel* campaign planner.
  - How to do it – Depending on what free tools you create, this could require a developer, designer or someone proficient in *Excel*, as well as a skilled copywriter. Consider the pain points of your buyer persona in order to determine how you can save them time through using your tool. Ensure that downloads and tools are hidden behind trackable data capture forms to gather user data for future campaigns.
  - When to use it – Much like interactive content, free tools can take a lot of time to create; hence these should be used for strategically important activities and can form part of a longer-term campaign.

- Podcasts

  - What it is – Podcasts are digital audio files that fulfil the same purpose as blog posts in that they are an audible way to discuss current events, news stories, interviews and opinion.
  - How to do it – Record an audio file and convert it into a podcast. You will need a good-quality microphone and solid editing skills. Consider branding this with theme music. Aim to get your podcast listed on *iTunes* or embed your podcast on your website or sound hosting platforms such as *SoundCloud*.
  - When to use it – Depending on your audience and your resources, consider adding podcasts on a weekly or a monthly basis for maximum pickup and engagement.

- Competitions

  - What it is – Competitions are giveaways of products, services and prizes, which can be relevant to your brand.
  - How to do it – Generating a landing page specifically for the competition details will give you an opportunity to easily share and track traffic to the page. Ensure you integrate a data capture form and sharing buttons.
  - When to use it – If you choose to host competitions and giveaways regularly, ensure that the prize giveaway is of high value. Be sure that you do not regularly carry out competitions irrelevant to your brand, as you will find your database grows with individuals only interested in your prize giveaways and with no longer-term value.

- Press releases

  - What it is – Press releases are official statements typically detailing product and service launches, issued to industry-specific online and offline newspapers, magazines and general press to raise awareness to their readers.

- How to do it – Press releases should follow a specific format, which requires a particular style of headline, opening statement, length, lay-out, quote and closing contact details. It is recommended that further research into press release styles and practice of press release writing is undertaken to fit with industry-specific journalists'/editors' exacting standards.

- When to use it – Press releases are a PR activity and should be used in conjunction with content marketing strategy.

• Email campaigns

- What it is – Emails are messages distributed to individuals within a targeted database containing images, newsletters and updates.

- How to do it – Ensure that your email headline is attention grabbing and the content is personalised to the reader. Consider adding links back to your website to encourage referral traffic back to your website. Ideally, special mail automation management software is used. A number of free versions such as *MailChimp* are available and can help you to trial this important and often underestimated strategy of communication. We also recommend the split a/b testing of email templates to test what drives the most interaction (http://kb.mailchimp.com/campaigns/previews-and-tests/best-practices-for-email-subject-lines).

- When to use it – Try not to send out too many emails unnecessarily, as the end reader could consider them 'spam'. Offer subscription options for monthly or weekly updates so that your audience can choose the frequency of communications. Make sure that you are only sending out truly relevant and targeted content. Be sure that you comply with opt-in and opt-out protocol and you are only sending your email content to those that are open to receiving it.

• UGC

- What it is – UGC includes reviews, opinion posts, testimonials and content generated via social media channels.

- How to do it – It is beneficial for creating natural content for your website, as well as other external sites, which can contain a link back to your website. It is also good for building brand reputation and user insight if managed correctly. Reviews are an essential trust-building process for your products and services. Actively encouraging your customers to create reviews, in particular those customers who are delighted with your products and services, helps you to guide the opinions about your brand online. Make it simple for your customers to create and post reviews. UGC is also helpful for engagement through competitions, for example asking people to submit a photograph or video as part of a prize draw. *My Starbucks Idea* is a good example of an organisation encouraging the buyer persona to help innovate the business – crowdsourcing ideas for innovation.

- When to use it – There is no constraint on UGC; just ensure that it is well written, is not duplicated from any other sites and does not damage your brand reputation.

As mentioned in the SEO chapter, generating links is important for SEO, so avoid spam tactics when engaging in content marketing. For example, avoid adding your website to online directories unless they are very well known, such as dmoz.org and www.google.com/business/, as many directories are not compliant with *Google*'s Penguin algorithm.

Using the right colours to convey the message

How you use colour in your content affects how your target audience engages with it. Colour helps you to convey your content messages and can guide your buyer persona towards key calls-to-action.

Your choice of colour also helps you to influence and emphasise attitudes and specific feelings towards your content, as each colour can trigger specific emotions. Interpretations of colours are likely to be subjective and can convey different messages based on the cultural background of the individual. For example:

Red communicates physical strength and warmth. It grabs your attention – that's why it is chosen for traffic lights all over the world. Whilst it is perceived as friendly, it can also be associated with aggression and danger.
Blue conveys intelligence, trust and efficiency. It is often used by politicians to convey their trustworthiness. However, it can be perceived as unemotional and unfriendly.
Yellow is associated with hope, positivity and optimism. Careful use of this colour in combination with others is advised, as it can trigger anxiety and depression.

Whilst the list above gives insight into emotional reactions related to the primary colours, lots of other colours and colour combinations can trigger specific reactions. As such, it is recommended that split a/b testing is carried out to determine which content style delivers the biggest impact.

Content tracking

It is important that you ensure you have proofed and tested all elements of your content, such as data capture forms and social sharing buttons, before launching your content and sharing it with your audience. Poor content can put your audience off interacting with your brand and can make it hard to track how well your content marketing campaign has performed.

In order to track the progress of your content marketing campaign to ensure it is performing and to justify the budget for future content marketing campaigns, you should have tracked all elements of your content, such as 'clickable' elements and 'thank you' pages. More details on tracking are in Chapter 12.

Content tracking tools and KPIs will be explored in section 9.5 of this chapter.

9.4 Content marketing implementation and delivery

Once you are happy that your content is fully integrated into your website or a website external to yours, and your tracking is correct, this is where you will look at sharing and amplifying your content to your buyer persona. The process of getting your content in front of your buyer persona is known as 'outreach'.

Research completed in stage one should have allowed you to construct a media list full of target publications, bloggers and key influencers who would be interested in hosting and sharing your content.

Outreach to contacts is a delicate, carefully considered process that requires a certain level of charisma to build a rapport and relationship with contacts in your media list. Remember that your contacts probably receive hundreds of requests per day, so ensure that your content pitch details the clear value and benefits of hosting or sharing your content. An automated email sent out to your list without any personalisation or thought will work against you and could sour the relationship for future content marketing campaigns.

To further amplify your content we recommend the following distribution channels, though the most appropriate channels for your business are entirely dependent upon what content you have decided to create and which channels your target audience are using:

- *YouTube/Vimeo* – a video content platform that can be optimised to encourage ranking of video content in search engines.
- *Google+* – Google's own social media platform that can be used to target specific communities.
- *Facebook* – a social media platform that is typically used for informal content and networking. Good for business-to-consumer (B2C) and consumer-to-consumer (C2C) content marketing.
- *Instagram* – a photo- and video-sharing social media platform that is particularly useful for showcasing visual products such as clothing and cosmetics.
- *Twitter* – a content-sharing and networking platform. Consider using a hashtag for ease of tracking and consistency in branding.
- *LinkedIn* – a platform typically used by professionals and career-driven types. Good for business-to-business (B2B) content marketing.
- Email – free emailing platforms such as *MailChimp* allow you to create email templates and track engagement rates.
- Paid media – paid-for content distribution channels such as PPC, display advertising and paid social advertising can be highly targeted and keyword/interest specific.

Further details of social media marketing channels, platforms and tactics can be found in Chapter 8.

Be sure to keep track of outreach progress using free management tools such as *Trello*, *Basecamp* or *Slack* and ensure all correspondence is saved for future content marketing campaigns. If there is a team of you working on the outreach of your content marketing campaign be sure to create a shared file of all contact made, related dates and status of communication to ensure there is no duplication of work and you are not continually disturbing your contacts. Should you be successful in placing your content, we also recommend that you request a link back to your website for SEO purposes and add this into your progress report. It is important to note that these inbound backlinks are a bonus of content marketing and not the driving motivation.

There are some automated tools to help you schedule your communication efforts such as *Hootsuite* and *Buzzstream*. The platforms also allow you to centralise your social marketing efforts by automatically tracking the pickup of your content.

We recommend that you continually test and optimise your outreach process (such as the time outreach occurred, key messages used in emails and tweets, which social profiles get the most traction – work or personal) to continually optimise and learn from your outreach and content marketing efforts.

9.5 Content marketing campaign evaluation

Assuming you have been very clear about your goals set in the early stages of your content marketing campaign planning, this is the point at which you determine how well your campaign has performed against the common KPIs listed in Table 9.1.

Whilst return on investment (ROI) can be notoriously difficult to outline, you can split your conversions into primary and secondary sales metrics:

Primary sales metrics – Those achieved through individuals landing directly on your website via your content landing page; a journey that is relatively easy to follow, should you have e-commerce and conversion tracking set up correctly, with a value assigned to each completed conversion.

Secondary sales metrics – As discussed in Chapter 1, the average consumer will come into contact with multiple content touchpoints over the duration of a campaign, which makes tracking the ROI of such journeys problematic. The recommended route adopted by various content marketers is to allocate an estimated monetary value to your marketing efforts, channels, goals and KPIs to build a clearer picture of how well your campaign has performed.

Free automated reporting platforms

Whilst it is recommended you monitor your *Google* Analytics and Social Media Analytics profiles on a daily basis, there are free automated tracking and reporting tools such as *Scoop.It* (http://business.scoop.it/) and *buffer* (https://buffer. com/) which remove some of the manual aspects of content marketing analysis from the reporting process.

Table 9.1 Content marketing goals, metrics and tools

Goal	Metrics	Tool
Brand Awareness	Traffic generated to content via referral, direct, paid and organic channels, traffic generated to website, click-through rate from content to rest of website, content views, time spent on content site/content	*Google* Analytics, using URL builder
Lead Generation	Subscriptions and downloads	*Google* Analytics, using URL builder
Sales & ROI	Sales generated, conversion rate percentage	*Google* Analytics, using URL builder
Retention	Number of returning visitors	*Google* Analytics
Social Engagement	Content views, shares, interactions, comments, followers (*Followerwonk*), time spent on content, in-page analytics, bounce rate	*Twitter* Analytics *LinkedIn* Analytics *YouTube* Analytics *Google+* Platform Insights *Facebook* Analytics Simplymeasured (for *Instagram*) *MailChimp* reports (for *Instagram*) AdWords (for PPC)
Link Building	Number of high-quality inbound links generated to content and website	Open Site Explorer, *SEMRush*, *linkdex*

Debrief

At the end of your content marketing campaign, we recommend a full campaign debrief is undertaken with all members involved in the content marketing campaign in question. This will allow you to constructively assess which elements of the campaign worked and which elements could be improved upon for future campaigns. Key learnings can be used to streamline future processes, as well as contributing to a crisis communication management plan for the benefit of managing your brand reputation in future campaigns.

Case Study 9.1　*Salford Business School* UGC

The *Salford Business School* blog (Figure 9.3) was created to increase brand awareness of the Business School and to engage students, alumni and external organisations. The blog was launched in January 2014 and had the following four KPIs for the first year:

- Be updated once per week.
- Recruitment of ten bloggers.

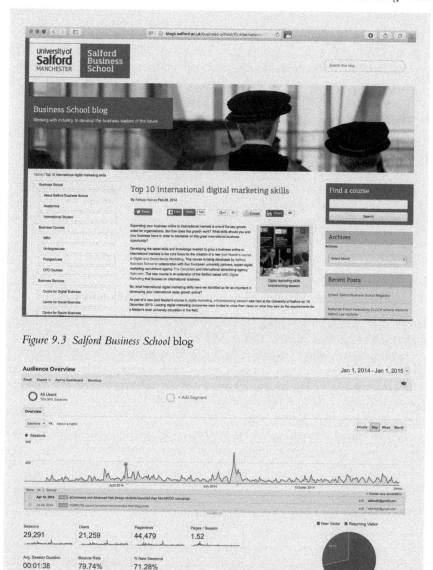

Figure 9.3 *Salford Business School* blog

Figure 9.4 Screenshot of *Google* Analytics for *Salford Business School* blog, 1 January 2014 to 1 January 2015

- Get 10,000 views.
- Get at least one student to apply as a consequence of blog content.

The KPIs were modest for a new blog, as it was the first year, it was a trial project and there was no central marketing resource allocated for this activity. As such, current students, business partners and academics were given the option to create UGC related to the Business School, as well as being encouraged to share and promote content via their preferred social channels.

For the students, content creation was part of their assignment brief. This assessment requirement encouraged blogging and enabled the development of content optimisation skills.

All the KPIs were met and superseded in the first year (Figure 9.4). Two distinctive days have been annotated on the *Google* Analytics timeline – 10th April 2014 and 24th July 2014 – which were when the student projects went live.

Source: http://blogs.salford.ac.uk/business-school/

9.6 Content creation and copywriting techniques and tips

Integrating your key messaging across platforms for brand consistency is not an easy task. You've defined who you are. Be it.

You'll have a mission statement or brand value proposition which captures your essence, and which talks to your audience in a language they understand. A language that appeals, that builds proximity. So take that spirit and the language that represents it. Thread it through all your communications across all platforms, clearly and consistently.

As mentioned above, emotion is important in reaching out to your buyer persona and it is a key ingredient in making your content go viral.

> Write with emotion – *'Don't tell me the moon is shining; show me the glint of light on broken glass.'*
>
> *Anton Chekhov*

It is important to appreciate the power of the six primary human emotions – anger, disgust, fear, happiness, sadness and surprise – as the driving force in eliciting a response to our writing. A seventh, often a component of the others, is yet more powerful still. More about that later, though.

Identifying both how your audience feels and how you want them to feel will dictate the language you choose to use. Here are some brief examples of language that you might use when appealing to the six primaries:

Happiness: Congratulations!
             The best time you ever had?
Sadness: There's no easy way to say this.
             For my daughter.

Disgust:	'I shoot people, they die, and it makes me laugh.'
	The stench of open sewers.
Anger:	Please help us find the monster that took these beautiful puppies.
	Widow cheated out of her life savings.
Fear:	48 hours to stop the next Chernobyl?
	How would you cope with a tax office inspection?
Surprise:	You don't need to be a millionaire to be treated like one.
	Someone likes you!!!

That seventh emotion that keeps people hanging on your every word?

Curiosity.

Tone of voice

A tone of voice represents your values, the reason you exist, what makes you different and the way you think.

Only once your values are clear (what you say) should you start to look at your vocabulary (how you say it) – the language you will need to express your values.

A good starting point is to look at the language your customers already use when they talk about your products and services.

Create a range of test writing and use it to identify what your tone is and, more importantly, what it is not. Use this comparative analysis to set tone-of-voice guidelines.

Be relevant

Deliver the right message to the right audience. Of course you will want your content to have a fabulous aesthetic and to provide plenty of share options. But unless the writing talks to your audience about their lives, and unless it addresses the problems they face, offers solutions, scratches itches, informs, educates and entertains – unless it is laser guided – your content is going nowhere. Slowly.

Anatomy of a good blog post

To quote the classic David Ogilvy line about headlines: 'On average, five times as many people read the headline as read the body copy. When you have written your headline, you have spent eighty cents out of your dollar.'

Best make your headline as compelling as possible: a headline that provokes curiosity, conveys news or promises a benefit – ideally a combination of all three.

Your first paragraph should open with a bang, your conclusion even. Think inverted pyramid.

- Use short sentences.
- And short paragraphs.

- Make the copy easily scannable.
- An arresting image helps.
- Be interesting.
- Be interesting and fiercely relevant.

Content for multi-platform content marketing campaigns

Multi-platform copy is modular copy. In effect, the components of a single high-quality piece are split up and repurposed across platforms. That's not to say that the piece needs to even exist as a single entity before being carved up, though. It's the principles that count.

Make your headline and subheads into tweet copy. Write your *Facebook* updates to lure. Your high-impact intro paragraphs and your conclusions can all be enticing leads. Your body copy is the basis for more in-depth, informative landing pages – they are the 'meat' on your social 'bones'.

If your ideas are strong and your copy supports with strength, with relevance, with humour, with empathy and with insight, you've already won.

9.7 Summary

This chapter focuses on the most important aspect of digital and social media marketing – content. Content comes in many formats – text, video, images – but one key message from this book is the need to understand the target audience and spend time identifying how they like to communicate and what is of interest to them. Only once the buyer persona is clearly understood is it possible to develop content that is relevant for them. The content is in the middle of the Buyer Persona Spring.

A range of processes and theoretical frameworks has been explored in this chapter, from viral marketing to the psychologies related to the content types and formatting. All these considerations should be used when developing high-quality content. Once quality content has been produced, the amplification process commences and here, effort and energy are invested to reach out to relevant stakeholders and influencers who can help to further amplify the content.

Content marketing implementation draws on all chapters of this book. The key challenge that you face when embracing content marketing is the ability to create high-quality content and having a sustainable routine of content creation and curation for community engagement which supports your strategic business objectives. Having a lot of views of your video is a good KPI, but what is important for your long-term strategy is how many of those individuals acted upon that content and if you were able to get your message across – generating results for your campaign.

9.8 References

Berger, J. (2013) *Contagious: Why things catch on*. Simon and Schuster.
Carnegie, Dale (ed.) (2010) *How to win friends and influence people*. Pocket Books.

Creative Commons (2016) *Licenses.* https://creativecommons.org/about/

Glennie, A. (2005) *Only half of young people's viewing is traditional scheduled TV.* www.theguardian.com/media/2015/jul/02/young-people-live-tv-bbc-iplayer-youtube-netflix

IAB (2015) *IAB / PwC study: Digital adspend up 14% to record £7.2 billion.* www.iabuk.net/about/press/archive/iab-pwc-study-digital-adspend-up-14-to-record-72-billion

Mintel (2016) *Company reports.* www.mintel.com/mintel-reports

Office for National Statistics (2016) *Statistics.* www.ons.gov.uk/ons/index.html

Survey System (2016) *Company website.* www.surveysystem.com/sscalc.htm

The Guardian (2016) *Data reports.* www.theguardian.com/data

10 Paid advertising – search, social and affiliate

Rimantas Gatautis and Elena Vitkauskaitė,
Kaunas University of Technology, Lithuania

10.0 Learning objectives

In this chapter you will learn how to:

- understand the range of paid search, social and affiliate advertising opportunities;
- plan and implement paid digital advertising across multiple profiles;
- evaluate and benchmark paid communications and affiliate advertising activities.

10.1 Paid advertising in context

In Chapter 7 you explored the benefits of working on the organic search engine optimisation (SEO) for your business. Here, we look at another way of directing traffic to your calls-to-action, either from external websites or via platforms such as search engines or social media networks – paid digital marketing communications.

Not only are paid digital marketing communications a way to have more control over the content and placement of your organisation's message, but, unlike organic SEO, they also offer instant results. As more users join social media platforms and spend increasingly longer periods of time socialising on them, paid social media marketing has become an increasingly important part of digital marketing.

But first, it is important to differentiate between 'paid display marketing' and 'paid search marketing', since the type of content and expectations on return on investment (ROI) tend to be different for each. Display marketing simply shows your ads when a user visits a certain website, which could be a social network site or a website that is taking part in the display advertising network. Display marketing provides more possibilities for advertisers to integrate their ads into the content of social communications between users and brands, as well as between users and other users. Although it is industry dependent, display marketing is generally better placed for brand awareness communications. In contrast, search marketing tends to be closer to the purchase decision, since once someone is searching for your product or services, chances are they want to know more about them and might be keen to purchase these.

Although most platforms offering paid marketing solutions claim that they can set up and get ads running in no time, understanding how advertising works on each platform is essential in order to save time and costs by avoiding the most common mistakes. There are also potential benefits to running parallel paid and organic campaigns in order to increase the exposure of a campaign and thus obtain synergies for content reach to a level that individual channels could not achieve in isolation.

10.2 Understanding paid advertising

Paid search marketing is also referred to as pay-per-click (PPC) search engine advertising or paid search, amongst other terms, and is part of search engine marketing. It differs from 'organic' or 'natural' SEO (discussed in Chapter 7) because it involves paid content placement.

In essence, search advertising is an advert that is triggered by a search engine user when they type a related keyword phrase into a search box. The ad copy is written by the advertiser and relates to their website offering in terms of what the user is searching for. Good ad copy will relay the benefits of the website to the user; if the ad is highly relevant to the search query, this should encourage the user to click the ad.

This ad is usually displayed on a search engine results page (SERP), either above the organic search results, below them or on the right-hand side (see Figure 10.1). The position of the ads always changes as search engines evolve. For example, *Google* removed its ads in early 2016 from the right-hand side

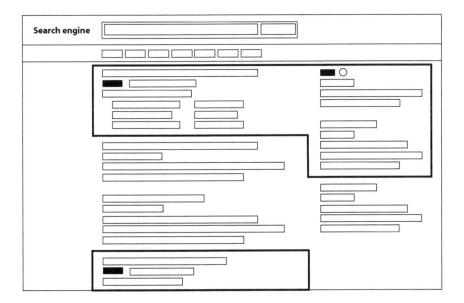

Figure 10.1 Paid search results on search engine results page

of the desktop search results in a move to make its web pages more mobile friendly. It is likely that other search engines such as *Bing* and *Yahoo!* might follow this direction in due course. Descriptions of paid search marketing provided in this chapter are based largely on *Google* AdWords, with details of the alternative systems covered separately later in the chapter.

A search engine's online advertising services might also provide the opportunity to place ads on third-party websites in their *display (content) networks*. Ads are posted on websites in relation to the content of those sites and relevance of these sites to the keywords defined by the advertiser. In this case the 'search' is conducted on behalf of the advertiser who wants to find a relevant platform for their content. Display advertising networks allow website owners to 'sell' space on their websites to display network management platforms such as *Google* AdSense. Display advertising is particularly popular amongst larger brands, but smaller organisations looking for targeted brand awareness can also reap the benefits of this method. Display advertising relies on creating message creative content such as images and video, which tend to be more labour intensive and require more resources and skills. This is particularly important, since the organic content reach on major social network sites such as *Facebook* and *Twitter* is in decline.

Generally, ads can be paid for on a cost-per-click (CPC), cost-per-mille or cost-per-thousand impressions (CPM) or cost-per-action (CPA) basis. Ads can include images and video content, as well as text (Table 10.1).

Video and image ads tend to be display ad formats, since video and images don't tend to appear on search engines, but they do appear on social media search results pages of various social network sites such as *YouTube*. Search ads appear when the user makes a search. Display ads appear when a user fits an audience profile or through remarketing, without the need for the user to search. However, some search engines serve display ads on SERPs too.

How does pay-per-click work?

The listing position of an ad in paid search results is decided through an *auction* that happens each time the ad is triggered by a keyword and other parameters (e.g. time of day, location of the user) that have been selected by the advertiser. Generally, the higher the ad position in SERPs, the more exposure it receives. As search engines strive to provide users with the most relevant search results, the maximum amount of the CPC bid is important, but is not the deciding factor in who wins the auction and is ranked in the top results. The relevance of the keyword is measured by another variable called *Quality Score* in *Google* AdWords, which is equally as important a factor as the keyword bid amount in determining the outcome of the auction.

Google AdWords introduced the Quality Score, and other search engines developed similar measures. Quality Score is defined as 'an estimate of the quality of your ads, keywords, and landing page' (*Google* AdWords Help Centre).

Table 10.1 Common types of paid advertisements

Figure 10.1.1: Text ads

Text ads

Contain only words. In *Google* AdWords they are made of four lines visible to users: a headline of up to 25 characters long, 2 x 35 character-long descriptions and a displayed URL address no longer than 35 characters (online advertising services of other search engines have different character limits).

Text ads can also be enabled across the display networks – in other words, websites that are not owned by *Google* can also display your ads.

Image ads

Ads use static or interactive graphics. They allow advertisers to showcase their product or service in a visual way, and to reach customers on websites in display networks.

In AdWords such ads can only be displayed across the *Google* Display Network. Some other search engines allow image ads on search results as well (e.g. mail.ru).

Figure 10.1.2: Image ads

Video ads

Online video advertising. Advertisers can run standalone video ads or insert them in streaming video content. These ads allow advertisers to deliver a rich and engaging experience to customers, and to reach customers on websites in display networks.

In AdWords such ads can only be displayed across the *Google* Display Network, as with image ads.

Figure 10.1.3: Video ads

Mobile phone ads

These are text or image ads for mobile phone devices. Usually, they have a smaller limit of characters to fit screens of non-smartphones.

They allow advertisers to connect with their customers on the go, targeting their ads based on customers' locations and offering different actions such as calling a phone number.

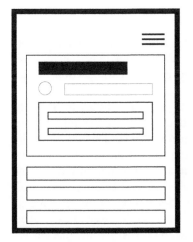

Figure 10.1.4: Mobile ads

(*Continued*)

Table 10.1 (Continued)

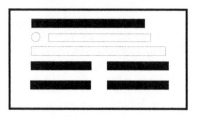

Figure 10.1.5 Ad extensions

Ad extensions

Ad extensions are not full ads on their own. They extend other types of ads (mostly text ads) with more information, such as additional links to the website (site links), store address (location extension) or phone number (call extension) and others. Call extensions used in mobile ads enable users to make a call directly without visiting the page.

In AdWords, ad extensions usually appear across the Search Network. However, location extensions and call extensions may also appear across the *Google* Display Network.

Quality score

| 6/10 |

Learn more

Expected click-through rate: Average
Ad relevance: Average
Landing page experience: Average

Figure 10.2 Example of AdWords Quality Score breakdown

In AdWords, each keyword targeted gets the quality score – a number from 1 to 10 where 1 is low and 10 is high. It is also a number that is shared with the advertiser as a feedback mechanism to improve the quality of the ad (Figure 10.2).

This shows that Quality Score is measured based on the expected *click-through rate*, ad relevance to the keyword targeted and landing page experience, as well as on other indicators such as historical performance of the account, which *Google* does not fully disclose.

Generally, if a website is ranking number 1 in an organic listing for the same keyword term, it is going to have a positive effect on the paid ad quality score (Ayanso and Karimi, 2015). Therefore, coordinating keyword selection is helpful for synergies between paid search advertising and organic SEO.

For example, keywords clearly reflected in an ad copy, which match the keyword term query of the user and lead to a highly relevant landing page, would get a higher Quality Score. A higher Quality Score leads to lower costs for the advertiser and a higher ad listing position (*ad rank*). A lower Quality Score results in higher costs and a lower ad rank. Moreover, keywords that do not reach the minimum Quality Score would not trigger ads to be shown at all, no matter how high the bids offered by advertisers are.

How does remarketing work?

Whilst the above is a basic overview of paid ad strategies, there are also a number of more advanced, personalised ways to set up bidding options. All search engines continue to innovate to offer you the best way to reach your buyer persona. One of the more advanced options for paid search engine advertising is remarketing.

Remarketing works on the principle that once someone has visited your website they are more likely to interact with your website again because they are already aware of you. Technically this works by creating tags for your web pages, which are then placed in cookies on the computer of your visitor. Then, when the visitor browses a website that recognises the cookie, and if your remarketing settings are valid, the ad is displayed to the user.

Remarketing can be used successfully for users that have not completed the desired action such as a purchase and who will benefit from a reminder of your product or service. It can also be used for those who have made a purchase and might be interested in a repeat or additional purchase.

There are several remarketing formats. *Google*, for example, currently allows (as of March 2016) the following five options:

1. Mobile apps, targeting users of your mobile website or app when they view apps of others. Also, video remarketing targets those who viewed your video content.
2. Remarketing lists for search ads (RLSA) is the term used by *Google* for customising search ads campaigns.
3. Standard remarketing displays your ads to known visitors when they browse related display network websites and use display network apps.
4. Dynamic remarketing allows for the content of the exact product or service that was viewed to be shown to the user. The setting up of such methods does take more time, since each product has to be appropriately tagged, but the results are much more powerful since the user is offered the exact product or service they were interested in during the first interaction.
5. Last but not least is video remarketing – this format allows you to display ads to those who interacted with your *YouTube* channel or videos when they browse *YouTube* and visit display network websites, apps and videos.

When should you choose the cost-per-mille model?

Paid search ads tend to be well placed to trigger click actions related to sales or website traffic building. It is useful to bear in mind that for brand awareness campaigns, serving ads on a display network (and bidding based on CPM or cost-per-thousand impressions) is a more suitable option.

The CPM model offers a good overarching campaign setting, where efforts can be measured by thousand impressions. The potential for fraud in CPM increases, since essentially all that the host of the ad has to do is prove that the page where your ad was placed was viewed. Therefore, regular monitoring of activities for CPM is important.

10.3 Differences in paid advertising on various search engines in Europe

Europeans mostly use the *Google* search engine for looking up information, with the popularity of other search engines lagging far behind (see Figure 10.3). On the other hand, Europe is not homogeneous, and popularity of search engines is not equally distributed across all countries. Therefore, it might be important to learn the peculiarities of advertising on different search engines popular in Europe, depending on the target markets that paid search marketing efforts are focused on. Reviewing these alternatives can offer potentially more cost-effective ways to reach out to your buyer persona, since the costs of ads can be cheaper when compared to *Google* AdWords due to fewer advertisers competing for the same keywords.

Advertising on *Yahoo!* and *Bing* is currently done via *Bing Ads*. It gives advertisers access to advertising on both search engines, which together are called *Yahoo! Bing* Network. Therefore, the peculiarities of advertising on *Google, Yahoo! Bing* Network, *Yandex, Mail.ru* and *Seznam* are what we will now focus on.

Google

Google is the most popular search engine in all European countries, with more than a 90 per cent market share of the search engine market in most countries, and losing over 20 per cent of the market only in the Russian Federation,

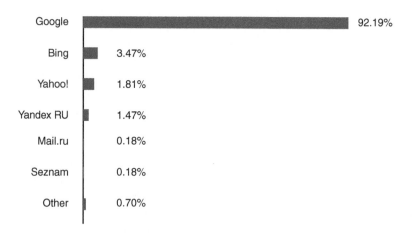

Figure 10.3 Search engine market share in Europe by leads to websites of organisations, February 2016 (source: StatCounter Global Stats)

Belarus, Czech Republic, Ukraine and the Faroe Islands (StatCounter Global Stats, February 2016).

Advertising on the *Google* search engine is done by using the online advertising service AdWords (https://AdWords.google.com), which provides advertisers with access to place ads in the *Google* Search Network (a number of non-*Google* websites (like Ask.com), as well as *Google* Maps, *Google* Video and other *Google* sites), and in the *Google* Display Network (websites that show AdWords ads). As most of the paid search marketing aspects discussed in this chapter are based on the AdWords service, they are not repeated here.

Yahoo! Bing Network

Yahoo! Bing Network serves over 5 per cent of search queries in Europe overall, reaching approximately 10 per cent of the search engine market in the United Kingdom and its territories (StatCounter Global Stats, February 2016).

Advertising on *Yahoo! Bing* Network is done using the online advertising service *Bing Ads* (http://advertise.bingads.microsoft.com), which is similar to *Google* AdWords and even enables importing AdWords campaigns. The most significant differences listed in the Help section of the service relate to different targeting options and a different approach to calculating the Quality Score.

Yandex

The Russian search engine *Yandex* is significantly important in several countries in Eastern Europe, most notably in the Russian Federation, Belarus and Ukraine. It might be an option for those advertisers targeting Moldova, Estonia and Latvia, though the market share of this search engine does not exceed 5 per cent there. The international version of this engine has a small search engine market share in Turkey (StatCounter Global Stats, February 2016).

Online advertising service *Yandex Direct* (https://direct.yandex.com/) is used for search advertising on the *Yandex* search engine. Its major differences from *Google* AdWords include: fewer opportunities to structure campaigns; higher limits for number of characters in the ads; a different approach to auctions and bidding (advertisers can bid for specific listing positions on SERPs, and auction happens only for positions they have bid for); less sophisticated reporting of campaign effectiveness; requires minimum order size to start campaign; and offers discounts for large-scope campaigns.

Mail.ru

Mail.ru is another Russian search engine, and could be an option for advertisers targeting Belarus, the Russian Federation, Ukraine, Moldova and Estonia.

The company owns a range of websites, their search engine being just one of many properties. Advertising on all those properties can be done using the online advertising service *Target* (https://target.mail.ru/). Significant differences between this and *Google* AdWords include: absence of text ads type (service mostly focuses on banner ads); ads are not related to keywords but placements; requires minimum order size to start a campaign; auctions depend on click-through-rate (CTR) and competition in same target market (in relation to targeting options); interface is only available in Russian; and offers advertising services directly.

Seznam

Established in 1996 as the first web portal in the Czech Republic, *Seznam.cz* was the most popular search service in the country for years. Currently, the search market in the country has been overtaken by *Google*, but *Seznam* is still the second largest search engine in the Czech Republic.

The company provides its *Sklik* service (www.sklik.cz/en/) to facilitate advertising on its properties. The service is similar to *Google* AdWords and provides similar functionalities. On the other hand, these functionalities are more limited in comparison (for example, ad copy extensions are limited to site links), the interface is only available in the Czech language and the company offers campaign management services directly.

Other search engines used by Europeans are *t-online* with 0.97 per cent of the German market, and *Kvasir* with 0.4 per cent of the Norwegian market (StatCounter Global Stats, February 2016). Even more search engines are available in European countries which do not have a critical mass of users at the time of writing, but might have become worthy of the attention of advertisers by the time you are reading this. Market shares of search engines can be checked on services like *StatCounter Global Stats* (http://gs.statcounter.com/).

10.4 Planning and managing paid search marketing

Since paid search advertising relies on the quality of the URL to which it is linked, it is recommended that the organic SEO of the web page, and ideally the entire website, be completed prior to commencing PPC experimentation. This will help in isolating the impact that paid search advertising has on the website, and will reduce the potentially negative impact of poor user experience. This book encourages you to experiment. Only with a trial and error approach and evaluation of the results will you be able to determine if paid search advertising works for your organisation.

The rapid nature of the paid search advertising setup process allows for quick experimentation and refinements of search engine marketing efforts, so it is essential to allocate regular times for monitoring paid search advertising activities. Unlike organic SEO, paid search advertising can very quickly use up a budget if not monitored closely, particularly if you are unfamiliar with the tools available to you. As with all other paid advertising options there is a risk of fraud (where, say, your competitors click on your ads to run down your advertising budget), and all search engines work on this click fraud management and mitigation.

The following steps detail good practice and are grouped to cover ad targeting, budget and bid management, creative testing and campaign optimisation, analysis of campaign results and communications integration aspects of paid search marketing.

Structuring your ads account

Similarly to organic SEO, the paid search advertising account needs to be structured to reflect the structure of your website and particularly the products and services offered. Within AdWords you have the option to divide your account into campaigns, and within each of these campaigns you have several ad groups. The budgets and targeting are set at the campaign level, but the individual keywords to be targeted are defined in the ad groups. Learning about the effectiveness of different campaigns – for example, by targeting display networks or only search engine users – can give comparative datasets and offer evidence for future campaigns.

> *Account*: Domestic appliances shop
> Within this account a number of different product types could be advertised, for example:
> *Campaigns*: Washing machines; Refrigerators; Cookers
> Within each of the campaigns there are different ad groups that allow you to target different user needs with a shared set of keywords. For example, the one for refrigerators could have campaigns based on the type of refrigerator:
> *Ad groups*: Refrigerators: Top Freezer Refrigerators; Compact Fridges; French Door Fridges

Within each ad group (Figure 10.4) you could have at least two ads which are interchangeably shared and constantly tested for their success. The ad rotation settings allow for optimising CTR or rotating evenly, which gives more feedback of A/B testing and data for identifying the more successful advertising creative. If manual bidding is set, make sure you review the results regularly.

When creating content for the display network, bear in mind that users are less likely to be in a research mindset, and therefore (similarly to social media

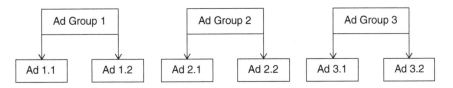

Figure 10.4 Grouping ads into ad groups

network sites), the creative message should be less sales focused. Monitor your ads' performance and revise, and if there is a theme related to a badly performing display network use the exclusion tool to refine where your ads appear. In the same way, review keywords and remove if a term is not performing – your aim is to only keep high-performing keywords.

Keyword alignment strategy

Overall organisational goals and business objectives can help in identifying specific ad groups. The number of keywords that are used to trigger a particular ad group depends on the granularity of the products and services being targeted. However, to make the ads relevant to what the user types into a search engine, using from 5 up to 15 keywords is a good benchmark to aim for and to keep to the lower numbers, otherwise the chance of your ad being irrelevant increases. Regular exclusion and deletion of keywords from ad groups can help to maintain a good Quality Score.

Around 20 per cent of keywords entered into a search engine are new and have not been used before – how can you capture these users? Using broad keyword match types allows your ad to be triggered when it contains a related term. But if you have a high-volume and high-value search term and are targeting it, then the exact keyword match type is more appropriate.

For websites where content related to their products and services is not updated daily, the Dynamic Search Ads can offer additional exposure. Unlike keyword targeting these ads are based on content that has been indexed in organic search results. As an advertiser, you still have control of some of the aspects, but the headline and the URLs are being generated automatically by AdWords.

Regular account maintenance requires identifying negative keywords, i.e. choosing those words which, should a user type them into a search engine, should not trigger your ad. Analysis of the Search Terms report and the Keyword Planner tool offers more insight into potential negative keywords for your AdWords groups.

Budget and bid management

Developing a budget for paid search advertising should be based on the profitability and the return in the investment calculations. Ultimately, the results generated by paid search advertising are trackable and these should inform whether it is worth investing in paid search advertising, and if so, how much. Paid search marketing is ideal as support for organic SEO efforts. Test paid search advertising by entirely switching it off and then monitoring the impact. The management of daily budgets helps to control the overall spend and understanding the buyer persona, and the hours and days they are likely to benefit from your ad can increase conversion rates. Have time-specific campaigns if necessary.

The *ad rank* for an ad based on a targeted keyword changes dynamically as the advertiser competes with other advertisers. It is a number from 1 to 10 and is expressed as an average such as 3.4 to reflect how it varies with time. Always having your listing rank as 1 might be expensive because you might have to bid higher than every other advertiser. On the other hand, the lower positions usually do not yield good click-through rates, though cost less. Therefore, it might be useful to have a balance in keyword portfolio, with both high- and low-ranking terms.

Ongoing testing and optimisation

Ad creatives – in other words, text, images or video where relevant – are the only parts of a paid search campaign visible to searchers and therefore of great significance to the success of the campaign. Because of their relevance, it is important to incorporate your targeted keywords in the ad creatives. What makes your content different? Highlight your unique selling points (USPs). Continuously run three or four variations of ads and learn what makes the better performing ads more appealing to your buyer persona.

Destination or landing pages are pages on your website where searchers land when they click on the ad. These pages have to be optimised for organic on-page SEO for the related search term. Using data from *Google* Analytics, regularly review if the content of the page follows the AIDA model and offers the user what they were hoping for when they clicked on the ad. User experience testing can help to refine these landing pages.

Campaign review and optimisation is a structured approach to reviewing an existing campaign and improving the paid search advertising results. The review should take into account paid search marketing performance in relation to other channels, relative performance to historic time period, competitor activity, etc. These reviews can take place on a weekly or – if needed – daily basis, especially at the critical points of a campaign. Learn through this data about your buyer persona behaviour and if necessary share the results to inform activities on other channels.

Case Study 10.1 *HIDROMOTAS*

HIDROMOTAS (www.hidromotas.lt), a small Lithuanian company established in 1997, specialises in repairs and sales of power steering systems and hydraulic components. The company mainly serves clients from Vilnius city and its surroundings. In 2008 the economic crisis forced the company to look for more effective means to increase sales with a small budget.

Paid search marketing using *Google* AdWords was the chosen trial campaign. By serving AdWords ads only to searchers located in Vilnius or in its vicinity, the traffic from regions that were not relevant to this organisation was avoided.

Using the insights gathered from *Google* Analytics, the keywords with high bounce rates and that were not converting to completed actions were removed from the list of keywords that trigger ads to appear.

As the company does not sell online, navigation to the Contact page was regarded as a conversion in this campaign.

With the initial budget of only 5 Lithuanian litas (approximately €1.45) per day for the AdWords campaign, the company experienced a 25 per cent increase in sales and profit. The campaign optimisation efforts resulted in a bounce rate drop to only 8 per cent, and 38 per cent of website users visiting by clicking on paid search ads navigated to the Contact page.

Google AdWords is especially attractive to small and medium-sized companies, as it allows tangible results to be achieved in a short time even with a very small budget. The campaign was regarded as a success according to Emilis Jarockis, *HIDROMOTAS* AdWords account manager and digital marketing consultant at digital marketing agency *Sinergija Verslui.*

The *HIDROMOTAS* example illustrates the need to regularly review and refine keywords for a paid search advertising campaign. The non-performing keywords can be deleted or paused. Your preference should be to pause keywords to avoid the chance of their reactivation during the same campaign. By pausing a keyword and not deleting it, the campaign data is preserved and is available for future reference. Your keywords and campaigns must be regularly monitored. Depending on your daily budget, smaller campaigns should be reviewed daily while larger budgets might be monitored hourly.

10.5 Paid social media marketing introduction

Social media marketing is an increasingly important part of digital marketing, as more users join social media platforms and are spending increasingly longer periods of time socialising on those platforms. Exactly because of this increase in using social media worldwide, it is no longer enough for organisations to rely on free organic engagement methods on social media. Organic content published by organisations on social media competes with ever-increasing numbers of contributions from other organisations and other users. Your content is not only competing with other content for the attention of followers. Social media platforms will filter content in order to only display what it regards as relevant material. Your content must also compete to pass through this filter.

Therefore, to reach the potential customers on social media, paid advertising (also called *paid social media marketing*, paid social media advertising and integrated social advertising) has gained increasing relevance, though organic engagement methods have lost none of their importance. Although paid social media marketing is used mostly to promote organic content, it is even more beneficial for organisations seeking to reach new potential customers from wider audiences rather than loyal customers who already follow the social media activities of the organisation.

Paid social media advertising is mostly related to content promotion, as mentioned above, and in this way it is similar to image or video ads used in paid search marketing. Despite this, it is important to discuss paid social media marketing separately from paid search marketing, as social media platforms provide more possibilities for advertisers to integrate their ads into the content of social communications between users and brands, as well as between users.

10.6 Overview of advertising on most popular social media platforms in Europe

Facebook remains the most popular social media platform in Europe (Figure 10.5). However, as with search engines, use of social media platforms varies across different European countries.

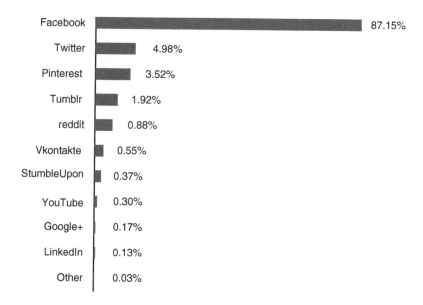

Figure 10.5 Social media market share in Europe by leads to websites of organisations, February 2016 (source: StatCounter Global Stats, February 2016)

252 Gatautis and Vitkauskaitė

Unlike search engines, various social media platforms are used for different purposes (i.e. *Facebook* is used for private social networking and sharing with friends; *LinkedIn* is used for professional networking; *reddit* is used for sharing news) and by various audiences (for example, *Pinterest* is significantly more prevalent among women). Some users are more likely to actively use several social media platforms, unlike in the case of search engines, which are switched more by accident than intention. Therefore, awareness of the different paid social media marketing opportunities on various social media platforms is even more important than in the case of paid search marketing.

Facebook

Facebook is the social networking platform most popular worldwide. However, in Europe it is the least effective in referring leads in Belarus, the Russian Federation and Ukraine where Russian social networking platform *Vkontakte* has significant popularity (StatCounter Global Stats, February 2016).

Paid advertising on *Facebook* can be done using a multitude of options. In the setup stage of an advertising campaign *Facebook* leads advertisers through a sequence of ordered steps to create a campaign based on its objectives:

- *Page Post Engagement*: Promote Page posts.
- *Page Likes*: Get Page likes to grow the audience and build the brand.
- *Clicks to Websites*: Get people to visit a website.
- *Website Conversions*: Get people to perform certain actions on a site (requires adding a *Facebook* pixel to the site).
- *App Installs*: Get people to install a mobile or desktop app.
- *App Engagement*: Get people to use a desktop app.
- *Local Awareness*: Reach people who are nearby.
- *Event Responses*: Increase attendance at an event.
- *Offer Claims*: Create offers for people to redeem in the store.
- *Video Views*: Get people to watch videos to raise awareness of the brand.
- *Lead Generation*: Get lead information from people who are interested in the brand.

In the next step, *Facebook* would take the advertiser to their choice of location for placing the ads: *Facebook* desktop News Feed, the *Facebook* mobile News Feed or the *Facebook* right-hand column. The latest data at the time of writing shows that the broader choice of placements is more beneficial to advertisers than targeting exclusively desktop users or mobile users (see Table 10.2).

On *Facebook*, advertisers can target their audience based on location, age, gender, language and other common demographic characteristics, though the most valuable possibility is to target the audience based on interests and behaviours. For example, a pet hotel company could target the ad to people interested in birds and intending to travel soon. Therefore, *Facebook* provides organisations

Table 10.2 Effectiveness of different placements of *Facebook* ads in Europe, fourth quarter 2014

	Desktop Feed	Combined Feed	Mobile Feed
CPM	€2.13	€2.57	€2.81
CPC	€0.31	€0.14	€0.17
CTR	0.68%	1.86%	1.65%

Source: Salesforce, 2015

with opportunities to reach exactly the right audience for their products or services.

The advantages of advertising on *Facebook* for small and medium enterprises (SMEs) include more opportunities to increase brand awareness and reach of the message, increasing foot traffic to physical premises or increasing web traffic to the website.

Shewan (2014) suggests that organisations with the potential to produce a lot of imagery may benefit most from advertising on *Facebook*. These could include photography services, e-commerce, travel agencies and caterers.

Twitter

Twitter is a microblogging service. In Europe it is the second most effective social media site in referring leads, and has significant importance in Turkey, Latvia, Ukraine, the Netherlands and the United Kingdom, where it has over 10 per cent social media market share (StatCounter Global Stats, February 2016).

There are three types of *Twitter* paid ads: Promoted Accounts, Promoted Trends and Promoted Tweets. Similarly to *Facebook*, *Twitter* ad campaigns can be categorised by objective (tweet engagement; website clicks or conversions; app installs or app engagement; video views; follower growth; and *Twitter* lead collection). Expected campaign costs will depend and vary greatly based on choices of objective (LePage, 2014).

On *Twitter*, advertisers can target their audience based on common demographic characteristics such as location, age, gender, language, etc. The most valuable feature of targeting on *Twitter* is an opportunity to target the audience based on their networks (LePage, 2014).

The advantages of advertising on *Twitter* for SMEs include: reaching a strong dedicated *Twitter* fan base who use it frequently, targeting the mobile market in a not overly intrusive way and extensively customisable targeting functionalities.

LinkedIn

LinkedIn is a social networking service for building and maintaining a professional network. Therefore, it is regarded as an important social media marketing channel in B2B, despite low popularity with the general public. The growing worldwide audience of *LinkedIn* offers a breadth of options for SMEs.

There are three main types of *LinkedIn* paid ads: Premium Display Ads, Email Marketing via Sponsored InMail and Direct Sponsored Updates.

Besides the opportunity to target ads based on common demographic characteristics, *LinkedIn* provides advertisers with more options to target based on business and position-related features, such as industry, company size, job title, job position and seniority.

Case Study 10.2   *Vaitiekūnų medelynas*

Vaitiekūnų medelynas (www.vaitiekunumedelynas.com) is a Lithuanian family owned nursery-garden business that has been operating since 1990. Marketing of the company is carried out by the sole daughter of the family – Martyna Vaitiekūnaitė. This micro-business initiated its online marketing activities in 2013 by creating a website and a *Facebook* page (www.facebook.com/vaitiekunumedelynas).

The *Facebook* page fan base grew slowly but steadily over the years, with somewhat larger boosts of interest during the sweepstake contests organised during tree-planting seasons.

By 17 February 2016, the *Facebook* page had 3,417 page likes with an average of four engaged page users per day. Martyna shared that day a link to the website with a promotion for an assortment of new saplings. After a few days she made the sapling offer a Boosted Post based on a recommendation by *Facebook*. She targeted Lithuanian 30–45-year-old female *Facebook* users interested in gardening, or the home and garden. The post was boosted for a total period of 16 days at a total cost of €23.20.

The boosted post was displayed 42,407 times, and reached 26,740 unique people of whom 1,016 engaged with the page or content on the page; 145 new page likes were made as a direct result of the boosted post (an increase of 4 per cent). However, during this period the average number of engaged page users increased to 99 per day, and the total number of page likes grew to 3,904 (an increase of 14 per cent).

The *Vaitiekūnų medelynas* example illustrates that even a small budget for a small organisation can have an impact on brand awareness. One of the examples illustrated here is that not all content should be boosted, but only that which shows signs of virality in its own right. A post which receives higher levels of natural engagement when compared to others that were not as active is likely to perform better when boosted through paid advertising. Therefore, don't boost every post, which can help you to make your budget go further.

10.7 Affiliate marketing

Affiliate marketing is a commission-based arrangement where referring sites receive a commission on sales or leads sent on to merchants' e-commerce sites. Commissions can be fixed per lead or action or an agreed-upon percentage of the purchase.

With the advent of paid search and social marketing, affiliate marketing is sometimes regarded as an outdated mode of paid advertising. However, in digital marketing, affiliate marketing is only as old as paid search marketing – both started in the mid-1990s. It can be regarded as another type of display advertising (together with image or video paid ads in paid search and social media). However, paid search and social ads could equally be regarded as a type of affiliate marketing. (Some affiliate marketing companies suggest dropping the word 'affiliate' and replacing it with 'performance', because of the negative attitude towards affiliate marketing by advertisers, who connect it to misleading, fraudulent, and 'making money online' sites that rip off advertisers and provide little, if any, return.)

An *affiliate* or publisher is a website that displays links (ads) to other websites, usually e-commerce ones, to its visitors. An affiliate network connects e-commerce websites (merchants) to affiliates.

Affiliate networks track and report all visitor activity to their clients (merchants) and usually make it available on their user interface. Visitor activities tracked include impressions, clicks, purchases, conversions, order value, shopping basket content and details of the referring publisher websites. Fees are charged for setting up a programme, a monthly licensing fee and a commission for successful sales. Figure 10.6 explains the basic affiliate marketing process.

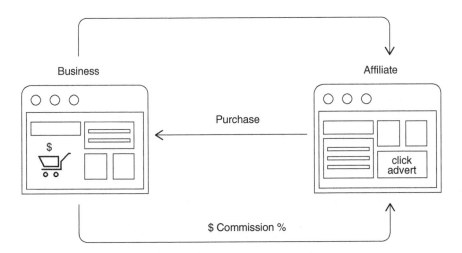

Figure 10.6 The affiliate marketing process

Following standard rules, an affiliate gets a commission fee only if 1) a user browses to an affiliate's site, 2) the user clicks the affiliate's specially coded link to the merchant and 3) the user makes a purchase from the merchant (Edelman, 2013). These performance-focused rules distinguish affiliate marketing from other forms of paid digital marketing.

Common types of affiliates include (PerformanceIN, 2015):

- *Cashback/Loyalty websites.* Users receive money back on purchases made. Cashback can be in the form of money, points or another virtual 'currency'.
- *Comparison websites* enable users to compare products and prices online. The price comparison site publisher receives commission when a customer clicks through to the advertiser's site and makes a purchase.
- *Content websites.* Websites of this type include blogs, where the content is written by a company or an individual. However, any site which carries information could be classed as a content site.
- *Email providers.* These publishers specialise in advertising to users via email. Email affiliates generally own, or have access to, lists containing thousands of email addresses. Merchants provide their creative materials that promote specific products and the publisher emails the promotion to their list(s).
- *Voucher code/Discount websites.* Publishers hosting money-off deals capitalise on consumers who increasingly seek vouchers and discounts before making certain types of purchases. Merchants have become a little savvier when using voucher code affiliates to drive sales, as they begin to push high-margin items or end-of-range clearance items as a priority.
- *Mobile publishers.* There is a diverse range of mobile publishers that operate within the performance marketing space, from existing publishers who have increased their portfolio with an application, to mobile-specific specialists such as 'discovery' and 'review' applications who work to a cost-per-download metric. They all drive sales via a mobile app to an advertiser's mobile-optimised site or app.

10.8 Benchmarking and monitoring paid advertising activities

The simplest way to measure paid advertising activities is through the comparison of financial investment into these activities and the corresponding benefits in terms of completion of calls-to-action.

Dependent on the budgets invested, paid advertising activities can have devastating results if left unattended. Paid advertising services are set up for ease of use and spend, and if your ad is not relevant to the user it's possible for you to bid for it without gaining any financial benefit at all, and in fact for this to be financially detrimental. The more times your ads are shown without a click-through by the user, the more expensive it will be for the same ad to appear next time, since it is a continuously dynamic calculations process. Therefore, ads should be reviewed regularly – ideally on a daily basis for a smaller budget campaign; if the campaign is new and involves high budgets (e.g. over €500 per day), ad performance should be monitored on an hourly basis.

When considering key performance indicators (KPIs) for paid advertising, the same rules apply as for any other digital activities – the last click is not always the one that generated the customer's interest in your products or services, so wider awareness of metrics is useful to evaluate the branding and exposure generated by a channel (Table 10.3).

These are just some of the tools to help with a number of paid advertising benchmarking efforts, together with a quick overview of these tools and how they could be used:

- *Google* Analytics – offers a free powerful tool for tracking paid activities related to a website. Using the free URL builder allows an extension of *Google* Analytics where each campaign can be specifically tracked even by the smallest organisation, without the need for an external software budget. It integrates particularly well with AdWords, where a paid search ad click can be tracked in terms of its conversions and revenue for e-commerce websites.
- KeywordSpy – offers an overview of the average cost being paid for a keyword by some of your competitors targeting the same market. This tool

Table 10.3 Sample KPIs and monitoring tools for paid digital marketing

Paid marketing type	Examples of KPIs	Example tools
Paid search marketing	Quality score for individual keyword Click-through rate Cost-per-click Conversion rate Conversions Impressions generated by the ad	Native paid advertising management tools, e.g. AdWords or *Bing Ads* KeywordSpy.com Wordstream.com *Weatherfit* *Google* Analytics
Paid social media marketing	Post reach of content Engagement with your ad Cost-per-click Conversion rate Cost per lead / customer	Native paid advertising management tools, e.g. Facebook.com or Twitter.com Wordstream.com SocialFlow *Google* Analytics
Affiliate marketing	Leads generated Conversions specific to your call-to-action Conversion rate Cost per acquisition Revenue Return on ad spend	Many affiliate network-specific tools such as Affiliate Window, LinkShare and Zanox *Google* Analytics

offers some free information and, for a premium, more advanced analytics on paid advertising performance.

- Wordstream – this advanced tool brings all your paid advertising accounts from AdWords, *Bing* and *Facebook* into one place and offers paid advertising grading reports and landing page grading, as well as advice on how to optimise your efforts.
- SocialFlow – allows for managing and reporting on multiple social media platforms such as *Facebook*, *Pinterest* and *Twitter* campaigns.
- Weatherfit – a weather-based AdWords management software that helps online retailers to link their weather-related paid search ads and automatically control campaigns based on the weather conditions and the specific location.

10.9 Summary

This chapter has outlined the different paid advertising opportunities available within the digital marketing mix, focusing on search engines, social media and affiliate advertising.

When reaching out to the buyer persona, it's important to bear in mind that the customer journey to the online purchase can involve a number of different online profiles. By reaching out through paid channels, a brand can increase its presence and its opportunities to remind the buyer persona of its products and services. It is important to remember that users of social networking sites are in different mindsets to those using search engines. When someone is searching for a product or a service on a search engine, they are more likely to make the decision to purchase; hence the content of the ads should be focused on the purchase decision. On social media, ads should be less direct, since the user is less likely to be focused on purchasing the product or service at the time.

Although paid advertising is fast to set up when compared to organic optimisation of content, it has the obvious drawback of relying on financial resources to achieve presence. However, in addition to the main payment models such as PPC, which relies on payment for every visitor, the affiliate payment model is much more flexible and acceptable to those who are able to sell in volume and essentially pay a referral commission. On the other hand, the affiliate model has its own drawbacks, such as the need for a product or services that would be acceptable by the affiliate network and a longer setup process compared to paid search marketing.

As ever, experimenting with the most relevant options, carefully monitoring the impact of your paid digital advertising efforts and then adjusting them accordingly – and continuing to do so as a regular practice – is the best way to discover the models which will lead to the most rewarding results for your individual business.

10.10 References

Ayanso, A. and Karimi, A. (2015) The moderating effects of keyword competition on the determinants of ad position in sponsored search advertising. *Decision Support Systems, 70*, 42–59.

Edelman, E. (2013) The design of online advertising markets. In Nir Vulkan, Alvin Roth and Zvika Neeman (eds), *The Handbook of Market Design*. Oxford University Press.

LePage, E. (2014) *A Beginner's Guide to Social Media Advertising*. http://blog.hootsuite.com/beginners-guide-to-social-media-advertising/

PerformanceIN (2015) *Performance Marketing Guide 2015*. http://performancein.com/resource/performance-marketing-guide-2015/

Salesforce (2015) *Social.com Advertising Benchmark Report*. www.salesforce.com/form/marketingcloud/socialcom-benchmark.jsp

Shewan, D. (2014) *Social Media Advertising: Which Platform is Right for Your Small Business?* www.wordstream.com/blog/ws/2014/09/24/social-media-advertising

StatCounter Global Stats (2016) *StatCounter Global Stats*. http://gs.statcounter.com

11 Mobile marketing

Bartłomiej Kurzyk, University of Lodz, Poland

Tahir Rashid, Salford Business School,
University of Salford, UK

Sayed Ali Hayder, Salford Business School,
University of Salford, UK

11.0 Learning objectives

In this chapter you will learn how to:

- understand the impact of mobile marketing;
- recognise how mobile marketing is influenced by consumer behaviour;
- identify tactics to achieve maximum potential for your mobile marketing;
- enable online content to suit web and mobile advertising;
- acknowledge the importance of mobile commerce and its business value;
- see the future of mobile marketing driven by the Internet of Things.

11.1 Introducing mobile marketing

Mobile marketing is marketing that involves the use of mobile devices, including smartphones, tablets, phablets and wearable technologies such as *Google* Glass. These new devices produce a new consumer who is technology-aware and expects continuous access to data networks while they are on the go. Mobile devices are very personal and often carried at all times. These same mobile devices are increasingly used to store personal and professional information, to communicate through social media, search for information, shop, work, read books and magazines, and, for some, to remotely control household gadgets such as fridges, lights and microwaves. Mobile technologies are increasingly becoming an integral part of a consumer's life. According to the eMarketer report, the United Kingdom (UK) is the world leader in terms of mobile phone adoption and mobile advertising. It has been predicted that by 2016, three out of four mobile owners in the UK will be using smartphones. Mobile penetration is even higher amongst the younger population (16–35 age group), who utilise smartphones less for call purposes and more to access mobile social media for texting, browsing and online purchasing (Ofcom, 2014).

One can assess the impact of mobile technology on the lives of its consumers by comparing the era of Internet-enabled mobile devices with the pre-mobile age. For instance, before the advent of Internet-enabled mobile devices, customers received product information through mass media or by visiting a nearby store for a required product or service. Mobile marketing taps into the understanding of how the buyer persona is engaged on a multitude of mobile devices and anticipates interacting with them. Using the data derived from mobile devices in the development of strategic plans introduces new market research opportunities and increases understanding of consumer behaviour. Association of mobile data with other social activities offers new ways for developing and promoting products and services, as well as acquiring new customers and maintaining relationships with existing ones.

Although mobile marketing requires very specific focus, it is productive to employ a standard toolset of questions for identifying and exploiting opportunities. These questions include: What are the objectives? Who is the audience? What are the relevant technologies and channels of communication? What content will achieve the objectives? How will it be implemented? What can be learned from the experience?

This chapter documents the uses of mobile marketing and discusses the hardware and software of mobile technologies, including mobile platforms, apps, social media, mobile search engine optimisation (SEO), m-commerce, pay-per-click (PPC), mobile payment systems, quick response (QR) codes and networked sensors and beacons such as Estimote stickers. The emphasis in this chapter is on how to maintain a meaningful dialogue with prospects and be continuously working to understand the consumer's journey, through mobile devices, to support the organisation's integrated marketing communication strategy.

11.2 Understanding mobile consumer behaviour

The recent revolution in mobile technology and its integration of the communication, information and entertainment industries has radically transformed the way consumers interact with products and services. The ubiquitous nature of mobile technologies has provided consumers with more options and more control over their buying behaviour. The use of smartphones and tablets has enabled these consumers to make informed decisions by giving them the freedom to share information with each other, regardless of time and space barriers.

Marketers used to have an upper hand over the purchasing behaviour of customers because of their ability to control the product information flow. However, mobile connectivity allows consumers to receive product information at any time and in any place by accessing social media and search websites such as *Google* and *Yahoo!*. This has given consumers an edge over marketers and has made them more proactive in their daily consumption habits.

According to Kaplan (2012), mobile communication technologies are better than traditional desktop-driven technologies such as online search engines and social media, since they act as a bridge between the consumer's physical and virtual worlds. Unlike traditional desktop search engines and social media, which are restricted to a fixed place, mobile-enabled social media allow more freedom to consumers in terms of accessing and sharing information anywhere.

Mobile communication allows consumers to search for, compare and exchange product information (such as price or quality) with fellow consumers and make organisations accountable for their actions. For example, more and more consumers are sharing the positive and negative experiences of airline travel with other potential and existing customers through mobile social media while sitting at the airport or in an aeroplane. In this way, the airline industry is more tuned in to the changing needs of consumers and allows consumers to have more influence on the airline's policies towards providing a quality experience.

The impact of mobile technology on consumers has changed the way the latter interact with the environment. The ubiquitous nature of mobile technology has allowed consumers to remain connected all the time. These consumers are using mobile devices to kill time while waiting to be served in a restaurant, looking for and comparing prices of the products in a store and finding their favourite food at a nearby location through apps like *Foursquare*. This gives these consumers the ability to become more organised in their daily lives and allows them to make effective and efficient decisions related to what they consume.

The unique features of mobile technology provide an authentic, engaging, relevant and personalised experience to customers and give them the freedom to make their lives less complex. However, the use of mobile technology also has some negative implications on their lifestyle. For example, the universal nature of mobile devices has seriously undermined consumer privacy. The consumption habits of consumers can be traced through their mobile devices, which is to some extent good for the consumer, but it also has the potential to reveal personal bits of information which the consumer does not want to share with a company. At times, consumers are bombarded with unwanted promotional ads

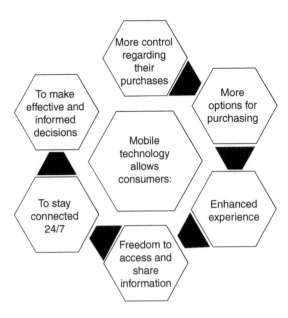

Figure 11.1 The impact of mobile technology on consumers

if they give their mobile phone numbers to companies which offer discounts and services. There are some organisations that are in the business of selling the phone numbers of consumers to other companies and indirectly contributing to a breach in consumer confidence.

Unfortunately, the growing use of mobile devices is having a contradictory effect on human relationships. The increased involvement of people with their mobile devices is giving them more control over their lives, but it is also causing them to spend more time with technology and less time with people, resulting in de-integration of human relations and self-isolation. For example, text messages amongst young adults are limiting their ability to have real-time conversations with other people, which are essential for their self-identity development.

In this context, one can argue that mobile technology also has the ability to limit communication with regard to products and services, since consumers are more focused on technology and using it as a multitasking device rather than for the sake of accessing consumption information alone.

11.3 Responsive mobile websites and applications

Since more and more consumers are using the World Wide Web on their mobile devices, owners of websites should take into consideration that visitors to their websites may be using the small screen of mobile phones. A website that works perfectly on a big monitor screen could be unusable on a small mobile screen.

Web designers have three major options for dealing with shifting consumer websurfing habits.

Option 1 – Create two versions of the website

The first version is created for visitors using standard computer monitors. The second, 'mobile version' is created and optimised for smaller screens. Usually these websites have two different addresses (normal version: www.address.com; mobile version: m.address.com). Users could select 'mobile version' from a menu when visiting a website or they could be automatically redirected to the mobile version when using a mobile device.

Option 2 – Use responsive web design standards

Responsive Web Design (RWD) refers to a web design process enabling content (including advertising) to resize, reformat, reorganise and reposition itself in real time so that it looks good based on the screen the user happens to be looking at (IAB, 2012). The web designer creates only one version of the website, but it is displayed differently on different devices, automatically readjusting itself to the different sizes of the screens. The readjustment of the size makes it easier for the mobile consumer to read and navigate content, something they cannot do easily with traditional websites designed primarily for desktop and laptop users (Zeng et al., 2014).

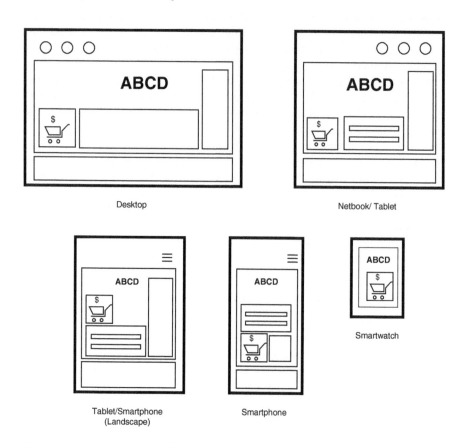

Figure 11.2 Your website on different devices

Option 3 – Build mobile applications

Mobile applications (apps) are software applications designed specifically for devices such as smartphones and tablets. They can be downloaded through a mobile web browser and can also come installed on the device (Wen et al., 2014). Mobile apps can mirror the functionality of a normal website, which could be either a simplified version of the core functionality of the website or an enhanced experience, providing additional functionality or usability specifically for the mobile app.

Nowadays, the technical difficulty and the cost of building responsive websites have been significantly lowered. This standard of web design has been widely accepted and is recommended as a default for building new websites, making option 1 (having a standard and a mobile version of a site) much less desirable.

The major differences between mobile responsive websites and mobile applications are stated in Table 11.1.

Table 11.1 Differences between mobile responsive websites and mobile applications

Criteria	Responsive web design	Mobile web app
Versions	Single version – build the website and optimise across mobile devices	Two separate versions – build one for website and another for mobile
Development cost	Higher. Cost increases with increase in number of elements in the website	Medium
Implementation time	Longer development cycle. Development complexity increases as the site map gets more complex	Less time if you know the exact features you need and you have planned your roadmap well
Design approach	Requires specialised knowledge of this new approach	Straightforward if you know the exact features and functionality you need in your mobile solution
User experience	Slightly lower user experience, since the app is designed for a website and optimised across mobile devices Does not require users to install additional apps Limited interaction with smartphones' native functions – photo camera, calendar or GPS. Navigation enabled from top to bottom by default. Left to right navigation requires additional customisation and modification in layout and code	Better user experience, specifically designed for mobile phone and improving further with HTML5 technology Requires users to find and install app on their mobile device Advanced interaction with smartphones' native functions – photo camera, calendar or GPS. Left to right navigation enabled to support carousel navigation
Performance	Potential bandwidth issues when server sends larger media than needed and text-heavy images	Better, more streamlined performance
Ongoing maintenance	Lower maintenance cost and effort Single version to maintain for the website and across a wide range of mobile devices Provides control and flexibility to make changes in website, which are reflected across all mobile devices	Medium Separate for website version and mobile web app version Requires changes to be made separately in website and mobile web app versions Apps should be updated regularly to meet requirements of new versions of mobile operating systems (OS)
SEO	Website content is indexed by search engines	App content is not indexed by search engines

Source: Adapted from Rapidvaluesolutions, 2013

11.4 Mobile advertising and promotions

Mobile advertising and promotion is one of the fastest growing sectors in the Western developed world, particularly in the UK. Smartphones provide marketers with an opportunity to target customers through personalised advertisements. Mobile technology makes it easier for marketers to develop long-term customer relationships by proactively anticipating and responding to the changing needs of the market and providing support in line with customer expectations.

Mobile promotions allow consumers to be aware of various new offers and discounts which are in line with customers' specific interests and help them make smart purchasing decisions. One of the main reasons for the growth of mobile advertising and promotion is the busy lifestyle of the modern-day consumer and the overflow of information which requires them to develop multi-tasking and time management skills.

The main purpose of mobile advertising is to provide quick and convenient access to information for consumers who are on the move or simply away from their desktop. It helps them enhance their multitasking skills by performing various actions simultaneously. For example, growing numbers of people not only use their smartphones to check on the whereabouts of their children, but also to access movie reviews while on their way to the movie theatre.

Unlike traditional mass media, mobile technology allows the consumer to receive advertising messages from companies that cater to their interests and to limit undesirable advertisements. Although customers occasionally receive unwanted advertisement messages from marketers, this is changing, as companies are finally realising the negative effect of sending text-based advertising messages from their brands without the consent of consumers.

The effectiveness of the mobile advertising and promotion mix does not mean that mass media (TV, radio, billboards) and traditional new media (online marketing through desktops/laptops) are losing their influence on the consumer. On the contrary, these technologies are still in demand, as consumers are simultaneously using them for daily consumption. For example, growing numbers of consumers are using their mobile phones or tablets while they are watching TV at home. This use of multiple media simultaneously by the consumer requires a more integrated marketing approach in terms of using both mobile and traditional marketing platforms to enhance the effectiveness of the promotional message.

11.5 Mobile pay-per-click advertising

Mobile PPC is a paid online marketing model that advertisers are increasingly employing to engage consumers. The growing numbers of mobile consumers are using search engines and websites to gain access to information about various products and services. This makes mobile PPC an essential tool in a company's marketing arsenal and gives them a competitive edge over other competitors in the market.

In mobile PPC, an advertiser pays the search engine or website owner a certain amount of money each time their ad is clicked by the consumer. The advertisers pay for the keywords which are relevant to what they are selling and are more likely to be used by consumers when they are searching for their products and services. Mobile PPC ads are not limited to paid ads on search engine results pages (SERPs); they also include banner ads on mobile websites, video ads and any other rich media text.

Mobile PPC advertising is one of the most effective ways to reach potential mobile consumers on the move at any place and time. It is also beneficial for creating a positive perception of the brand in the mind of the consumers, improving brand awareness and increasing mobile visibility. This form of advertising is valuable for local businesses, since the majority of mobile consumers use their mobile devices to identify products and services which are close to their location.

Mobile PPC is different from traditional PPC advertising in various ways. For instance, the screens of smartphones and tablets are smaller than monitors and laptops, and this requires the marketer to keep their advertising content brief and customised to individual mobile screen sizes. Another difference is in the intent of consumers, since desktop consumers spend more time in searching and comparing the product information online, while mobile consumers are more interested in making instant purchase decisions and spend less time performing research. In addition, since mobile PPC is a new technology, it is less costly than desktop PPC advertising and yields higher click-through rates, resulting in more companies investing in mobile PPC campaigns.

11.6 Mobile search engine optimisation

The latest data shows constant growth in multi-screening, a behaviour where customers use multiple devices with different screen sizes at the same time to achieve their goals. More and more customers are using mobile devices to access websites and online stores and are expecting a consistent experience across all platforms. This is a key reason to invest in a mobile-friendly version of your website.

Probably the most important factor that can influence your mobile SEO strategy is the model of website configuration used. Both *Google* and *Bing* have stated that they recommend RWD as the preferred choice for building mobile sites. One can expect that this choice will influence the SEO ranking of a website in those search engines.

This design decision is the most difficult to implement for existing businesses. Websites designed non-responsively may have to be rebuilt in order to meet this criterion, which may be a long and expensive process, depending on the extensiveness of the website. New businesses should invest in RWD from the start, and existing businesses should seriously consider rebuilding their websites according to this standard.

Other mobile SEO recommendations concentrate on the common errors that can hinder user experience in mobile environments. *Google* (2016) published a list of common problems to avoid:

- Blocked JavaScript, CSS and image files.
- Unplayable content (such as Flash).
- Faulty redirects (including irrelevant cross-links between desktop and mobile-friendly web pages).
- Mobile-only 404s (missing pages, dead links).
- App download interstitials (heavy promotion of the app version of the service that lowers the user experience).
- Slow mobile pages.

There are also certain rules that set apart local SEO strategy from other SEO activities:

- *Local profiles* – a company should claim and create a local profile, not just on *Google* but also *Yahoo! Local* and *Bing Places*.
- *Citations* – a citation is any place online that uses your company name, address and phone number all on the same page; they should be in the same format as your local listing.
- *Address management* – using the same address format is important; it should be used on every page within the site (the footer may be the best location).
- *Reviews* – these are especially important on *Google* Places profiles, but are also important on other websites or social media.
- *Metadata fields* – use your local city in metadata tags and descriptions, and within the content of your website.

11.7 M-commerce

More and more people are using mobile devices to help them shop. There are two interesting effects that link the Internet and physical sales:

- ROPO (Research Online, Purchase Offline) – before making any purchase, customers are browsing the Internet, finding information about the product, finding deals, etc. Equipped with this information, they make the sale offline.
- Showrooming (research products offline, purchase online) – consumers are visiting shops and researching products offline. Then they go online and purchase the product (usually for a lower price) in one of the online stores.

Both scenarios contribute heavily to the already complicated landscape of online and offline retailing, and both can be either beneficial or harmful to different shops depending on factors such as their online presence and the similarity of their online and offline prices. Both scenarios have been known and accounted for in the world of traditional e-commerce.

The rise in popularity of mobile devices further blends the intermixing of the online and offline retail experience. Right now:

- Consumers can research products and compare prices on the go using their mobile devices, regardless of whether they are at home or at the shop, the bookstore or the supermarket. There are even apps that help consumers find the best deals by simply scanning the barcode of the product. This directly influences the purchasing process and can result in no sale on the spot.
- Consumers can purchase products they see in a store directly using mobile shops and mobile payment systems.

Both of these effects, combined with rising numbers of smartphones, tablets and mobile-enabled stores, have resulted in the growing importance of m-commerce.

M-commerce is the act of shopping on a portable device rather than a traditional desktop or laptop computer, and this portable device is most commonly a smartphone or tablet (www.sage.co.uk/blo/index.php/2014/02/what-is-mcommerce-and-what-does-it-mean-for-your-business/).

Case Study 11.1   *Listonic's* mobile shopping app benefits brands

Listonic is a Polish start-up that created a mobile shopping list app. Users can easily create, share and use shopping lists on the go. It is an easy solution for people to help them with their shopping, but it's also a great tool for advertisers to reach their prospective customers. Advertisers can:

- attach their recommendations non-intrusively within shopping lists (e.g. next to 'milk', users are presented with recommendations for a specific brand of milk);
- run banner campaigns targeted at customers with specific products on their shopping lists, and link the banners to landing pages with direct response buttons such as 'add to shopping list'.

By using advertising options within the *Listonic* app, advertisers are able to show their message to prospective customers at the exact moment of making a specific product purchase.

One such campaign was made with MobextPolska (Havas Media) for *Durex* (manufacturer of condoms and other mainstream sex-related products) in 2013 for Valentine's Day. On 14th February, users that had certain products (e.g. 'whipped cream') on their shopping lists were presented with additional context-based recommendations (e.g. 'for dessert, not only in the kitchen'). The campaign resulted in:

- 450,000 impressions of banner ad with CTR 0.69 per cent;
- 45,000 impressions of context ad with CTR 2.32 per cent;
- 1,162 per cent growth of month-to-month brand occurrences within shopping lists across all users;
- 202 per cent growth of popularity of product category on shopping lists.

Source: http://tylkofmcg.pl/reklama-mobilna-durex-performax-intense-case-study/

More and more customers are using mobile devices to visit online stores. In recent research (August 2014) conducted among shops that use the Shopify platform, 50.3 per cent of traffic came from mobile devices (40.3 per cent from mobile phones, 10 per cent from tablets) and just 49.7 per cent from desktop computers and laptops (Shopify, 2014). It is expected that the traffic from mobile devices will continue to grow, making m-commerce channels essential to any company selling products or services online.

If your company wants to run both a mobile online shop and a regular online shop, you can use one of three solutions:

- Design separate versions for the e-shop and the m-shop using responsive web design rules.
- Design a single mobile-friendly online shop using responsive web design rules (there are numerous ready-to-use e-commerce platforms with m-commerce functionality that can be used as a solution here).
- Design an m-commerce app that uses native m-commerce functionality.

All three options would allow consumers to browse a selection of products using their mobile device. There is, however, one significant difference – payments. For desktop computer/laptop shopping, submitting credit card data to purchase products online is a viable option. In a mobile environment, however, no one would be willing to input credit card data on the go. A company wanting to set up an m-commerce channel should carefully consider using a standard mobile payment system.

11.8 Mobile payment systems

Mobile payments (m-payments) combine payment systems with mobile devices and services to provide users with the ability to initiate, authorise and complete a financial transaction in which money or funds are transferred over mobile network or wireless communication technologies to the receiver.

Since users generally have mobile devices with them almost all the time, there is a certain expectation that mobile devices will act as mobile wallets.

Companies that are willing to use mobile devices for mobile payments have four options:

1) Mobile register apps – an integrated point of sale that uses mobile devices as a centre for the financial operations of a storefront. From the perspective of a customer, the transaction looks normal. From the perspective of a seller, a mobile integrated register app can provide significant benefits such as sales tracking, inventory management and financial data management, all synced through the cloud. To use it to its full potential, some investment is needed for additional mobile device compatible credit card readers, receipt printers and related products, such as those provided by squareup. com, for example. It has to be noted that this option does not provide a full m-payment system because, from the perspective of a customer, a transaction is usually performed in standard fashion.

2) Near Field Communication (NFC) – in countries where PayPass and Pay-Wave credit/debit cards are popular, mobile phones can be used as a credit card. The easiest option is to issue a special sticker that can be placed on a mobile phone, which has an integrated microprocessor that acts as a normal NFC card. The main disadvantages of this system are that there are only a limited number of credit card issuers and there is a lack of support for NFC SIM cards by *Apple* products.

3) Integrated mobile payment systems – since *Apple* is not accepting NFC SIM cards, in 2014 a similar concept was introduced under the name of *Apple* Pay. By using its own proprietary system of NFC terminals and *Apple* PayPass, where users can keep their credit card data, users can pay using their iPhone, iPad or *Apple* Watch. At the time of writing, the system is still in its infancy and is just being rolled out in the USA. It is expected, however, that it will be introduced in Europe soon.

4) Mobile payment apps – a seller can choose to integrate payment options within its own application, usually by enabling a way for the customer to pre-configure credit card information so it is easy to choose it as a payment method during mobile checkout. Alternatively, a pre-paid system can be used to finalise transactions on mobile devices, and users can use normal online payment methods to top up the balance on their accounts. An app can confirm transactions up to this balance. Two examples of this are:

   - *Skycash* – a payment system operating in Poland where users can install the *Skycash* app on their mobile device and pay for tram, bus, rail tickets and parking.
   - *Starbucks UK* – offers users a mobile device app that can be used for paying for orders using a pre-paid balance.

In order to use mobile payment apps, a seller must either build their own mobile payment system – which may be difficult and expensive – or join one of the existing systems. As with normal credit card transactions, these systems usually operate by charging a fee for each transaction, which the seller must accept as the cost of meeting customers' expectation of convenience.

11.9 2D and QR codes

The need to link the physical and digital worlds together, so that computers could interact with physical objects, presented a very specific problem for information technology.

One of the first applications that gained widespread acceptance was in the form of barcodes. They were popularised in the 1970s and allowed products to be scanned quickly at store checkouts.

For its time, barcode scanning technology was a perfect solution for a very specific need. By placing barcodes on physical items, a computer 'learned' a way to identify objects and link them to additional data, such as product name or price.

The technology was cheap. The barcode is very simple, and you don't need very sophisticated image recognition technology to make it work. Placing barcodes on objects is also very easy – you just need to add the additional graphical element to the product packaging.

Nowadays, barcodes are ubiquitous, but using them in a mobile environment has many limitations, the most noted being limited capacity. A typical barcode can contain only 20 alphanumeric characters of information. It is enough to help catalogue the products available at any given store or market, but with the growth of the Internet it was not enough. For example, if one would like to link a physical object to a URL or email address, that could very easily go beyond the 20-character length of a barcode.

The answer to this problem was the introduction of 2D codes in the 1980s and 1990s. With normal barcodes, information is coded only in one dimension.

QR code

Data Matrix code

Figure 11.3 Encoding your messages

2D codes use coding in two dimensions, allowing them to store over 4,200 alphanumeric characters of information. Moreover, 2D codes can be read from any direction and can be recognised even when partially obscured or even destroyed. Depending on the error correction capacity level, up to 30 per cent of the information stored within a 2D code can be restored.

The invention of 2D codes marked a natural progression for barcodes – it allowed for increased capacity without increasing the cost of 'tagging' objects. More advanced software is needed, but no sophisticated image recognition system is required. Moreover, 2D codes are much easier for mobile phone cameras to read than standard barcodes.

There are two popular forms of 2D codes in use: QR (Quick Recognition) codes and Data Matrix codes.

The main difference is that since QR codes were developed in Japan, they can embed kanji (Japanese characters). Data Matrix codes, being a US standard, have no such functionality. This results in QR codes having greater popularity worldwide, especially in Europe, where adoption rates are rapidly growing.

Since the 1990s, QR codes have evolved into many different types, each of which has a specific application (Denso Wave Inc., 2016):

- Micro QR codes – this type of code can be printed in a smaller space.
- iQR codes – these can be printed as square or rectangular shapes.
- SQRC – these have reading restriction implemented, so they can be used to store secure information.
- LogoQ – these can incorporate logos, illustrations and letters in the code design.

In order to generate 2D codes, a special application is needed. Since most of the common ways of encoding information in 2D codes use open standards, there are many free-to-use Internet applications that can be used to generate these codes for marketing purposes. Most of these applications can generate both QR codes and Data Matrix codes. Many applications give users the option to generate either static or dynamic 2D codes.

For static 2D codes, the generator creates an image into which is encoded the data that was provided by the user. If the 2D code includes a URL, scanning it will take the user directly to the desired landing page. Generating a static 2D code is usually free; however, if something in the encoded information needs to be changed, such as the target URL, a new 2D code image must be generated.

For dynamic 2D codes, the generator creates an image which is encoded with a link to a landing page, with information provided and managed by the user. If the 2D code includes a URL, scanning it will link to a page from the service provider and then be redirected to the desired landing page. If the user wants to change something in the encoded data – the target URL, for example – they can log in to the service provider and update this information without changing the image for the 2D code itself.

Dynamic 2D codes are provided by companies that offer not only 2D code generators, but also 2D codes campaign management services. Using such a service usually allows:

- tracking of 2D code scans, allowing for analytics and campaign optimisation;
- dynamic changes of landing pages used for the same 2D code;
- coupon code management;
- multiple URLs encoded in a single 2D code.

The core concept of using the 2D codes for mobile marketing purposes is directly linked to the ability to be recognised and scanned on mobile devices.

There are three main barriers for the widespread use of 2D codes:

1   Use is limited to owners of smartphones. Most traditional mobile phones don't have the necessary camera and software to scan QR codes.
2   In order for a customer to use a code on their mobile device, special software needs to be installed. Such software is available for major mobile operating systems (especially iOS, Android and Windows), but not all devices have it pre-installed. Most notably, in order to scan 2D codes on an iPhone, a third-party application must be downloaded.
3.   Although they are becoming more and more popular, there is still a substantial part of the population that do not know what 2D codes are and what they can do with them.

Both types of 2D codes are used by many companies for marketing purposes. Typical areas of usage are:

- Advertising – using 2D codes on promotional material such as posters, banners, printed ads and leaflets can help customers get additional content that is connected with the advertised brand. 2D codes can link to websites or social media profiles for the brand. Research shows that including a 2D code in an ad changes the attitudes towards the advertisers favourably.
- Coupons – companies can distribute coupons with 2D codes that will offer customers benefits such as free products and discounts.
- M-commerce – a company can use advertising or catalogues with 2D codes that link to its m-commerce shop, allowing for fast and easy purchase of the advertised products.
- Enhanced shopping experience – retailers can display 2D codes beside the products in their store, where they can be scanned by customers who want additional information.
- Product/service enhancements – museums and art galleries can display 2D codes next to exhibits to give visitors additional multimedia content.
- Event experience enhancement – 2D codes can be used on invitations and name tags.

In order for the use of 2D codes to be successful, there are certain rules that need to be adhered to:

- Scanning the code should give value to customers. Scanning a 2D code takes time; customers have to bring their phone out, load the application, position the phone in order to scan the code and wait for the linked content to load. In order to go through the process, customers should know what to expect after scanning the code and see value in the result.
- Scanning the code should be easy and problem free. Using the codes on billboards, vehicles or electronic displays, for example, would not work.
- The landing page should be optimised for the mobile device experience. Scanning the code in order to be linked to a desktop version of the landing page will frustrate the customer.

11.10 Internet of Things

Linking the online and offline worlds via 2D codes has its benefits, but it also has serious limitations. Most notably, it requires activity on behalf of the user – a conscious action to pull out their smartphone and scan the code. Moreover, the link is just a one-time event. The 2D code is scanned and then the interaction goes between the user and mobile device.

The concept of the Internet of Things aims at getting rid of those limitations. It is a vast, invisible, global network in which nearly every product and physical object, including toasters, trees, milk cartons, shopping centre parking spaces, cars, roads, wristwatches and medical equipment, will be tagged with sensors that will gather and transmit data about people's consumption, usage patterns and location.

The Internet of Things manifests itself in two major trends.

The first trend is enabling Internet connectivity to various products that, as well as fulfilling their main function, also connect themselves to the Internet and transfer data about their usage. These types of products include wearables (such as watches and fitness trackers), security cameras, thermostats, smoke detectors and weights. This trend is becoming more and more visible. The 2014 Accenture State of the Internet of Things showed that 4 per cent of surveyed US citizens own at least one such device, and predicted that this number will reach 69 per cent in 2019 (Accenture, 2014).

The second trend is closely connected with the introduction and growth in popularity of beacon technology. Beacons are low-cost, Bluetooth, low-energy sensors that can send push notifications to enabled smartphones or tablets.

At the time of writing, the popularity of beacons is just starting to grow. Introducing a Bluetooth low-energy standard in 2010 enabled beacons to work for a reasonable time counted in years. Another important factor influencing the beacon adoption rate was the introduction of the iBeacon communication standard by *Apple* in 2013 to all iOS 7 devices. The popularity of iPhones and iPads helped to introduce the concept of beacons to the general public.

So far, the widespread application of beacon technology is just starting. There are several companies producing beacons and publishing their software development kits to help application developers make use of them.

Similar to 2D codes, there are barriers for widespread beacon use:

1   Use is limited to owners of smartphones that are compliant with the Bluetooth low-energy standard.
2.   In order for a mobile device to properly interpret beacon data, and deliver the expected content and functionality, the customer has to install the appropriate app. Companies have to promise enough value to give their customers a reason to install their apps, and then deliver the expected result.

Expected uses of beacons are:

•   Promotion (walk-by promotion) – customers can get notifications about promotions and special offers when they walk by the store.
•   Enhancing shopping experience – showing recommended routes, displaying ads and information on in-store monitors with displays targeted to specific customers, recommending additional products based on the customer's profile or the path taken in store.
•   Coupons and loyalty programmes – customers can be identified automatically when in store by their mobile device app, without even pulling their phones from their pockets. Loyalty benefits can be triggered not only by purchases, but also by visits or by time spent in establishments.
•   Service enhancement – menu enhancement and museum guides. In comparison to 2D codes, beacons allow for a much more seamless experience. For example, in a museum, a visitor doesn't have to scan any code to get additional information on the exhibits – data is pushed to their mobile device as soon as the customer gets close to them.

11.11 Wearable technology

The recent phenomenon in mobile marketing is wearable technologies, which are becoming increasingly popular among consumers. Wearable technologies are devices that one is able to wear on their body. They are considered to be more sophisticated than mobile devices because they have the ability to outperform some of the tasks of mobile devices through sensors and screening functions.

There are many types of wearable technology gadgets trending in the market today in the form of glasses, watches, jewellery, wristwear and skin patches. They come in a variety of shapes and forms, and carry out various functions simultaneously. What impels these popular technology gadgets is that they allow people to access their data and information and connect worldwide through broadband connectivity.

Two of the most well-known wearable brands trending in the market are the *Google* Glass and the *Apple* Watch. *Google* Glass is a device shaped like and worn as regular eye glasses, but which carries out as many functions as a smartphone (Google, 2014). It has the ability to deliver actions based on motion and sensors, from navigation to tracking your health performance and from text messaging to listening to your favourite music, all hands free. Interacting on social media and sharing your pictures and videos is made easier due to this hands-free device. One can share any information on *Facebook* and *Twitter* just by motioning the Glass, without having to take out a device and carry out the action manually.

Apple Watch carries out the same functions as the *Google* Glass, but is worn on your wrist rather than on your face (Apple, 2014). With *Apple* Watch the user can take pictures, navigate, connect to the Internet or watch movies. In the context of marketing, an organisation could take advantage of the positive aspects of both devices – such as the hands-free and motion signal features – to promote its products in a new way. For example, Evernote lets the user send their grocery lists to *Google* Glass so they can access it while they are shopping. As for *Apple* Watch, it can help users keep track of their health and fitness. Wearable data can also be used by employers, health care providers and medical insurers to better manage the health of their clients and provide them with quality health at a reduced cost.

Another way to market a brand or a product is by using one of these products' best features – picture and video capturing. For example, sellers such as cosmetics companies or travel agencies could market their products by giving the consumer the idea of life made easy, in which they, the consumer, could be applying make-up or travelling to exotic locations while applications are running on these gadgets in the background, making their experience more exciting.

11.12 Summary

Mobile technologies are becoming an integral part of a consumer's life. Mobile penetration is rising as users start to utilise smartphones less for call purposes and more to access mobile social media for texting, browsing and online purchasing. To this end, the mobile sector has become a critical environment for marketing.

With such growth, it is crucial that marketers are fully aware of the mobile marketing concepts that have been covered in this chapter, from mobile marketing as a key emerging trend, to how mobile marketing is influenced by consumer behaviour; from how to enable online content to suit both web and mobile users, to how best to adopt mobile payments; and finally, to the future of mobile marketing – the Internet of Things and wearable technologies – knowledge and understanding of which will ensure that your organisation stays up to date with new advancements.

11.13 References

Accenture (2014) *State of the Internet of Things Study from Accenture Interactive Predicts 69 Percent of Consumers Will Own an In-Home IoT Device by 2019.* http://newsroom.accenture.com/industries/systems-integration-technology/2014-state-of-the-internet-of-things-study-from-accenture-interactive-predicts-69-percent-of-consumers-will-own-an-in-home-iot-device-by-2019.htm

Apple (2014) *Apple Watch.* www.apple.com/watch/

Denso Wave Inc. (2016) *Types of QR Code.* www.qrcode.com/en/codes

Google (2014) *Google Glass.* www.google.com/glass/start/

Google (2016) *Google Developers.* http://developers.google.com/webmasters/mobile-sites/mobile-seo/common-mistakes

IAB (2012) *Responsive Design and Ad Creative: An IAB Perspective. A Report Prepared by the IAB Mobile Marketing Center of Excellence.* www.iab.net/media/file/ResponsivePerspective Final.pdf

Kaplan, A. (2012) If you love something, let it go mobile: Mobile marketing and mobile social media 4x4. *Business Horizons, 55*(2), 129–39.

Ofcom (2014) *The Communication Market Report, August.* http://stakeholders.ofcom.org.uk/binaries/research/cmr/cmr14/2014_UK_CMR.pdf

Rapidvaluesolutions (2013) *The New Design Trend: Build a Website; Enable Self-optimization Across All Mobile Devices.* http://rapidvaluesolutions.com/whitepapers/responsive-web-design.html

Shopify (2014) *Mobile Now Accounts for 50.3% of All Ecommerce Traffic.* www.shopify.com/blog/15206517-mobile-now-accounts-for-50–3-of-all-ecommerce-traffic

Wen, D.M.H., Chang, D.J., Lin, Y-T., Liang, C.W. and Yang, S-Y. (2014) *Gamification Design for Increasing Customer Purchase Intention in a Mobile Marketing Campaign App. Proceedings of the 2014 International Conference Held in Heraklion, Crete.* Crete, HCI.

Zeng, Y., Gao, J. and Wu, C. (2014) *Responsive Web Design and Its Use by an E-Commerce Website. Proceedings of the 6th International Conference held in Heraklion, Crete.* Crete, HCI.

12 Measuring brand awareness, campaign evaluation and web analytics

Alexander Christov, University of National and World Economy (UNWE), Bulgaria

Verena Hausmann and Sue Williams, Universität Koblenz-Landau, Germany

12.0 Learning objectives

In this chapter you will understand:

- why it is important to measure brand awareness;
- what indicators to use for campaign and brand evaluation;
- how to correlate indicators with business objectives in order to make decisions;
- web analytics and its relevant tools and concepts;
- concepts of conversion.

12.1 Introduction

One of the key reasons why Digital and Social Media Marketing is gaining such popularity is because the data that can be obtained through digital campaigns is both rich and transparent. However, intelligent use of campaign data needs to go beyond simply the measurement of 'clicks' through websites or social media channels – it should associate these simple and readily obtainable metrics with the overall purpose and intent of the campaign, as well as the wider strategic position of digital marketing within organisations. This chapter advocates an approach to brand development and campaign management that is informed by evidence-based decision making.

The chapter will outline the main reasons and techniques for evaluating and tracking the online consumer journey and their connection to the effective use of business-specific key performance indicators (KPIs). The techniques discussed will cover those most commonly used, including tracking, physical response metrics, campaign reporting and user experience evaluation.

Understanding basic metrics and their correlations with business objectives will enable you to remain focused and purposeful in your decision making and actions. The exploration of paid, owned and earned KPIs shapes the discussion around the 'bigger' issues of building and maintaining brand awareness in European and international contexts, and the development of sustainable conversion-orientated strategies.

12.2 Digital marketing = conversions + brand awareness

Measurement is an essential aspect of the marketing process. The measurement and assessment of the success of your marketing activities, including campaigns and brand building, is the feedback mechanism through which these activities can be improved. It's also how marketers learn and expand their practical knowledge. The more extreme view takes this statement even further to claim that marketing without measurement cannot be considered marketing at all. Although this claim may appear obvious to the more experienced marketer or overly clichéd to a student of the subject, it remains a truism for all forms of digital marketing.

In fact, digital marketing and its intimate link to the technologies of client/server systems – but especially web servers and browsers – provide access to far larger volumes of accurate and precise quantitative data at greater levels of detail than was ever possible within traditional marketing strategies. The ready availability of the right tools and the right data means there is little excuse for a lack of campaign measurement or a failure to assess the value of an activity. The challenge for a marketer when measuring the success of their actions, however, is to make sense of what can very quickly become a mountain of impenetrable 'big data'.

From the analytical perspective, the meaning and purpose of digital marketing can be practically broken down and understood as the sum of conversion and brand awareness activities. Both concepts themselves are the sum of many parts, and any judgement of marketing success may well not consider – or even need to consider – every single element that comprises each of these concepts. Measurement and any evaluation of success that is extrapolated from the data received as a result of marketing activity must be done contextually with an holistic awareness of organisational and situational conditions. In optimal organisational situations any evaluation of success will utilise mixed methods that consider both qualitative and quantitative inputs.

the push of conversion → ← the pull of brand

Brand awareness and conversion activities exert force on the consumer from two different directions. Brand awareness and reputation pull a consumer through a journey that results in a final concluding transaction. Conversion activities actively push consumers through the journey to a final transaction. Traditionally, these two processes are a powerful combination that, when done well, produce loyal regular consumers who act as advocates and perpetuate the success of a brand. However, in a digital economy organisations with little brand awareness can successfully compete with popular traditional brands by building a positive conversion experience, and for e-commerce organisations a brand can ultimately be built around this positive experience. *Amazon's* emergence as a recognisable global brand is at least in part due to its pioneering 'One Click' checkout system – itself an early but crude form of conversion tool.

Conversion

Conversion – in the most general sense – is a progression from a beginning action to a different, separate and concluding action. From a conventional e-commerce perspective the most common form of conversion is based on pushing users who are prospective customers and visiting a website – the beginning action – through to a completed sale – the concluding action. This final action produces revenue for the business and brings a tangible bottom-line benefit as a result of this conversion. In e-commerce, it is also the conversion that can be most readily measured. A coarse conversion ratio can be derived by simply dividing the total value or volume of sales achieved over a period of time by the total number of website visits during the same time period.

More nuanced measurements employing additional tracking technologies can bring greater precision to calculating a conversion ratio when resources allow. This further sophistication will, for example, recognise and discard visits by web robots as well as duplicate visits. When a conversion progresses from action to action without any intervention of a third party – such as the marketer, peers or other external influences – the conversion can be regarded as 'natural'. When external forces – including those of the marketer – are required to push a consumer to undertake the final action, the conversion has required some form of interaction and can be described as a 'transacted' conversion. Natural conversions are a double-edged sword for the marketer, who is ever conscious of the importance of measurement to improve and refine their actions. Natural conversion occurs with no additional marketing action or direct costs, but these benefits in themselves result in a potentially restricted capacity to explain the reasons or motivations for a consumer's actions.

Initial Trigger Action → Final Action (natural conversion)
Initial Trigger Action → Intersecting Marketing Action → Final Action
    (transacted conversion)

However, more sophisticated e-commerce operations that are conscious they are interacting with increasingly informed and discerning consumers have recognised the need to break down this coarse view of conversion into smaller and more refined units of conversion. This can minimise the number of conversions being identified as natural and potentially baffling, and also enables the marketer to plan more precise and tightly focused interactions that promote conversion. In this way the consumer's journey to a final planned outcome is directed and guided through a series of small conversion activities in which the final action of one conversion becomes the trigger action for the next conversion activity.

Initial Trigger Action → Intersecting Marketing Action → Concluding
    Action (becomes) Trigger Action → Intersecting Marketing Action →
    Final Action

There is a vast range of marketing actions that can move the consumer from an initial action to a final action. Retargeting is a good but controversial example of a technique that is increasingly used to convert a visitor – who is presumed to be a suspect through their actions – into a buyer after they have abandoned their initial visit to an e-commerce site. *Amazon* uses this technique, prompting its visitors to return to specific items by showing banner and block advertising on other websites that are visited after leaving the *Amazon* domain.

More precise understanding of the chain of conversion activities can also be used to iteratively improve the design of the user experience through each action. For the tangible properties such as websites and apps, this involves initial design testing followed by gathering ongoing feedback from consumers using the properties.

Brand awareness

Brand awareness encapsulates a more complex combination of factors than those represented by conversion. The concept and importance of brand is well documented and almost synonymous with the development of marketing as a discipline and as a professional practice. The promotion of brand and brand awareness has also been the focus and vehicle for much of traditional marketing practice. The result is that traditional marketing and the focus on brand primarily benefit larger organisations with the ability to invest significantly in traditional broadcast media advertising. This relationship of brand to large-scale advertising investment – and without necessarily direct measurement and consideration of success – has the self-fulfilling consequence of building brand awareness. However, it is essential to recognise that high levels of brand awareness do not always directly correlate with higher levels of conversion.

Digital marketing practice challenges the primacy of brand awareness and reflects the attitude that online businesses can compete with bigger 'brands' through a balance of good conversion tactics and engaging brand collateral. In fact, the influences of the 'social' and the 'open' in digital business act as a disincentive to being – or being perceived as – a big brand that has connotations of being impersonal, disconnected and solely motivated by achieving the next sale. These connotations also contrast with perceptions in some national markets – including the US, the UK and Australia – that independent brands are better for their quality, service and attention to detail. In effect, this reversal in the relative perceptions of brands from the 1980s and 1990s is also a retreat from modernist concepts of the mass consumer and the associated positive principles of mass consumption techniques.

Brand awareness and brand perceptions shape the way in which a consumer is pulled towards a purchase. In extreme negative cases the purchase may be made despite a resistance to the brand, for example, because the conversion process is so easy, the price is so low or the alternatives are so limited. In extreme positive examples of brand pull the purchase is made irrespective of price, the complexities of a checkout system or a vast range of alternative options in the marketplace.

Building an appropriate and long-term sustainable brand takes time, requires investment and above all, will only succeed when it is linked to the overall strategic direction of the business. These prerequisites towards building a brand – while arguably common sense – offer a significant explanation as to why small businesses have traditionally struggled to compete with larger businesses. More importantly, and obversely, it is not solely a lack of financial investment that prevents small businesses from competing – and this is where opportunity lies for small businesses. Increasingly customers expect a degree of transparency to be associated with a brand, and a close integration and alignment between the claims of the brand and the actual conduct of its business. This is a relationship that traditional brands struggle with when they are still led by their brand and branding. Examples of this disconnection of brand and practice in traditional businesses can be seen in *McDonald's* high-calorie salad debacle. A small business with patience and strategic foresight that is prepared to be transparent and open can compete with the traditional brands.

12.3 Calculating return on investment and customer lifetime value

Just as brand building has traditionally been the form of marketing activity preferred by large businesses, so too do the preferred methods of calculating success differ between traditional businesses and digital businesses.

Return on investment (ROI) is regularly used for assessing a campaign against specific objectives. This approach favours large-scale brand-building techniques where a coarse measure of success can be readily obtained from calculating the total sales against the marketing investment over a given time period. The assumption implied by this approach is that all marketing investment will produce a positive consumer response that can be entirely captured and represented in the form of sales. Using ROI also presumes that there is a continuous level of marketing activity over a greater period of time than the one inspected by the ROI calculation that returns a consistent base level of positive consumer responses in the form of sales.

Customer lifetime value (CLV), as the title suggests, takes a longer-term and arguably more strategic view of a business's relationship with each individual customer. CLV calculates the average value of transaction from a customer over the period in which that customer continues to interact with the business. Because CLV measures the strength and value of long-term relationships, this tends to encourage focus on the widest parameters of service, extending beyond conversion tactics that produce a single immediate sale and instead aiming to convert the initial engagement of a prospect into them becoming a lifelong loyal brand advocate. This recognition of the need for vision to create a sustainable business is increasingly found in many truly digital businesses, and contrasts with the traditional brand-building actions of businesses that have relied on broadcast media as part of their business strategy. Using CLV as a means of judging the impact of marketing activity enables recognition of the distinctiveness of customers and their different behaviours in relation to individual goods and services. This is acknowledged with varying values in the cost per acquisition and the varying duration of interaction with the customer, depending on the nature of goods or services. CLV can also introduce consideration of the effect of churn among customers (when existing customers stop doing business with you).

12.4 Web analytics

Why web analytics?

The digital world, including websites and social media, has become a key communication channel for organisations (Norguet et al., 2006). With the opportunity to quickly reach millions of potential customers in an easy way, the Web has become one of the most powerful marketing vehicles available (Burby and Atchison, 2007), which should be reason enough to take a closer look at web analytics.

Web analytics has its origin in Data Mining (Cooley et al., 1997), which deals with the analysis of big data in order to find patterns and rules. Web analytics is specifically aimed at the 'objective tracking, collection, measurement, reporting, and analysis of quantitative Internet data to optimize websites and web marketing initiatives' (Digital Analytics Association, 2006).

Thus, the goal is to both understand and track what users or customers are doing while they are interacting with your digital profiles such as an app or a web page, and then to use that intelligence to design effective websites which meet users' needs and also to shape or improve online marketing initiatives.

ROI in marketing initiatives is important for marketers. In many organisations marketing is one of the single largest investments. Without some kind of analytics to assist in evaluating the effectiveness of online marketing initiatives, the outcome of this investment is often unclear. Web analytics can bring insight to this aspect of ROI. For example, the volumes of customers coming to a website as a direct consequence of a specific marketing campaign can be tracked and specific consumer groups can be identified. Web analytics also plays an important role in improving website design to improve customer satisfaction, for example, by making it easier to find information and generally improving the user experience.

How do we use web analytics?

The data we can obtain through web analytics does not itself tell a story. This data must be brought into context in order to provide transparency and assist in identifying, for example, marketing or website usage problems. The data which could lead to improving a website or campaigning or assisting in making business decisions requires skilled and sensitive analysis to enable interpretation and action taking (Hendriyani et al., 2013). Using a web analytics tool is only one part of the process and must be complemented by effective analysis and interpretation in view of business objectives or those set out by a digital marketing campaign. Nevertheless, we need to understand the tools in order to get appropriate data for analysis. Therefore, the following section will give an overview of the web analytics market and its tools before an example for a web analytics implementation plan is outlined. Important measurables as well as reporting insights are given in the following sections.

Web analytics tool market

In the past, web analytics was usually achieved by analysing a website's log files, and it was only capable of capturing basic data such as the number of times a page was viewed. Today, a more common way for web analytics tools to collect data is to use the quantitative method of JavaScript tagging. When using JavaScript tagging, a short piece of JavaScript code must be included on the web page. With the help of this tagging code it is possible to capture a wide variety of data. Web analytics tools offer the possibility to log various user actions and events on websites. In addition, there are many tools which allow the tracking of social media actions. By analysing the logs, user interactions become observable and can be used for improvements in developing and maintaining a website, marketing campaigns, etc.

At the end of the 1990s the software tool WebTrends was one of the first commercial web analytics tools on the market. Since then, much has happened. Today, the number of different web analytics tools is enormous and at first glance it is difficult to distinguish between the different offerings, since they all cover similar development scenarios and are capable of tracking a wide range of similar things. The most obvious aspects for separation are the differences in where the data is stored, who has control of the data, whether the software is open source or commercial, if the software is acquired as Software as a Service (SaaS) or an in-house installation and whether or not additional support is needed.

Even though many web analytics tools are available, only a few tools dominate with a market penetration of more than 75 per cent (Lovett et al., 2009). Looking globally, we can find *Adobe*, *Google*, *IBM* and *Webtrends* currently at the top (Gassman, 2011). *Google* Analytics Standard, which was launched in 2005, is the most used web analytics tool in the world, counting more than 10 million registrations. Among organisations, *Adobe* Analytics is leading the market (Kart and Kihn, 2014).

The following list includes the most widely used web analytics software products:

- *Adobe* SiteCatalyst (Omniture)
- Analyser NX (AT Internet)
- Click Tale
- comScore Digital Analytix
- Etracker
- *Google* Analytics
- *Google* Universal Analytics
- *IBM* Digital Analytics
- KISSmetrics
- NetInsight
- Netmind GO
- Open Web Analytics (OWA)
- Piwik
- SiteCensus
- Sitestats
- StatCounter
- Webtrekk Q3
- Webtrends Analytics
- *Yahoo!* Web Analytics

According to Gartner, 90 per cent of the potential users are already using some kind of web analytics. However, less than 60 per cent use advanced features such as targeted email or search engine marketing. Many companies are using more than one software tool at the same time and the market around web analytics is still growing, expanding in areas such as mobile and social analytics, targeted digital advertising and market automation. The software offerings are therefore becoming more powerful analytics software suites encompassing all areas (Kart and Kihn, 2014).

How to design and implement a web analytics plan

Why do we need a plan for web analytics?

As with most tools and initiatives, web analytics is not just done by choosing a tool and implementing it. Web analytics should be seen as an ongoing programme including different phases, each of which should be carried out at different intervals. Goals need to be defined in order to be able to measure success and each output from web analytics can and should be used as input for another cycle.

What does a web analytics plan look like?

A web analytics process can be described in five different phases:

- Phase 1 – Business requirements – the information needs should be analysed and an information architecture audit conducted in order to gain a clear understanding of the business needs.
- Phase 2 – Planning for web analytics – includes the building of knowledge about Web Analytics metrics and analysis possibilities, as well as the identification of needs and the mapping to a suitable tool.
- Phase 3 – Developing a data collection capability – contains the activities of implementing and setting up the selected tool so that the relevant data is kept.
- Phase 4 – Generating value through web analytics – contains two activities and is the most important phase. First, the pattern analysis and reporting. In this activity statistics and reports are created and evaluated in order to gain an understanding of the website usage. The second activity is the action taking. Based on the results of the previous steps and bringing together web analytics aims and actual results, a clear pathway for possible changes as well as future measurements should be developed.
- Phase 5 – Evaluation of actions – everything that has been done before should be evaluated and monitored. After several rounds of using the framework, it might be possible to benchmark metrics. This phase should help you to see if the web analytics process has resulted in positive outcomes.

Figure 12.1 shows the web analytics framework, which includes the five phases described above, and further outlines the different process phases by dividing them into different actions and including questions to ask in each step.

At the beginning of each web analytics programme you should ask yourself what you want to do with your website, what problems you currently have and what you look for within web analytics. Then you need to set clear objectives and goals for your programme. Furthermore, you need to identify the status quo of your website and your users in order to understand your business requirements (Phase 1). For example, the design of a website normally undergoes a major review every two to five years and new technologies might be used, so this phase should be repeated each time a big change has happened.

Phase 2 centres around the requirements for the tools, the metrics that should be captured and on identifying the output you want, so that you can plan for web analytics and decide on a specific tool.

The implementation and customisation of the tool is the major activity in developing a data collection capability (Phase 3). Only good data can help in improvements. In addition to the action taking, this can be seen as the most important action.

After the data is captured, we know nothing more than before. That's why the most important activity is to translate this data into usable information and

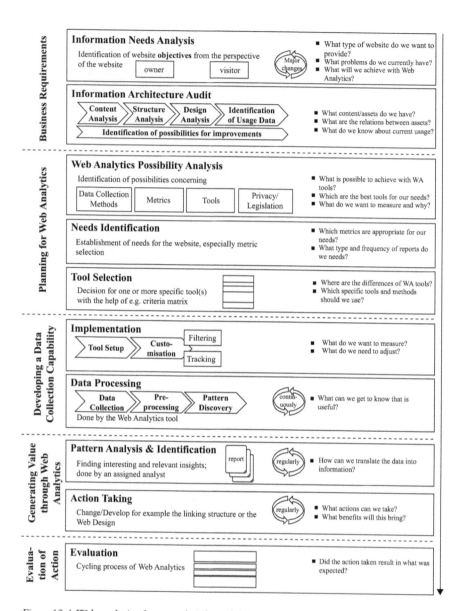

Figure 12.1 Web analytics framework (adapted from Hausmann et al., 2012)

generate reports for visualisation. Only when taking actions from the results is it possible to benefit from web analytics (Phase 4).

In order to evaluate your initiatives – such as marketing campaigns, website developments or your web analytics programme itself – you should compare expectations with results, and start the whole process again by identifying changes and setting a new goal for the next round.

12.5 Key performance indicators for small and medium enterprises when using *Google* Analytics

Why key performance indicators?

The goal of web Analytics is to get insights into the usage behaviour of your potential customers on websites and social platforms, so that you can then adapt your own digital offerings according to customer needs. Defined measurable attributes can be used to gain these insights. In Web Analytics these attributes are called metrics (Hassler, 2010, p. 90), and the most important metrics for your organisation are called KPIs.

How do you find and use key performance indicators?

Your KPIs depend on the goals of your organisation, and they might change over time as your company changes or sets new goals. KPIs can and should be quite different depending on the kind of website you are looking at. For example, personal, commercial, organisational, informational and political websites all have different purposes in what they want to achieve (Crowder and Crowder, 2008). Most common for organisational marketing are organisational websites, where information about the organisation itself is given, and commercial websites, which include online shops and/or are set up to generate profit. For those websites, KPIs are often very financial in nature and take into account the revenue. Nevertheless, all organisations are asking the same challenging question:

What should be measured and how do you measure success?

By looking into the literature and testing different web analytics tools, you will find hundreds of different metrics. Very basic, well-known and commonly used metrics include the following:

- Page view: the number of times an individual page was visited.
- Most viewed page: most popular page.
- Visitors: number of people visiting the site; difference between total visitors, unique visitors and session and cookies.
- Visit duration: time spent on the website per visitor.
- Referrer: shows the source where user came from to visit the site.
- Entry and exit page: shows the starting and the leaving page of a visit.
- Completion/order conversion rate: percentage that conducted a purchase.
- Path analysis: shows how a user clicked through the links on a site.

However, depending on the website type you will have more specific KPIs such as conversion rate, customer loyalty or bounce rate for commercial websites. The list of metrics is long, and the above only gives a sample. In addition, the names as well as the calculation of the different metrics vary according to the specific tools. However, as long as you understand what is included in the metrics, and as long as the numbers you compare over time are from the same tool, this does not really matter.

In order to give more details on how to use KPIs we will concentrate on *Google* Analytics. Why *Google* Analytics? As outlined before, *Google* Analytics is the most used web analytics tool in the world. It is free of charge and thus easy to use for small and medium enterprises (SMEs), for whom financial resources are often limited. It is not the aim of this chapter to outline all available KPIs for web analytics, but instead to offer an impression of how you can find out which metrics are available and work out which are best for you.

General information and support for *Google* Analytics can be found on the *Google* Support page (Google Support, 2016). When starting web analytics with *Google* Analytics you will get first measurements directly after you have registered and placed the snipped code onto your website and the first users have visited your website.

NOTE: Dependent on your website content management systems (CMS), this process could be as simple as pasting your GA code into a *Google* Analytics setup on your system. For example, a commonly used CMS is *WordPress*, and to enable *Google* Analytics on it is simply a case of pasting the GA number, which updates the code on each web page.

You will then have the possibility to customise your own dashboard and/or use the predefined structured metrics and reports:

*   Audience – who is looking at your site?
*   Behaviour – how are they browsing?
*   Acquisition – where did your users come from?

If, later, you have defined website conversion goals, etc. you can find them within the section Conversions. All sections are customisable. Figure 12.2 shows an example of the standard *Google* Analytics layout and menu, and Figure 12.3 shows a behaviour flow of an example website.

When using *Google* Analytics you will come across Universal Analytics as well. Universal Analytics enables you to gather customer data across multiple platforms and devices, and it increases the possibilities for metrics. However, all data is imported into your *Google* Analytics accounts, which by now are completely integrated with each other.

When defining KPIs, there are a few general things which should be kept in mind:

*   KPIs are quantitative and often have a monetary value, e.g. turnover.
*   As long as you are not comparing to your own historical data, try to avoid absolute numbers; KPIs should be ratios or percentages.
*   KPIs should be time-based.
*   Different stakeholders might be interested in different KPIs, e.g. e-commerce, webmaster, customer support.
*   The KPIs should be aligned to your business goals.
*   KPIs should meet the following characteristics: relevant, well defined, understandable, usable, comparable, testable, cost effective and efficient.

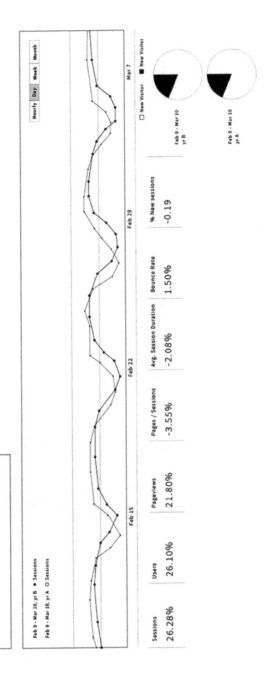

Figure 12.2 Google Analytics design

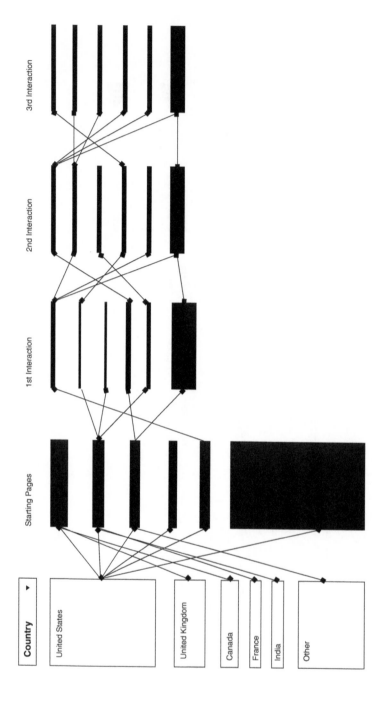

Figure 12.3 Behaviour flow

12.6 Designing web analytics reports that meet business needs

Custom reports help you to filter your gathered web analytics data.

Case Study 12.1 *Enterprise 2.0* uses web analytics to redesign starting page

The website www.e20cases.org is a platform which presents case studies around the topic *Enterprise 2.0*. The publishers and editors of the site are various groups from universities within Austria, Germany and Switzerland. The goal of the website is to document case studies in which social software is used in organisations in order to transfer and enrich the developed knowledge into research, and across and between interested organisations.

The website is an informational website and has no commercial aims. It is set up with the open source CMS *WordPress*. Even though web analytics was running on the site for a while, no one was examining the data until a student project took over responsibility for the web analytics data.

By analysing the gathered data, it became obvious though an in-page analysis that many links on the starting page were not used at all, and the ones which were used often were further down the page. In order to provide a better overview, and to better show which topics are included on the page, a restructured starting page was designed and tested for two months.

The data collected in the testing phase of the new design of the website was then compared to the previous collected data in order to see the differences. Two significant results were found: 1) within the testing period several links were used which previously had not been clicked on for the two years that analytics was tracking the site, and 2) the descent rate was reduced by 12.63 per cent.

Source: www.e20cases.org

12.7 Meaningful reporting and campaign tracking

Nowadays, businesses use digital media advertising in order to increase the awareness of their brand. It is vital to track those campaigns in order to understand whether the resources invested in a particular digital campaign are having efficient results and are contributing towards the realisation of business goals (Chaffey and Ellis–Chadwick, 2012).

The first aspect to be considered is having proper campaign tracking and reporting. Without this, it is impossible to accurately collect campaign data that will allow the occurrence of analysis and optimisation. Beginning to use campaign tracking across the entire organisation will provide significantly better data about the age, gender, cultural background, needs and wants and opinions of potential customers, as well as how many people click on the particular digital marketing page. In order to achieve this, some KPIs that could be established include search engine ranking, site traffic, new/returning traffic and mobile traffic (Rowles, 2015).

There are various tools available for campaign tracking. One of these is *Google* Analytics, which provides audience demographics to referral sources, and gives you a solid breakdown of how people are finding the particular website, what's getting the most attention and the amount of time they spend on your website. *Google* Analytics even tracks the traffic patterns people take within the website.

Another popular tool is *Facebook* Insights. This monitors how many people view particular social media posts, the number of clicks each post receives and how many times people are sharing the posts with others. It also gives a breakdown of the different demographics of the page's *Facebook* network (Rowles, 2015). Similar popular tools include *LinkedIn* Insights, *YouTube* Analytics and *Hootsuite*.

Proper campaign tracking will give the company reports about its most valuable networks, how much social media contributes to the overall visits of the website and information about landing pages, which will allow the company to gain significant knowledge of the market and build a competitive advantage (Linnell, 2011).

12.8 Digital campaign tracking – UTM codes

Urchin Tracking Module (UTM) parameters (UTM codes) are short texts which are added to the end of a URL in order to depict and track the success of particular marketing campaign content on the Web. There are five parameters of UTM:

- Campaign (utm_campaign): Identifies a specific promotion or a strategic campaign, and groups all of the content from one campaign in your analytics.
- Source (utm_source): Which website is the source of the traffic (e.g. search engines, newsletters, etc.).
- Medium (utm_medium): The type of marketing medium that the link is used in.
- Content (utm_content): Used to track the different types of content that point to the same URL from the same campaign, source and medium codes. Often used in pay-per-click (PPC) or with two identical links on the same page.
- Term (utm_term): Used to identify the keywords you've paid for in a PPC ad.

Once a particular link is clicked, the tags are sent to different tracking tools. Using these codes allows companies to assess the effectiveness of digital campaigns and identify how to increase the number of visitors to the website. For example, UTM parameters can be used to see how much traffic came from a particular *Facebook* post rather than the general website traffic. On a particular *Twitter* account the companies can tag the tweets and compare these to the overall website referrals (Chaffey and Ellis-Chadwick, 2012).

However, UTM parameters have some drawbacks, one of which is parameter order. The UTM URL has to come before any additional tracking parameters, and if the order is mixed up the performance will not be properly accessed. Another disadvantage is 301 redirects. These can strip the particular tracking of URL and categorises PPC into organic or direct (Polivka, 2014).

Regardless of the drawbacks, UTM codes are irreplaceable in tracking digital marketing campaigns, and provide sufficient information about minimising costs on advertising and reducing time spent on campaigns (Ellsworth, 2013).

Useful tips and tools to consider are:

- *Google* Analytics – if the content appears on your own website, ensure that all content is tracked using *Google* Analytics to be able to easily and effectively monitor traffic sources and volumes, as well as bounce rates and time spent on the site.
- Event Tracking/Thank You Pages – ensure your link elements have been tracked with event tracking and that any thank you pages have tracking on them also (Seoweather, 2016).
- UTM Tracking – You can generate custom campaign parameters for your URLs to easily isolate your campaigns in *Google* Analytics (Google Support, 2016).

12.9 Ethical dilemmas in marketing research and data collection

Marketing research, measurement and evaluation in the digital environment raise even more sharply the issue of ethics, related to the interaction between the communicator and consumer. Now companies and organisations possess new and developed tools both for data collection and marketing research, and some of them are definitely not ethical, and at the very least can be seen as controversial. Therefore, the constantly developing practices in this field need to be structured, and some limitations should be implemented – this is usually done by professional associations in digital marketing and/or in marketing research on a country level.

The ethical considerations in digital marketing research are closely related to the concept of privacy – currently the hottest issue when talking about consumer protection in the digital environment. In order not only to protect the interests of people from misuse of their personal data but also to motivate them to engage and interact online, it is becoming even more important for digital marketers to follow ethical behaviour and to protect consumer privacy.

Therefore, four aspects of information exchange (interactions) between marketers and consumers where ethical dilemmas can arise can be highlighted (Milne, 2000):

- Information requests and disclosure statements: made by marketers – explicitly asking for information by registration and others.
- Information provision and marketing contact: volunteered information exchange by consumers with subsequent contact by marketers – filling in surveys, participation in campaigns, etc.
- Information capturing without consent: observed information gathered by marketers that is not volunteered by consumers – collecting information for visits and online behaviour, including leaving cookies.
- Information practices: uses of information by both marketers and consumers – personalisation software and others.

To summarise, consumer privacy can be seen as enhanced when consumers are aware of information practices and given a choice over information provision and use. On the contrary, consumer privacy can be seen as decreased and ethical issues emerge when there is unwanted marketing contact of information gathering without consent.

The ethical dilemmas in marketing research, like all ethical dilemmas in marketing, are being solved based on the professionalism and personal attitude of marketing or research specialists. However, to contribute to this process, three main aspects can be outlined – informed consent, access and data protection. Consumers and respondents should be properly informed about everything that might influence their decision to get involved. Regarding the access, it is clear that digital marketing research tools provide more opportunities to get involved in a particular study or campaign. However, it should not be discriminative or designed in such a way as to give preferences to people with better access than others. And finally, data protection is perhaps the biggest ethical consideration to be taken into account. The researcher should ensure that everything is password protected and encrypted, so as to avoid misuse of information.

12.10 Quantitative data analysis methods

Moving forward from the point where marketers have their hands on the data collected through web analytics, it is of high importance to understand the several statistical methods that can be used in order to interpret such massive amounts of quantitative data. Nevertheless, even with the big amounts of data collected through analytics, the limitations of quantitative data analysis are still sufficient to prevent one from properly understanding the buyer, and this is why extra qualitative approaches are required. To this end, this subsection will focus on quantitative methods and topics, while the next will present several qualitative methods that can be used to triangulate with the quantitative methods in order to lead to more accurate buyer-related observations/facts.

Regression analysis

Regression analysis is divided into two categories: linear and multiple regression. Linear regression analysis is used to identify the value of a variable while the value of the other variable is known (example: identify the effect of buyer preference for a specific buyer age group). Multiple regression analysis is used to identify the value of a variable when two or more other variables are known (also called predictors). To achieve this, a hypothesis for the type of relationship is made, and proximate values are assessed in relation to the parameters in order to establish an estimated regression equation. The multiple regression equation can be tested using the coefficient of determination (r^2), which always ranges between 0 and 1 (Lind et al., 2010).

Correlation analysis

Correlation analysis is a technique that examines if two variables are related to each other and to what extent they are related. To examine this, the correlation coefficient (r) is used. The value of (r) represents the strength of the relationship (i.e. -0.1 to 0.1 means there is no relationship or the relationship is very weak). However, it should be noted that the correlation coefficient only measures linear relationships between variables (Lind et al., 2010).

Sample size

Sample size refers to the individual units of data collected in a survey. It is crucial to determine the accuracy and reliability of a survey's outcomes (Anderson et al., 2010). However, the sample size can never reflect the real values unless a census of the population is conducted. This is not just expensive, but also impossible. Therefore, surveys are usually based on a small proportion of the population, which makes them less reliable. This is called sampling error. Non-sampling errors occur when due to systematic or random factors (i.e. selection bias) the outcomes do not reflect the 'true' value for the entire population (Anderson et al., 2010). Nevertheless, in the case of web analytics, the sample size is generally large and thus this should not be considered a primary area of concern.

Hypothesis testing

Hypothesis testing is a statistical process for determining if a null hypothesis should be accepted or rejected in comparison to an alternative hypothesis related to a survey or test result (Aczel, 2009). In order to determine the significance level of the test, the null hypothesis is tested at 5 per cent. If null hypothesis is rejected at 5 per cent, the test moves to 1 per cent. If the null hypothesis is still rejected, then the result is 'highly significant'; if it is not rejected, the test result is 'significant'. If the null hypothesis is rejected at 5 per cent, the test moves to 10 per cent, and if it is still rejected, then the result of the test is 'weakly significant'; if not, the test result is 'not significant' (Aczel, 2009).

12.11 Qualitative data analysis methods

Focus groups

Focus groups refer to groups of individuals who are assembled to provide feedback on the plausibility of a product, service or campaign. Although this might be effective in some cases, it may also not reflect the opinion of the larger target population (Onwuegbuzië et al., 2009). However, focus groups may be used as an option to validate (from an expert's point of view) the findings of quantitative analysis of web analytics, for example.

Interviews

Interviewing includes asking questions and receiving responses from the participants in a survey. Interviews can be structured, semi-structured or not structured, and can be either face-to-face individual or group interviewing or via other communication channels. Although interviews can lead to extracting valuable amounts of information, the quality of the responses can be questionable, as participants might offer responses they consider the interviewer will appreciate. This is called 'the interviewer effect' (Edwards and Holland, 2013). However, as with focus groups, this technique can prove useful to cross-validate quantitative findings.

Online ethnography

Cyber-ethnography refers to the adaptation of ethnographic methods to the research and analysis of the communities and cultures created through computer-mediated social interaction. There are several methods to conduct cyber-ethnography, including observation, field diary, participatory choices, storing conversations, content and discourse analysis (Murthy, 2008; Akturan, 2009). This can prove useful to cross-check quantitative findings; however, such a technique might be biased towards the attitudes/opinions of the performer.

12.12 Summary

This chapter has highlighted the wealth of data about your customers that is now available through evaluating and tracking the online consumer journey. By understanding basic metrics and their correlations with business objectives, by using the techniques discussed above and by taking action to apply them to your business, SMEs are now in an ideal position to develop successful brands and campaigns that are constantly evolving and improving in line with their customers' needs and expectations. To the same extent, adopting, in an ethical manner, research methodologies and practices towards analysing/tracking consumer behaviour is also presented as a core objective of today's digital marketers.

12.13 References

Aczel, Amir D. (ed.) (2009) *Complete Business Statistics*. McGraw-Hill Higher Education.

Akturan, U. (2009) A Review of Cyber Ethnographic Research: A Research Technique to Analyze Virtual Consumer Communities. *Bogazici Journal*, 23(1–2), 1–18.

Anderson, D., Sweeney, D. and Williams-Rochester, T. (eds) (2010) *Statistics for Business and Economics*. South-Western Cengage Learning.

Burby, J. and Atchison, S. (2007) *Actionable Web Analytics: Using Data to Make Smart Business Decisions*. Wiley Publishing.

Chaffey, Dave and Ellis-Chadwick, Fiona (eds) (2012) *Digital Marketing Strategy Implementation and Practice*. Pearson Education Limited.

Cooley, R., Mobasher, B. and Srivastava, J. (1997) *Web Mining: Information and Pattern Discovery on the World Wide Web*. IEEE.

Crowder, P. and Crowder, D.A. (2008) *Creating Web Sites Bible*. Wiley Publishing.

Digital Analytics Association (2006) Description. www.digitalanalyticsassociation.org/mission-vision

Edwards, R. and Holland, J. (2013) *What Is Qualitative Interviewing?* Graham Crow, University of Edinburgh.

Ellsworth, J. (2013) *Marketing on the Internet*. John Wiley & Sons, Inc.

Gassman, B. (2011) *Web Analytics Market Update*. Gartner Group.

Google Support (2016) http://support.google.com/analytics/

Hassler, M. (2010) *Web Analytics: Metriken auswerten, Besucherverhalten verstehen, Webseiten optimieren*. MITP-Verlags GmbH & Co.

Hausmann, V., Williams, S.P. and Schubert, P. (2012) *Developing a Framework for Web Analytics*. http://aisel.aisnet.org/bled2012/11

Hendriyani, J., Ceng, L., Utami, N., Priskila, R. and Anggita, S. (2013) Online Consumer Behavior: Confirming the AISAS Model on Twitter Users. In the *Proceedings of the International Conference on Social and Political Sciences* (ICSPS) 2013, Karawaci, West Java, 25–26 February.

Kart, L. and Kihn, M. (2014) *Market Guide for Web Analytics*. Gartner Group.

Lind, D., Marchal, W. and Wathen, S. (eds) (2010) *Statistical Techniques in Business and Economics*. McGraw-Hill Higher Education.

Linnell, N. (2011) *Campaign Tracking: A Vital Analytics Tool for Marketers*. Chlickz Group Limited.

Lovett, J., Doty, C., Sehgal, V., Vittal, S. and Murphy, E. (2009) *US Web Analytics Forecast, 2008 to 2014*. Forrester Research.

Milne, G. (2000) Privacy and Ethical Issues in Database/Interactive Marketing and Public Policy: A Research Framework and Overview of the Special Issue. *Journal of Public Policy and Marketing*, 19(1), 1–6.

Murthy, D. (2008) Digital Ethnography: An Examination of the Use of New Technologies for Social Research. *Sociology*, 42(5), 837–55.

Norguet, J.-P., Zimányi, E. and Steinberger, R. (2006) *Improving Web Sites with Web Usage Mining, Web Content Mining, and Semantic Analysis*. Springer, pp. 430–9.

Onwuegbuzie, A.J., Dickinson, W., Leech, N. and Zoran, A. (2009) A Qualitative Framework for Collecting and Analyzing Data in Focus Group Research. *International Journal of Qualitative Methods*, 8(3), 1–21.

Polivka, J. (2014) *Introduction to UTM Parameters and Best Practices.* The Hangar.

Rowles, D. (2015) *Digital Marketing Toolkit, Target Internet.* www.targetinternet.com/resources/DigitalMarketingToolkit.pdf

Seoweather (2016) *Google Analytics Event Tracking Code Generator Website.* www.seoweather.com/google-analytics-event-tracking-code-generator/

13 Future users, content and marketing

Gordon Fletcher, Salford Business School, University of Salford, UK

Alexander Christov, University of National and World Economy (UNWE), Bulgaria

13.0 Learning objectives

In this chapter you will learn how to:

- consider the future of digital business;
- recognise activities in an organisation that will make them become fully digital;
- understand future trends;
- recognise future business models that will respond to future trends.

13.1 Introduction

In this chapter we explore the future of digital marketing with a discussion of the Digital Business Maturity Model. This model can be applied to any organisation and any of its operations.

Positioning an organisation within the Digital Business Maturity Model recognises its current levels of digital activities – including marketing – as well as its future potential. Identifying an organisation's current digital business maturity in relation to its current strategic position also offers a clear understanding of the progression route required to achieve even greater levels of digital maturity. Digital maturity should itself be considered a desirable, if not essential, development trajectory for any organisation. The relationship that the Digital Business Maturity Model introduces between strategic perspectives and the combined threats and opportunities of digital technologies for an organisation is significant. Holding and maintaining a strategic understanding of your current situation is as much a challenge for many organisations as keeping pace with technological change. However, in a world that is increasingly digital, a strategic perspective will serve the combined beneficial purposes of avoiding short-term decision making and preventing fire-fighting approaches to the day-to-day management of your organisation. Being strategic also lifts your perspective above a desire to just 'use' the current, favourite social media channel or newest technological devices towards a recognition of the need to continuously engage your buyer persona through digital channels. Overall, the Digital Business Maturity Model presents the need for greater integrated use of technology within your organisation as part of wider, more systemic change to processes and management. In the long term, this approach will give you new efficiencies, redefine your employees' roles (if you have any) and present your entire organisation as an engaged component of the global digital economy.

13.2 The Digital Business Maturity Model

Informally, your digital maturity can be measured through the regularity with which your actions and your organisation's functions – including marketing – are prefixed with a label indicating that they are 'digital' (or 'e', 'i' or even 'cyber'). As a rule of thumb, the greater the digital maturity of an organisation, the less often a special case needs to be made for being digital. An extreme example of this can be experienced when friends or colleagues insist on using the term 'electronic mail' rather than 'email' or even 'mail', which shows how the process of embedding technology within an organisation occurs over time. Positioning your organisation's strategy for greater levels of digital maturity also allows for management reflection. More specifically, this reflection can reveal how far your organisation's digital maturity is ahead of your current buyer persona. This reflection will, in turn, assist in explaining why an organisation cannot always immediately reap the rewards of its current investment in technology or its commitment to organisational change. Organisations that are lagging behind the experience, knowledge and expectations of their current buyer persona risk losing to more dynamic, newer and potentially more aggressive competitors.

There are five stages of the Digital Business Maturity Model (Figure 13.1). At the base of the model there is no digital activity or engagement. The organisation is effectively off the Web, cannot be found through social media and does not conduct any of its functions through digital channels. A proxy for these organisations having their own web presence can be found in online directories that are analogous with the traditional *Yellow Pages*. But, as with this older form of print media, online directories are of little value to these organisations. These presentations are automatically created for organisations through common simple templates that primarily benefit the business creating the directories rather than those being represented. In many cases these businesses have only minimal involvement in the creation of their own entry, further reducing the benefits of any messaging. The business of online directories currently exploits organisations that are at this base level of digital maturity. As more organisations leave this level of digital maturity behind, the value of the business model of online directories will also fall away. However, with up to 50 per cent of small businesses still offline in the UK – and higher proportions elsewhere – the demise of online directories as a proxy for web presence is still many years away.

The next stage of digital maturity sees an organisation become visible online through, for example, a website, a blog or a *Facebook* page. This second stage

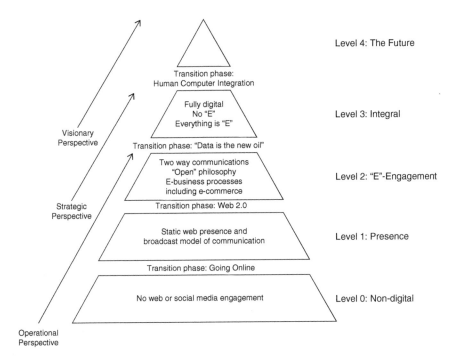

Figure 13.1 The Digital Business Maturity Model

of the Digital Business Maturity Model is described as having 'presence'. At the core of presence activity is a 'broadcast' view of the relationship between an organisation and the buyer persona. Broadcast modes of communication involve sending messages out to the world with only minimal differentiation or consideration for the differences that exist between the many types of customers and prospects. In the Buyer Persona Spring, organisations at this level of maturity equate the buyer persona with all users. If some knowledge and understanding of customers *does* exist within the organisation, there is no differentiation in the messages being broadcast.

The limited capability and capacity of early information and communications technologies (ICTs) was originally a barrier for creating and managing differentiated engagement with multiple buyer personas. The earliest movers in digital business, who now have a presence that stretches from the 1990s, had to recognise these early limitations, and worked around them or produced innovations as a response. However, both the technology of the Internet and those early adopters have now moved on significantly from these early and tentative starting points. Conventional web presence can now be supplemented by more recent technologies, including the use of Quick Response (QR) codes – presented as static devices on printed media that link consumers to an online presence and primarily equivalent in purpose to a printed URL.

More commonly within Level 1 of the Digital Business Maturity Model there are many examples of traditional methods of brand building being translated into a digital realm. For example, *Google* AdWords, with its obvious and direct analogy to traditional display advertising in broadcast and print media, is a hallmark of a broadcast-focused web presence. *Facebook*'s advertising model also conceptually exploits this same business model. The advantage of *Google* and *Facebook* advertising is the built-in capacity to target prospective customers with a greater degree of accuracy and to produce reports that are more accurate than traditional forms of advertising.

All these forms of technology enhance straightforward presence without extending the form of interactions. A solely broadcast presence simply amplifies the reach of your content. Organisations that recognise the limitations of a broadcast presence and the low level of engagement with the buyer persona that conventional advertising brings are also organisations that are ready to progress to higher levels of digital maturity. In contrast to straightforward broadcasting techniques are those technologies that can be added to a current web presence and can extend the type and volume of interaction with the buyer persona. At the same time, moving towards two-way conversation and engagement is a hallmark of an organisation's move to the next level of digital maturity.

The third level of the Digital Business Maturity Model consciously designs and embeds two-way interactions between the organisation and its buyer persona. The organisation is also engaging with more of its stakeholders, including suppliers, regulatory bodies and potentially competitors, through digital communications, even if this engagement may initially be confined to emails. Interaction between the buyer persona and the organisation at this stage of digital maturity is most commonly recognised as a form of e-commerce – it is also regularly described in technology terms as Web 2.0 – with the conscious 'designing in' of engagement with a clearly defined buyer persona. The key step forward at this stage of digital maturity is epitomised by the difference between a *Facebook* page that solely communicates information and a constantly staffed *Twitter* account through which two-way (and three-way) communications happen rapidly and openly with genuine, trusted responses from the organisation.

At this stage of digital maturity there is at least some recognition that 'the digital' in the form of different ICTs has had a significant impact on all aspects of the organisation. The buyer persona is increasingly regarded as an active participant in the organisation's activities and not solely a passive consumer. This level of digital maturity also brings an awareness of, if not full engagement with, an 'open' business philosophy and the practices of co-creation and co-production at the overall level of the brand, as well as through individual goods and services. Considering this definition, it is evident that many organisations have a level of digital maturity that sits between simple presence and genuine engagement. Having recognised the limitations of only maintaining a presence, these organisations must build their capacity and alter their view to fully enter the engagement level of digital maturity.

There is a challenge to becoming a fully engaged digital business and it is not without its hazards. For many organisations there is a tendency to drift back to 'old ways'. Traditional multinational brands that have already attempted to engage customers through co-creation have shown a tendency to reduce the process to familiar marketing techniques and to present the process as, for example, a superficial time-limited competition. *Walker's Crisps* in the UK have regularly run large-scale television advertising and social media campaigns to promote a competition that allows customers to design their own flavour of crisps. The 2014 winner received £1 million for proposing 'Pulled Pork in a Sticky BBQ Sauce'. However, there are indications that the process is not one of co-creation. The corporate website that announced the winner prevented cutting and pasting content, and featured a large warning announcing that the website's content is copyright protected. These are not the sentiments of a company open to adopting an engagement level of digital maturity.

There is also a tendency to regard businesses built entirely around an e-commerce model as being fully engaged digital organisations. For example, *Amazon*, *Spreadshirt* and *Etsy* have all been described in terms which suggest they are to be regarded as fully engaged digital businesses. However, this misleads other organisations seeking engagement and their buyer persona as a co-creator. For each of these aforementioned businesses the mechanism that enables customer customisation and co-creation occurs through a model of structural franchising. *Amazon* stores take advantage of both the technical infrastructure and the brand the company has built up in order to present goods within the systematised *Amazon* framework. *Amazon* stores are, in effect, tenants in an online shopping centre, and so how, or whether, *Amazon* engage with their customers will vary from experience to experience, though everything is mediated by the *Amazon* system, which requires a certain level of service that is monitored through feedback services.

Apparel company *Spreadshirt* also offers a technical infrastructure that allows individuals and small businesses to present their own products. However, this means that the mechanisms for customer engagement and co-creation are entirely mediated by the predefined infrastructure of the *Spreadshirt* system. *Etsy*, too, works on a similar model, except that the franchise holders of *Etsy* create their own products.

In contrast, organisations that understand co-creation is a more comprehensive and longer-term relationship with customers and suppliers take advantage of external stakeholders to reach the next stage of the Digital Business Maturity Model. Examples of genuine engagement of customers by small organisations can readily be identified. Many of these examples – perhaps unsurprisingly – are based around a social enterprise or charitable mission. This engagement necessitates that the customer is actively involved in the functions of the organisation in a way that goes beyond their participation in a single straightforward purchase.

The Moss Cider Project (http://themossciderproject.org/) in the south Manchester suburb of Moss Side brews cider from apples gathered from across

Manchester by future customers. Those who bring in apples or help with the production process are rewarded with credits against the final products – either apple juice or brewed cider. Customers and local residents are engaged through a dedicated website and *Facebook* presence, and the project has received considerable amounts of local press coverage. Importantly, the project web pages include statements asserting openness about the ingredients and process used to produce the cider. The project requires a digital model to function, as the number of apples required to produce viable quantities of juice or cider requires a vast geographic range for gathering raw ingredients that extends beyond what more traditional methods of community communications could achieve.

The fourth level of the Digital Business Maturity Model embraces the adage that 'data is the new oil'. The recognition in this statement is that all interactions with internal and external stakeholders are opportunities to accumulate and aggregate data. This level of digitally mature business attempts to extract intelligence and actively learn from the volumes of data that are being gathered. This 'integrated' stage of the Digital Business Maturity Model finds and stores data from every interaction and engagement and regards this data – irrespective of its current meaning and understanding – as being valuable to the organisation. The large-scale collection of data can already be evidenced in many organisations, where it precedes the recognition or understanding of the value of what is being gathered. Early examples of data-driven business actions are the various supermarket loyalty card schemes, particularly schemes that span multiple businesses such as the *Nectar* card in the UK. However, these schemes are themselves not representative of this level of digital maturity, but instead should be considered an early vanguard towards complete business integration and awareness.

Examples of organisations that have recognised the importance of data and its flow between traditionally separate business functions are more difficult to recognise when these organisations are small or the data they manipulate has a degree of sensitivity, e.g. if it is primarily personal data. St Patrick's College in London (www.st-patricks.ac.uk/) is a small private college of further and higher education that has operated for many years. The UK Government heavily regulates private education providers and places significant data-gathering and management requirements upon each of these colleges to track and monitor individual students. The significant administrative burden that this places on what are generally small business operations has contributed to the demise of many providers.

St Patrick's is noteworthy in that it expanded in a period of heavy scrutiny. This expansion was due, in part, to an early recognition of the pivotal importance of data in day-to-day operations. Data was everywhere at St Patrick's, including the student registry, learning managements systems and external-facing web and social media presences. As a result, St Patrick's utilises a fully integrated business and information system, where prospective students making an enquiry through the website have their data stored in the same system from their initial point of enquiry through attendance monitoring until they become an alumni. This not only brings efficiencies for the college in its registration and monitoring processes, but also enables the potential for comprehensive reporting about any individual student from the date and time of their individual enquiry through to the day they arrived at the college, the grades they received for individual assessment items and the award with which they left.

In recognising the way that data flows continuously throughout the organisation, the organisation at this level of digital maturity has moved far beyond straightforward transactional relationships. Communication between stakeholders is integrated with the systems that require the data, and systems that were intended for external customers might now also be deployed for internal use – and vice versa. St Patrick's College is again an indicative example of the conceptual breakdown in what were traditionally separate business functions and the decoupling of an individual business function from a specific mechanism for that function. For the college, all online enquiries flow through a single web portal. Prospective students, current students, prospective lecturers and other business enquiries all utilise the same contact point, which is then routed through the college's system to the most appropriate respondent. Other examples of this blurring of intended usage and application include the use of wiki systems for corporate knowledge management or microblogging systems for internal business communications. The popularity of *WordPress* as a platform for content management systems (CMSs) for small businesses also breaks down the distinction between external and internal communications and information needs. An organisation with this degree of digital maturity will inevitably be affected by organisational change. The results are seen in changes in employee role and in management hierarchy, as well as efficiencies, both planned and unexpected, being recognised and embraced by the organisation.

There are inevitably negative impacts in this development of digital maturity, too. The negative impacts of digital maturity can be seen within the human factors of an organisation, and specifically within the change in business culture that such a business – one that has progressed through the earlier stages of digital maturity – must experience. Effective business systems can reduce the need for tasks currently completed by employees, but they can equally raise the need for other, new and higher-level tasks. The impact of digital maturity will require some employees to re-skill or re-train entirely. More challenging within a business is the need for employees to give up existing practice and the certainty of regularised work patterns and well-defined regular work outputs in exchange for degrees of flexibility and, consequently, uncertainty.

13.3 Future work

Greenhill and Fletcher (2013) describe the difference between the demands and expectations of semantic and syntactic labour. Syntactic labour is the regularised, repeated work that is best represented by factory work, but can be seen in many work environments. The digitally mature business has released the need for human labour to complete day-to-day syntactic labour tasks. In place of this work comes the requirement for additional semantic labour – the processing of complex and incomplete data to a conclusion. Digital technology can deliver incomplete information and potentially even recognise this data as being incomplete, but the ability for a system to efficiently manage this incompleteness is limited and requires human intervention. This changing requirement reflects the need for new job roles and also offers at least a preliminary explanation as to why call centres are rightly and increasingly described as the factories of the digital era.

With the Internet of Things, the need for humans to complete syntactic labour is further reduced, as inanimate objects autonomously interrelate with systems and aggregate the data of an organisation in the same way that people can retrieve business intelligence. From an organisational perspective, the Internet of Things is not simply reduced, for example, to a smart light bulb. The Internet of Things enables simple two-way communication and a range of interactions directly between different things, as well as between individual things and employees or your buyer persona. The future prospect is that these relationships with things will reach a form of transparency allowing two-, three- and more-way engagements between connected things and connected people.

An example of this prospect is the driverless delivery van that will directly communicate with a customer's house and the business's warehouse to facilitate delivery arrangements. The planned delivery might be interrupted in transit by a sudden change in the client's diary that now requires alternative delivery arrangements to be made to their home instead of to their place of work. Similarly, in a domestic setting, a dinner meeting might be moved back 30 minutes to allow the host to visit a virtual wine shop and arrange immediate delivery, as the home cellar has reported that there are no suitable bottles of wine available for the planned menu. The integrated stage of digital maturity still remains at least partially speculative on a day-to-day level.

The greatest challenge to the achievement of this level of digital maturity is the twinned preparedness by an organisation to reduce the constraints created by current practices and processes, and equally to avoid 'cargo cult' responses to the observable activities of competitors. The Theory of Constraints paradigm identifies that an organisational constraint within the existing system can be turned into an opportunity that can be exploited to gain competitive advantage. Cargo cult thinking, in contrast, acts as a warning, particularly to smaller organisations, to avoid assuming that imitating external observable factors and readily identifiable features of success in another organisation will automatically impart the same levels of success in their own. Small businesses are particularly prone to this combination of allowing existing constraints to override their ability to innovate and change, and of assuming that copying the practices of others will bring tangible benefits to themselves. For example, a local corner store in Salford brands itself in blue and red and is named *Tecco* in an obvious imitation of the more familiar international *Tesco* brand. Another overly simple example of this combined tension is the race among more digitally conscious small businesses to have their own 'app', even though the strategic purpose or immediate benefits of an app may be of marginal advantage at best. Here, cargo cult thinking is used as a substitute for having a clear strategy.

Beyond the integrated third level of the Digital Business Maturity Model – with its incorporation of the exploitation of the Internet of Things – the model becomes more speculative. The final stage of the Digital Business Maturity Model represents the visionary future of an organisation with still greater degrees of uncertainty. If we extrapolate from the current trajectories of technology development, it points to closer human–computer integration, with the prospect of an Internet of Connected Humans and, more speculatively, a completely clickable world.

At this final level of digital maturity, a range of technologies will offer new opportunities, including:

- virtual reality;
- augmented reality;
- wearables and implantables;
- telepathic technologies.

All of these technologies will first fire the imagination of games developers before having a more nuanced impact on business functions and operations. Already, the expectation of young people born into our digital age is that everything is responsive to the clicks or swipes pioneered through current touchscreen interfaces, and that all 'things' will necessarily respond positively to this type of regularised interaction. These current trajectories of development will increasingly have a significant impact on marketing strategy. Marketing will become ever more personalised through algorithms and data matching, a trend that has first been explored through cookies and retargeting in web-based interactions. The true personalisation of the customer experience will be focused around individual preferences rather than – as is currently the case – the accumulated histories and cookies stored on each connected device or through the stored actions of logged-in users.

To manage the complexity of buyer persona behaviours, their traits and behaviours will be classified around typical and atypical actions. This is a subtle but pivotal distinction between current marketing and future marketing. Technology still remains a limiting factor in fully engaging with customers when each of their potentially many devices are disconnected and disjointed from one another. Ultimately, the behaviour of the buyer persona is, for the moment, a best guess of actions conducted on a range of separate devices.

Marketing, as a particular set of online practices, will become more closely allied with co-production. This will be distinct from the broader association that it currently has with sales and public relations. Individuals will be capable of designing their own goods and services to such an extent that individual businesses will only offer the templates and frameworks within which individualised production can safely and functionally operate. Perhaps unsurprisingly, software engineering has already recognised the advantages of this approach, with object-oriented methodologies, design patterns and reusable code librar-ies all providing robust building blocks for high-level customisation.

The approach has developed still further with the wide availability of public Application Programming Interfaces (APIs) for a range of services including *Facebook*, *Google* and *Twitter*. The result is that at least some of the success of all these services can be connected to the preparedness of these businesses to release some control over the way in which the services are presented to cus-tomers in favour of enabling other businesses to re-package and re-present their data in multiple different ways. Some 3D design and printing services already hint at this potential for fully customisable consumer products in relation to physical objects, by presenting catalogues of functional designs that can be cus-tomised in at least some way by the consumer before final print production.

In this newly emerging environment of digital business some functions will be reduced to the process of data transfer and will require data manipulation without any direct human intervention. With this resultant shift in organisa-tional processes and functions, new roles will emerge for employees that could be described as information curation tasks – the necessary addition of human semantic context as meaning making onto datasets in order to create informa-tion. The key change for an organisation, irrespective of its size, will be the degree of preparedness that exists internally to give up control of some of its business processes and functions. Control in this sense is not the action of outsourcing a function – the control relationship in this case is simply regu-larised, reduced and systematised into a contractual or service-level agreement. More importantly, it is control that is released towards the consumer and, more broadly, all external stakeholders. This release of control can only be satisfac-torily achieved when there is clear strategy and a clarity around the relation-ship of this strategy to a vision that directs and drives the organisation. Those operational processes and functions of the organisation that do not now con-tribute to creating a pathway towards the vision are superfluous. The functions of the business that do build the pathway to the vision require close and careful management. The aspects of the organisation that already represent part of the vision are prime opportunities to release control, but only to the extent that their manipulation does not distort the purpose and intent of the final vision.

Despite these many radical changes, a fully mature digital organisation of the present is (simply) what all organisations will look like in the future.

13.4 Future marketing ethics

Being digital and being a digital organisation is also transforming ethics. The most significant ethical issue for digital businesses will be the management, con-trol and security of personal data. Despite the discussions throughout this book about needing to connect more closely with your buyer persona, one of the main challenges for any organisation is overcoming the dehumanising aspect of technology and avoiding the temptation to reduce your buyer persona to a dataset that can be manipulated, measured and even experimented upon. The relationship between face-to-face interactions and computer-mediated interactions is not simple. In the early era of digital communications much time was spent arguing for its effect of distancing individuals from one another. However, computer-mediated communications increasingly draw people together as much as other forms of interaction. In this context, several important trends for future marketing ethics can be outlined.

Attention, authenticity and truth. Since your buyer persona's attention is becoming a dynamic variable and the competitive environment is increasing, organisations are being forced to act faster and more efficiently. This pressure produces a tendency for shortened and louder messaging. This pressure equally places a challenge on the organisation to remain fair and authentic. Expressing the truth, keeping a high informational value in each message and respecting the data privacy of consumers require time and space. In a high-pressure environment you should make even more effort to remain efficient and ethical. In order to maintain the prevalent advertising business model of the Internet, your marketing strategy must remain resolutely respectful and consider the experience of your buyer persona rather than viewing online activity as the achievement of a marketing strategy (Quigley, 2015).

Privacy and requests for consent. Increasing interaction online will continually raise the issue of user privacy. Gaining consent from your buyer persona to make two- and three-way interactions possible will become an increasingly important aspect of your strategy, campaigns and tactics. Content will remain 'king', but without consent your content will be heavily lopsided and appear very broadcast orientated – and ultimately be damaging to your authenticity.

Extreme opinion and user-generated content. The means to publish opinions, thoughts and streams of consciousness is now in the hands of any user. Web 2.0, the Interactive Web or the User Web – whichever term you prefer – encourages user-generated content. This content can represent a major challenge in the context of your owned channels – you cannot control this, but you must manage it. Various social media channels have also become a forum for expressing extreme opinions, including those directed to specific organisations. These opinions can spread virally. The ethical challenge for your organisation now, and in the future, will be to manage opinion. This will be achieved, in part, by maintaining a consistent image while remaining fair and transparent.

13.5 Interactive everything and the Internet of Things

The digital landscape presents a culture of interaction between people and between organisations. The tools for this interaction continue to expand in form, e.g. watches, phones and embedded devices. Simultaneously the forms of interaction also expand, e.g. car sharing, dating and room rental. The range of mechanisms, channels and forms of potential interaction will continue to expand outwards.

This expansion of channels and devices will create an exponential increase in the structured data that is captured from all online activities. The 'everything of everything' is now being created, as a network of structured data is leading to 'everything' being connected to 'everything' else. *Google* is increasingly a multimedia engine by indexing images, videos, apps, tweets and *Facebook* pages. While you cannot predict the future, using structured data for content publishing can prepare your organisation to move into the future without significant legacy problems.

The Internet of Things presents a very near future in which the objects of everyday life will be digital and able to communicate with one another, with your organisation and with your buyer persona. The Internet of Things will make marketing and interaction ever more immersive and pervasive. By enabling access and interaction with a wide variety of devices such as, for instance, home appliances, surveillance cameras, monitoring sensors, actuators, displays and vehicles, new services will emerge (Zanella et al., 2014). Undertaken correctly, the Internet of Things will improve our quality of life.

This is both a challenge and an opportunity for your organisation and your marketing strategy (Patel, 2015):

- On-demand services will be expected everywhere.
- New relationships will develop through improved data-driven decision making.
- Nothing will remain unmarketable.

The Internet of Things will shape the near future of your organisation, your buyer persona and your digital strategy.

13.6 Future business models and structures

As data becomes the new oil in an increasing number of organisations, the management and structure of the business will increasingly be informed and directed by its data. For the majority of organisations, data will become the most important asset. For some, data has already become their primary asset, but they are yet to recognise this pivotal fact and yet to base their strategies upon this recognition.

The framework for a future information strategy (Figure 13.2) does not explicitly identify marketing functions. This is, in part, because what are currently labelled as marketing processes and functions permeate the entire model. The future information strategy also removes the assumption that your organisation is both large and structurally divided into discrete departments with hierarchical management structures.

Management in small businesses can also defy neat mapping in a meaningful two-dimensional organisation chart. The challenge of being small in the era of digital business is to gain the understanding and perspective of larger brands and businesses without committing to the requirement for a long evolution through the Digital Business Maturity Model from pre-digital to higher levels. No organisation of any size wants to become involved in massive infrastructure

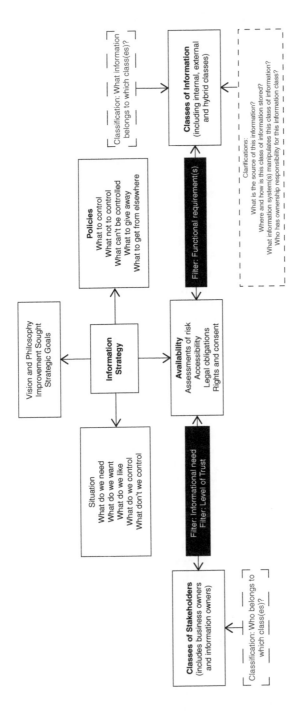

Figure 13.2 A model for a future information strategy

purchases or become tied to syntactic labour processes that can be undertaken through outsourcing or be completely automated. Smaller organisations have the additional incentive and advantage of becoming a digital business, as they are less encumbered by burdensome commitments to particular technology contracts or large-scale investment in rapidly aging infrastructure. Building an information strategy also provides a smaller organisation with the tools to 'design in' their digital maturity and circumvent long and slow development phases.

From a governance perspective, the interactions between availability, accessibility and rights to specific classes of information will be regarded as the points at which information can be controlled in relation to specific classes of stakeholders. A marketing perspective on the same information and stakeholders would regard these same points of interaction as key touchpoints. What information is drawn from which classes of information and what mechanisms are employed to interact with consumers – who are a specific form of external stakeholder – become the primary questions for any business function, whether it is marketing, accounting, human resources or strategic management. This framework for an integrated information strategy also embeds internal marketing as an interchange that exists between people – internal stakeholders – and information, and is of equal importance to external interactions.

Just as the Digital Business Maturity Model acknowledges the imminent demise of digital as a primary point of distinction within organisations (Evans and Wurster, 1997), so too can a fully articulated and comprehensive information strategy be regarded as a perfectly functional business strategy – at the broadest level. The need to identify and manage the interactions between classes of information and classes of stakeholders, and, by implication, the definition of who belongs to which classes, takes an organisation into a strategic, if not visionary, perspective and moves it away from day-to-day operational and reactive decision making. The advantage of a strategic perspective is often recognised in small businesses but difficult to realise against the backdrop of day-to-day operational necessity. An 'information strategy first' approach – bringing together this book's emphasis on marketing strategy and data – shifts the place and perspective of information in an organisation and, in doing so, offers a mechanism for achieving an always strategic approach.

Clear vision and visionary management are pivotal to the success of an information strategy. The key to a vision of a digitally mature business is to not be bound by current technologies but rather to be informed by what is currently possible.

New business models will be shaped by well-articulated visions of transparent information flows within the organisation. The information strategy of the organisation will be the realisation of a vision that permeates all aspects of a digitally mature business. The most challenging and exciting example of a new business model that takes up this perspective is described as Decentralised Organisations (DOs) and Decentralised Autonomous Organisations (DAOs). The latter concept has found particular favour among cryptocurrency advocates, particularly bitcoin evangelists. This is largely due to the fact that the backbone of existing bitcoin technology, the blockchain, provides an underlying solution to the financial and, by extension, contractual arrangements required in a DAO, where the operations are primarily conducted as functions of autonomous artificial intelligence. The exchanges between autonomous (computing) agents in the DAO are conducted technically through the blockchain network and are built on codified business rules and logic. In the fully realised DAO, human interaction with the organisation is primarily as external stakeholders – with the single exception of shareholders. The organisation conducts its business functions entirely through computing power and the application of artificial intelligence. It is possible to envision a future for DAOs in which higher and higher levels of business functions become reduced to effectively syntactic tasks for artificial intelligence. In a DO, people still figure within the organisational structure for their labour contribution. The distinction between syntactic and semantic labour offers a clear explanation as to why and when this contribution will be required, but at the same time increased processing speed and computing ability have the potential to shift currently semantic (higher-level interpretative) tasks to syntactic (mundane and repetitive) work. The analogy here is with the utopian claims of 1960s office automation, which attempted to engineer the paperless office – a vision never fully realised despite the ability of technology to enable the prospect. Similarly the future vision of a humanless office is also extreme because, despite the prospect that technology will enable this capability, there will be at least residual social and cultural reluctance to fully accept this seemingly dystopian prospect.

From the perspective of digital marketing, DAOs represent a challenge to existing marketing thinking and concepts. The DAO removes much of the emotive aspects of decision making to exchanges formed as a contract and visible on the blockchain. Digital marketing of the future will need to engage with autonomous agents and things – as part of the Internet of Things – alongside the shareholders and developers of these systems. But as this digital maturity evolves, the systems employed for marketing will themselves become more automatic. Many marketing actions will be reduced to syntactic labour functions completed through artificial intelligence and codified business rules and managed by the blockchain as part of a distributed autonomous organisation.

The information strategy first approach (Figure 13.2) commences with interrogation of the vision and philosophy for the use of information within the organisation. Businesses with a digital maturity will position data as their primary asset, and questions of vision are consequently questions regarding the organisational mission and purpose. These 'big' questions are necessary to ensure that strategic viewpoints overarch and drive operational necessity. Within the information strategy, by asking questions of classification and clarification regarding the stakeholders and information within the system – effectively the entire organisation – the operational reality of business can then be recognised and incorporated into a forward-thinking approach that can respond to changing circumstances, including new technologies, without the organisation itself becoming unviable.

The future of business is entirely digital. The future of marketing is entirely digital. These observations build on the recognition that we will inevitably interact with each other through the mediation of technology, including the rise of smart machines. This is not a new observation. Neanderthals communicate to us with cave paintings and Egyptian pharaohs communicate with us through their tombs. What is constantly changing is the speed and amplification of our communications, made possible through newer, more sophisticated technologies. To manage and keep pace with this change we must ourselves inevitably make use of the same new technologies – in whatever forms they eventually take.

13.7 Summary

This chapter provided insights into the future through discussion and development of the five-staged Digital Business Maturity Model, as well as a model Information Strategy. Both models can be applied to any organisation and encourage the application of a consistently strategic perspective.

Positioning an organisation within the Digital Business Maturity Model recognises its current levels of digital activities – including marketing – as well as its future potential. Identifying an organisation's current digital business maturity in relation to its current strategic position also offers a clear understanding of the progression route required to achieve even greater levels of digital maturity. The Digital Business Maturity Model provides a mechanism for measuring an organisation's current and future prospects for participating in the global digital economy.

An information strategy takes digital marketing to a holistic position by embedding it within a single data-oriented view of the organisation. The marketing function is everywhere in the organisation and an integral part of every action – as are all business functions and processes.

13.8 References

Evans, P. and Wurster, T. (1997) Strategy and the new economics of information, *Harvard Business Review*, Sept–Oct, 75(5), 70–82. https://hbr.org/1997/09/strategy-and-the-new-economics-of-information

Greenhill, A. and Fletcher, G. (2013) Labouring online: Are there any 'new' labour processes within virtual worlds? *Journal for the Association of Information Systems (JAIS)*, 14(11).

Patel, N. (2015) *How the Internet of Things is changing online marketing.* www.forbes.com/sites/neilpatel/2015/12/10/how-the-internet-of-things-is-changing-online-marketing/#690d55456e2f

Quigley, C. (2015) *The ethics of attention and the inevitable future of digital advertising.* In *WallBlog*. http://wallblog.co.uk/2015/11/13/the-ethics-of-attention-and-the-inevitable-future-of-digital-advertising/#ixzz3ycFhMRri

Zanella, A., Nicola, B., Angelo, C., Lorenzo, V. and Michele, Z. (2014) Internet of Things for smart cities, *IEEE Internet of Things Journal*, 1(1), 22–32.

Index